No. 1056
$10.95

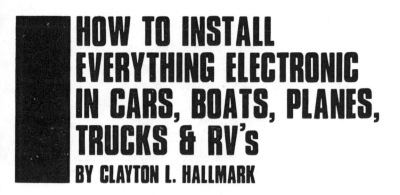

HOW TO INSTALL EVERYTHING ELECTRONIC IN CARS, BOATS, PLANES, TRUCKS & RV's
BY CLAYTON L. HALLMARK

TAB BOOKS
BLUE RIDGE SUMMIT, PA. 17214

FIRST EDITION

FIRST PRINTING—JUNE 1978

Copyright © 1978 by TAB BOOKS

Printed in the United States
of America

Library of Congress Cataloging in Publication Data

Hallmark, Clayton.
    How to install everything electronic in cars, boats, planes, trucks & RV's.

    Includes index.
    1. Motor vehicles—Electronic equipment. 2. Boats and boating—Electronic equipment. 3. Airplanes—Electronic equipment. 3. Airplanes—Electronic equipment. I. Title.
TL272.5.H29   629.04   78-5116
ISBN 0-8306-9902-3
ISBN 08306-1056-1 pbk.

Cover aircraft installation photo courtesy of King Radio Corporation

Preface

Where people go, electronics goes, too. People keep in touch with CB radio, entertain themselves with stereo tape decks, put radar in their boats and radar detectors in their cars. All of this has created a huge demand for mobile and portable electronic accessories—also a huge need for information about how to install them. Perhaps you have a boat in which you are considering the installation of a depth sounder or direction finder. Or perhaps you are not satisfied with the features or performance of the factory-installed radio or tape player in your car. Or perhaps you are a private pilot and wish to know more about the avionics equipment available and piloting techniques such as area navigation that are based on it. Maybe you want to know what's available for your recreational vehicle to make mobile living more safe, comfortable, and enjoyable. Or maybe you would like to install electronic accessories for others as a sideline. This book, then, is for you.

The book is divided into two parts. Part 1, roughly speaking, is the *basics and vehicles* part, and Part 2 is the *installations* part. Part 1 takes up such matters as electricity, electrical systems, vehicle designs, radio, and working with tools. Starting at the most elementary level with the atom, it then provides all the background needed for making installations quickly and successfully. Laid bare are all the hidden intricacies of the automobile which can make installations difficult for the uninitiated. Also discussed fully are the special problems encountered in making installations in trucks, boats, and recreational vehicles.

Part 2 is an alphabetical index of accessories for cars, recreational vehicles, boats, planes, trucks—even bicycles. It covers all kinds of accessories from A to Z. (Well, almost. The entries range from *Antennas* to *Windshield-Wiper Delay*.) Complete, specific, accurate, step-by-step instructions tell how to install almost any electronic accessory. This is probably the most complete assemblage of installation procedures in print. It is also an extensive *detailed* catalog of mobile electronics equipment, one that is sure to assist you in selecting accessories. Part 2 also provides extensive guidance in operating the equipment covered—more than the operating instructions that come with some equipment.

There are many advantages to do-it-yourself installations as opposed to factory installations. Doing it yourself is satisfying, thrifty, and informative. It allows you to select just the equipment you want, with just the features you want. And it allows you to install your accessories for your convenience, according to your preferences. It may even lead to a profitable sideline. Now is the time to get started—with this book as your guide.

For their invaluable assistance in providing data, photographs, drawings, and other material, I am indebted to the following:

Heath Company
    Robert Gernand
    Coy Clement
    Marge Streit

Radio Shack
    Hy Siegel

Antenna Specialists Company
    Jerry Kuchinski

King Radio Corporation

Chrysler Corporation

Ford Motor Company

General Motors Corporation

RCA Corporation

Pace Two-Way Radio Products

Hy-Gain Electronics Corp.

Turner Division of Conrac Corp.

Amphenol

Clayton L. Hallmark

Contents

Other TAB books by the author:

Part 1
Principles of Electronics and Mobile Installations

Chapter 1
Electrical Principles and Systems

To know what you are doing when you make an electronic installation in a car, recreational vehicle, truck, boat, or airplane, it is necessary to know something of electrical matters. Fortunately the principles of conductors and insulators, current and voltage, resistance, Ohm's law, magnetism, opens and shorts, batteries and generators, and grounding are the same for whatever you are installing or wherever you are installing it. It is also fortuitous that the charging and ignition systems of these vehicles are often similar. Airplane and large boat motors, for example, use the same type battery ignition system developed by Charles Kettering for the automobile in 1914. Small outboard motors and diesel engines employ magneto ignition and compression ignition, respectively; but the same principles of electricity, magnetism, and electromagnetism apply to the smallest boats and the largest diesel trucks. Knowing these principles and understanding the operation of battery charging and ignition systems will help you to avoid the most common mistakes in electronic installation.

COMPOSITION OF MATTER

To understand electricity, let us first study *matter*, which is the name for all material substances. We find, if we study the world about us, that everything (solids, liquids, and gases) is made up of tiny particles called *molecules*. These molecules are made up of *atoms*, and these atoms can be further subdivided. When we divide atoms, we get smaller particles with electrical charges.

The basic particles that make up all the atoms and thus all the universe, are called *protons, electrons,* and *neutrons*. A proton is a basic particle having a single positive charge. An electron is a basic particle having a single negative charge. A neutron is a basic particle having no charge. A group of

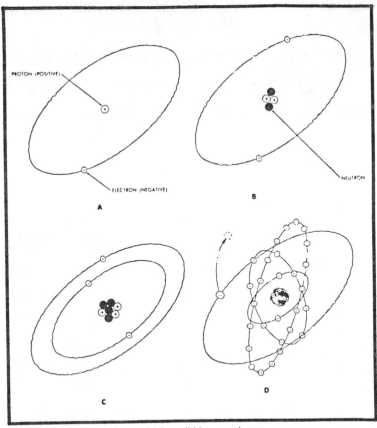

Fig. 1-1. Atoms of hydrogen, helium, lithium, and copper.

protons produces a positive electrical charge. A group of electrons produces a negative electrical charge. A group of neutrons would have no charge.

Let us examine more closely the construction of atoms of the various elements, starting with the simplest of all, hydrogen (A, Fig. 1-1). The atom of hydrogen consists of one proton around which is circling one electron. There is an attraction between the two particles, since negative and positive electrical charges always attract each other. Opposing the attraction between the two particles, and thus preventing the electron from moving in to the proton, is the centrifugal force on the electron, caused by its circular path around the proton. This is the same sort of balance we get if we were to whirl a ball tied to a string around our head. The centrifugal force exerted tries to move the ball out of its circular path, and is balanced by the string (the attractive force). If the string should break, the centrifugal force would cause the ball to fly away. Actually, this is what happens at times with atoms. The "string," that is, attractive force, between the electron and proton sometimes is not great enough to hold the electron in its circular path, and the electron gets away.

A slightly more complex atom is shown in B, Fig. 1-1. This is an atom of helium. Notice that there are now two protons in the center and that two electrons are circling around the center. Since there is an additional proton in the center (or nucleus) of the atom, an electron must be added so as to keep the atom in electrical balance. Notice also that there are two additional particles in the nucleus. These two additional particles are neutrons and are necessary in order to overcome the tendency of the two protons to move apart from each other. For, just as unlike electrical charges attract, so do *like* electrical charges *repel*. Electrons repel electrons. Protons repel protons, except when neutrons are present. Neutrons have no electrical charge (some scientists think they are actually an electron and a proton combined in perfect electrical balance), but neutrons have the ability to cancel out the repelling forces between protons in an atomic nucleus and thus hold the nucleus together.

A still more complex atom is shown in C, Fig. 1-1. This is an atom of lithium, a light, soft metal. Notice that a third proton has been added to the nucleus and that a third electron is now circling around the nucleus. Notice also that there are two additional neutrons in the nucleus; these are needed to hold the three protons together. We could also picture the atoms of other elements in a similar manner. As we did so, we would find that as we go up the scale in atomic complexity, we find protons and neutrons added one by one, to the nucleus, and electrons to the outer circles. After lithium comes beryllium with 4 protons and 5 neutrons, boron with 5 protons and 5 neutrons, carbon with 6 and 6, nitrogen with 7 and 7, oxygen with 8 and 8, etc. In each of these, there are normally the same number of electrons circling the nucleus as there are protons in the nucleus.

ELECTRON THEORY OF ELECTRICITY

We have mentioned that electrons occasionally break free of their atoms. When numerous electrons do this and gather in one area, we call the effect a *charge of electricity*. When the electrons begin to move in one direction (as along a wire, for example), we call the effect a *flow of electricity*, or an *electric current*. Actually, electric generators and batteries could be called *electron pumps*, since they remove electrons from one part of an electric circuit and concentrate them in another part of the circuit. For example, a generator takes electrons away from the positive terminal and concentrates them at the negative terminal. Since the electrons repel each other (like electrical charges repel), the electrons push out through the circuit and flow to the positive terminal (unlike electrical charges attract). Thus, we can see that an electric current is actually a flow of electrons from negative to positive.

CONDUCTORS AND INSULATORS

The electrons, in order to flow, must have a path or circuit in which to move. Copper wire forms a good circuit because it has many free electrons in it. In D, Fig. 1-1, an atom of copper is shown. It has 29 electrons circling about its nucleus in four different orbits, or paths. The outer orbit has but one electron. This electron is not held very strongly and it can get away from the nucleus rather easily. As a result, it can become a free electron. In a copper wire, made up of countless copper atoms, there are tremendous numbers of these free electrons. Thus, when a copper wire is connected to a generator, the free electrons on the negative terminal can easily push into the copper wire. As they do this, they repel free electrons farther along in the wire (like repels like). These electrons then repel other electrons ahead of them, and so on along the wire. Almost instantly, as the wire is connected, free electrons are pushed along the wire, and the free electrons in the wire at the positive terminal are pushed off and also attracted into the positive terminal.

An insulator is made up of a substance that does not have many free electrons. Without free electrons, a flow of electrons cannot be set up, for the flow depends upon repelling free electrons along the circuit. If an insulator blocks the circuit, free electrons cannot push through. Insulators are used to cover and protect wires and other metal parts of electrical devices. The insulators keep the free electrons (or current) from going off in the wrong direction (wandering) and taking a short circuit. For instance, the insulation on the cord and switch of a lamp keeps the current from wandering into the hand of a person turning the lamp on and giving them an electric shock. It also prevents the current from taking a short circuit instead of going through the lamp. Insulators include rubber, porcelain, glass, certain kinds of enamel, varnish (baked or air-dried on wire, for instance), Bakelite, fiberboard of certain types, etc.

AMPERAGE AND VOLTAGE

Current flow, or electron flow, is measured in amperes. While we normally consider that one ampere is a rather small current of electricity (it is about what a 100-watt light bulb would draw), it is actually a tremendous flow of electrons. More than 6 billion billion electrons a second are required to make up one ampere.

Electrons are caused to flow by a difference in electron balance in a circuit; that is, when there are more electrons in one part of a circuit than in another, the electrons move from the area where they are concentrated to the area where they are lacking. This difference in electron concentration is called *potential difference*, or *voltage*. The higher the voltage goes, the greater the electron unbalance becomes. The greater this electron unbalance, the harder the push on the electrons (more electrons repelling each other) and the greater the current of electrons in the circuit. When there are many electrons concentrated at the negative terminal of a generator (with a corresponding lack of electrons at the positive terminal), there is a much stronger repelling force on the electrons and, consequently, many more electrons moving in the wire. This is exactly the same as saying that the higher the voltage, the more electric current will flow in a circuit (all other things, such as resistance, being equal).

RESISTANCE

Even though a copper wire will conduct electricity with relative ease, it still offers resistance to the flow. It takes force (or voltage) to move the electrons along the wire. This resistance to electron (or current) flow is expressed in ohms. The resistance of a wire varies according to its length, its cross-sectional area or diameter, its composition, and its temperature.

A long wire offers more resistance than a short wire of the same cross-sectional area. The electrons have further to travel.

A small wire (in thickness or cross-sectional area) offers more resistance than a large wire. In the small wire there are fewer free electrons (because of fewer atoms), and thus fewer electrons can push through.

Some elements can lose electrons more readily than other elements. Copper loses electrons easily, so there are always many free electrons in a copper wire. Other elements, such as iron, do not lose their electrons quite as easily, so there are fewer free electrons in an iron wire (comparing it to a copper wire of the same size). Thus, with fewer free electrons, fewer electrons can push through an iron wire; that is, the iron wire has more resistance than the copper wire.

Most metals show an increase in resistance with an increase in temperature, while most nonmetals show a decrease in resistance with an increase in temperature. For example, glass (a nonmetal) is an excellent insulator at room temperature, but is a very poor insulator when heated to red hot.

OHM'S LAW

The general statements about voltage, amperage, and ohms can all be related in a statement known as *Ohm's law*, so named for the scientist (Georg Simon Ohm) who first stated the relationship. This law says that voltage is equal to amperage times ohms. Or, it can be stated as the mathematical formula

$$E = I \times R$$

where E is volts, I is current in amperes, and R is resistance in ohms.

This formula is a valuable one to remember, because it helps you understand many of the things that happen in an electric circuit. For instance, if the voltage remains constant, the current flow goes down if the resistance goes up. An example of this would be the lighting circuit that is going bad in a truck. Suppose the wiring circuit between the battery and the lights has deteriorated due to connections becoming poor, strands in the wire breaking, switch contacts becoming dirty, etc. All of these conditions reduce the electron path or, in other words, increase resistance. And, with this increased resistance, less current will flow. The voltage of the battery stays the same (for example, 12 volts). If the resistance of the circuit when new (including light bulbs) was 6 ohms, then 2 amperes will flow. To satisfy the equation, 12 (volts) must equal 12 (amperes times ohms resistance). But if the resistance goes up to 8 ohms, only 1.5 amperes can flow. The increased resistance cuts down the current flow and consequently the amount of light produced.

A great majority of electrical troubles on automotive vehicles result from increased resistance in circuits due to bad connections, deteriorated wiring, dirty or burned contacts in switches, etc. With any of these conditions, the resistance of the circuit goes up and the ampere flow through that circuit goes down. Bad contact points in the ignition circuit will reduce

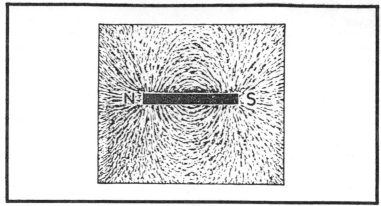

Fig. 1-2. Magnetic lines of force of a bar magnet as shown by iron filings.

current flow in the circuit and cause weak sparks at the spark plugs. This will result in engine missing and loss of power.

If the resistance stays the same but the voltage increases, the amperage also increases. This is a condition that might occur if a voltage regulator became defective. In such a case, there would be nothing to hold the generated voltage within limits, and the voltage might increase excessively. This would force excessive amounts of current through various circuits and cause serious damage. If too much current went through the lightbulb filaments, for example, the filaments would overheat and burn out. Also, other electrical devices probably would be damaged.

On the other hand, if the voltage is reduced, the amount of current flowing in a circuit will also be reduced if the resistance stays the same. For example, with a rundown battery, battery voltage will drop excessively with a heavy discharge. When trying to start an engine with a rundown battery, the voltage will drop very low. This voltage is so low that it cannot push enough current through the starter motor for effective starting of the engine.

MAGNETS

We have learned that electric current is a flow of electrons and that the unbalance of electrons in a circuit (that causes electrons to flow) is called *voltage*. As a first step in learning what causes a generator to concentrate electrons at the negative terminal and take them away from the positive terminal, magnets will be discussed.

Magnetic Field

If we were to take a bar magnet, lay a piece of glass on top of it, and then sprinkle iron filings on the glass, we would find that the filings would become arranged in curved lines (Fig. 1-2). These curved lines, extending from the two poles of the magnet (north and south), follow the *magnetic lines of force* surrounding the magnet. Scientists cannot fully explain magnetism, but they have formulated certain rules for these lines of force. These rules are listed below.

1. The lines of force (outside the magnet) pass from the north to the south pole of the magnet.
2. The lines of force act somewhat as rubber bands and try to shorten to a minimum length.
3. The lines of force repel each other along their entire length and so try to push each other apart.
4. The "rubber band" characteristic opposes the "push apart" characteristic.
5. The lines of force never cross each other.
6. The magnetic lines of force, taken together, are referred to as the magnetic field of the magnet.

The magnetic fields of a bar and of a horseshoe magnet are shown in Fig. 1-3. In each, note how the lines of force curve and pass from the north to the south pole.

Effects Between Magnetic Poles

When two unlike magnetic poles are brought together, they attract. But when like magnetic poles are brought together, they repel. These actions can be explained in terms of the rubber band and push apart characteristics (Fig. 1-4). When unlike poles are brought close to each other, the magnetic lines of force pass from the north to the south poles. They try to shorten (like rubber bands), and therefore try to pull the two poles together. On the other hand, if like poles are brought close to each other, lines of force going in the same direction are brought near each other. Since these lines of force attempt to push apart, a repelling effect results between the like poles.

ELECTROMAGNETISM

An electric current (flow of electrons) always produces a magnetic field. In the wire shown in Fig. 1-5, current flow causes lines of force to circle the wire. It is thought that these lines of force result from the movement of the electrons along the wire. As they move, the electrons send out the lines of force. When many electrons move, there are many lines of force (the

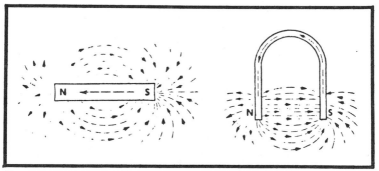

Fig. 1-3. Magnetic fields of a bar and of a horseshoe magnet.

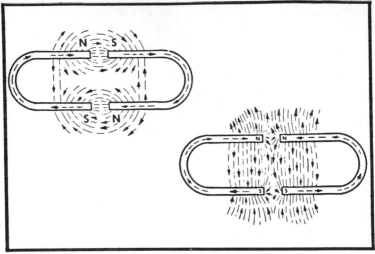

Fig. 1-4. Attraction and repulsion between magnetic poles.

magnetic field is strong). Few electrons in motion means a weak magnetic field or few lines of force.

Electron movement as the basis of magnetism in bar and horseshoe magnets can be explained by assuming that the atoms of iron are lined up in the magnets so that the electrons are circling in the same direction. With the electrons moving in the same direction, their individual magnetic lines of force add to produce the magnetic field.

The magnetic field produced by current flowing in a single loop of wire is shown in Fig. 1-6. The magnetic lines of force circle the wire (Fig. 1-5), but here they must follow the curve of the wire. If two loops are made in the conductor, the lines of force will circle the two loops (Fig. 1-7). In the area

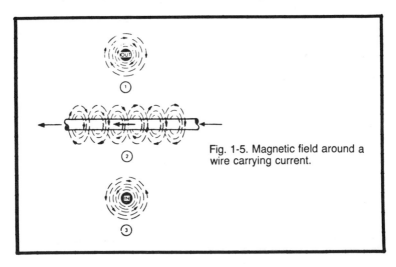

Fig. 1-5. Magnetic field around a wire carrying current.

between the adjacent loops, the magnetic lines are going in opposite directions. In such a case, since they are of the same strength (from same amount of current traveling in both loops), they cancel each other out. The lines of force, therefore, circle the two loops almost as though they were a single loop. However, the magnetic field will be twice as strong since the lines of force of the two loops combine.

When many loops of wire are formed into a coil as shown in Fig. 1-8, the lines of force of all loops combine into a pattern that greatly resembles the magnetic field surrounding a bar magnet. A coil of this type is known as an *electromagnet* or a *solenoid*. However, electromagnets can be in many shapes. The field coils of generators and starters, the primary winding in an ignition coil, the coils in electric gauges, even the windings in a starter armature, can be considered to be electromagnets. All of these produce magnetism by electrical means.

The north pole of an electromagnet can be determined, if the direction of current flow (from negative to positive) is known, by use of the left-hand rule (Fig. 1-9). The left hand is held around the coil with the fingers pointing in the direction of current flow. The thumb will point to the north pole of the electromagnet. This rule is based on current, or electron, flow from *negative to positive*.

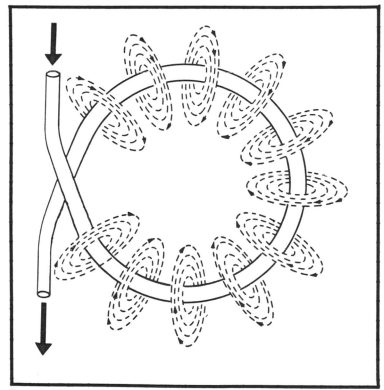

Fig. 1-6. Magnetic fields in a loop of wire carrying current.

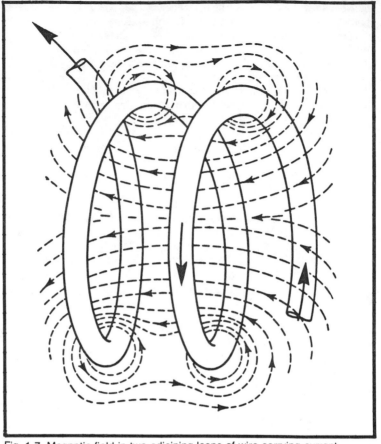

Fig. 1-7. Magnetic field in two adjoining loops of wire carrying current.

The left-hand rule can also be used to determine the direction that lines of force circle a wire. Try this with Fig. 1-5.

The strength of an electromagnet can be greatly increased by wrapping the loops of wire around an iron core. The iron core passes the lines of force with much greater ease than air. This property of permitting lines of force to pass through easily is called *permeability.* Wrought iron is 3000 times more permeable than air. In other words, it allows 3000 times as many lines of force to get through. With this great increase in the number of lines of force, the magnetic strength of the electromagnet is greatly increased, even though no more current flows through it. Practically all electromagnets use an iron core of some kind.

ELECTROMAGNETIC INDUCTION

Current can be induced to flow in a conductor if it is moved through a magnetic field. In Fig. 1-10, the wire is moved downward through the

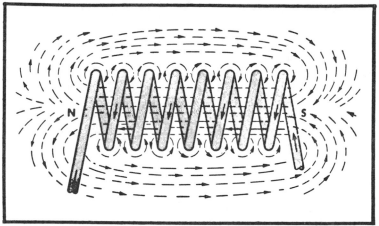

Fig. 1-8. Magnetic current produced by current flowing in an electromagnet.

magnetic field between the two magnetic poles. As it moves downward, cutting lines of force, current is induced in it. The reason for this is that the lines of force resist cutting and tend to wrap around the wire as shown. With lines of force wrapping around the wire, current is induced. The wire movement through the magnet field produces a magnetic "whirl" around the wire, which pushes the electrons along in the wire.

If the wire is held stationary and the magnetic field is moved, the effect is the same; that is, current will be induced in the wire. All that is required is that there be relative movement between the two so that lines of force are cut by the wire. It is this cutting and whirling, or wrapping, of the lines of force around the wire that produces the current movement in the wire.

The magnetic field can be moved by moving the magnet or, if it is a magnetic field from an electromagnet, it can be moved by starting and stopping and current flow in the electromagnet. Suppose we had an elec-

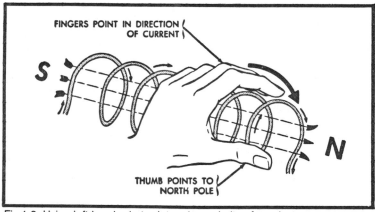

Fig.1-9. Using left-hand rule to determine polarity of an electromagnet.

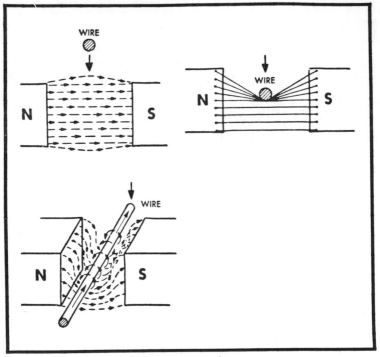

Fig. 1-10. Current induced by electromagnetism.

tromagnet, such as the one shown in Fig. 1-8, and held a wire close to it. When we connected the electromagnet to a battery, current would start to flow through it. This current, as it starts to flow, builds up a magnetic field. In other words, a magnetic field forms because of the current flow. This magnetic field might be considered as expanding (like a balloon, in a sense) and moving out from the electromagnet. As it moves outward, its lines of force will cut through the wire held close to the electromagnet. This wire will therefore have current induced in it. The current will result from the lines of force cutting across the wire. If the electromagnet is disconnected from the battery, its magnetic field will collapse and disappear. As this happens, the lines of force move inward toward the electromagnet. Again, the wire held close to the electromagnet will be cut by moving lines of force and will have current induced in it. This time, the lines of force are moving in the opposite direction and the wire will, therefore, have current induced in it in the opposite direction.

It can thus be seen that current can be induced in the wire by three methods: the wire can be moved through the stationary magnetic field; the wire can be held stationary and the magnet can be moved so the field is carried past the wire; or the wire and electromagnet can both be held stationary and the current turned on and off to cause the magnetic field buildup and collapse so the magnetic field moves one way or the other across the wire.

GROUND

The reference point of a circuit is always considered to be at zero potential. Since the earth (ground) is said to be at a zero potential, the term *ground* is used to denote a common electrical point of zero potential. In Fig. 1-11, point A is the zero reference, or ground, and is symbolized as such. Point C is twelve volts (12V) positive, and point B is four volts (4V) positive in respect to ground.

In most equipment the metal chassis (car body) is the common ground for the many electrical circuits. The value of ground is noted when considering its contribution to economy, simplification of schematics, and ease of measurement. When completing each electrical circuit, common points of a circuit at zero potential are connected directly to the metal chassis, thereby eliminating a large amount of connecting wire. The electrons pass through the metal chassis (conductor) to reach other points of the circuit. An example of a grounded circuit is illustrated in Fig. 1-12.

OPEN CIRCUITS

A circuit is said to be *open* when a break exists in a complete conducting pathway. Although an open occurs any time a switch is thrown to deenergize a circuit, an open may also develop accidentally, due to abnormal circuit conditions. To restore a circuit to proper operation, the open must be located and its cause determined.

Sometimes an open can be located visually by a close inspection of the circuit components. Defective components, such as burned-out resistors and fuses can usually be discovered by this method. Other opens, such as a break in wire covered by insulation or the melted element of an enclosed fuse, are not visible to the eye. Under such conditions, the understanding of an open's effect on circuit conditions enables a technician to make use of a voltmeter or ohmmeter to locate the open component.

In Fig. 1-13, the series circuit consists of two resistors and a fuse. Notice the effects on circuit conditions when the fuse opens. Current ceases

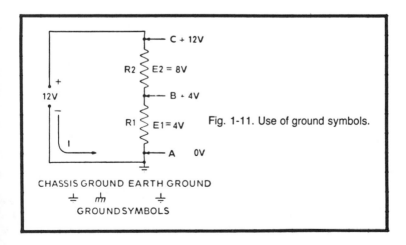

Fig. 1-11. Use of ground symbols.

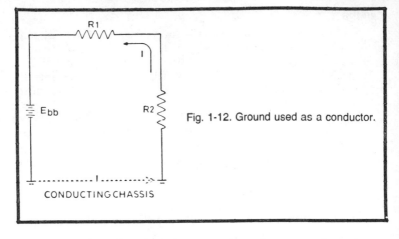

Fig. 1-12. Ground used as a conductor.

CONDUCTING CHASSIS

to flow; therefore, there is no longer a voltage drop across the resistors. Each end of the open conducting path becomes an extension of the battery terminals, and the voltage measured across the open is equal to the applied voltage.

An open circuit such as found in Fig. 1-13 could also have been located with an ohmmeter. However, when using an ohmmeter to check a circuit, it is important to first deenergize the circuit. The reason is that an ohmmeter has its own power source and would be damaged if connected to an energized circuit.

The ohmmeter used to check a series circuit would indicate the ohmic value of each resistance it is connected across. The open circuit, due to its almost infinite resistance, would cause no deflection on the ohmmeter, as indicated by the illustration (Fig. 1-14).

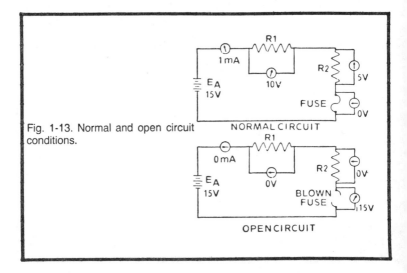

Fig. 1-13. Normal and open circuit conditions.

NORMAL CIRCUIT

OPEN CIRCUIT

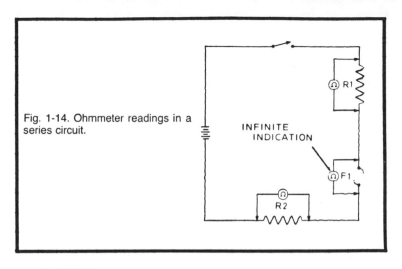

Fig. 1-14. Ohmmeter readings in a series circuit.

INFINITE INDICATION

SHORT CIRCUITS

A *short circuit* is an accidental path of low resistance, which passes an abnormal amount of current. A short circuit exists whenever the resistance of the circuit or the resistance of a part of a circuit drops in value to almost zero ohms. A short often occurs as a result of improper wiring or broken insulation.

In Fig. 1-15, a short is caused by improper wiring. Note the effect on current flow. Since the resistor has in effect been replaced with a piece of wire, practically all the current flows through the short, and very little current flows through the resistor. Electrons flow through the short, a path of almost zero resistance, and complete the circuit by passing through the 10-ohm resistor and the battery. The amount of current flow increases greatly, because its resistive path has decreased from 100 ohms to 1 ohm.

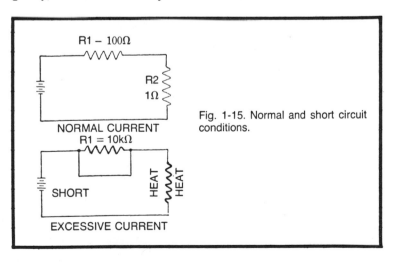

Fig. 1-15. Normal and short circuit conditions.

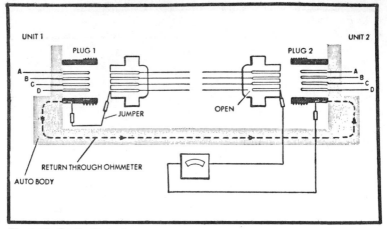

Fig. 1-16. Continuity test.

Due to the excessive current through the resistor, the increased heat dissipated by the resistor will destroy that component.

CIRCUIT TESTS

Open circuits are those in which the flow of current is interrupted by a broken wire, defective switch, or any means by which the current cannot flow. The test used to check for opens (or to see if the circuit is complete or continuous) is called *continuity testing.*

An ohmmeter (which contains its own batteries) is excellent for a continuity test. In an emergency, a continuity tester can readily be made from a flashlight. Normally, continuity tests are performed in circuits where the resistance is very low (such as the resistance of a copper conductor). An open circuit is indicated by a very high or infinite resistance. Such a condition would be an open conductor.

The diagram in Fig. 1-16 shows a continuity test of a cable. Notice that both connectors are disconnected and the ohmmeter is in series with the conductor under test. The power must be off. When you are checking conductors A, B, and C, the current from the ohmmeter will flow through plug No. 2, through the conductor and plug No. 1. From this plug it will pass through the jumper to the car chassis. The chassis will serve as the return path to unit 2, completing the circuit to the ohmmeter. The ohmmeter will indicate a low resistance.

Checking conductor D (Fig. 1-16) will reveal an open. The ohmmeter will indicate maximum resistance because current cannot flow. With an open circuit the ohmmeter needle is all the way to the left since it is a series-type ohmmeter (reads right to left).

Where conditions exist that the chassis cannot be used as the return path, one of the other conductors may be used. For example, to check D (Fig. 1-16), a jumper is connected from pin D to pin A of plug No. 1, and the ohmmeter leads are connected to pins D and A of plug No. 2. By the process of elimination, this technique will also reveal the open in the circuit.

Grounded circuits (shorts) are caused by some conducting part of the circuit making contact either directly or indirectly with the metallic body of the car. Shorts may have many causes. The most common is perhaps frayed insulation allowing the bare wire to come in contact with the metal ground.

Shorts are usually indicated by blown fuses. Blown fuses, however, may also result from a short other than to ground. A high-resistance ground may also occur where sufficient current does not flow to rupture the fuse.

Use the ohmmeter to test for grounds. By measuring the resistance to ground of any point in a circuit, it is possible to determine if the point is grounded. One possible means of testing a cable for grounds can be seen at Fig. 1-16. If the jumper is removed from pin D of plug No. 1, a test for grounds can be made for each conductor of the cable. This is accomplished by connecting one meter lead to ground and the other to each of the pins of one of the plugs. A low resistance indicates that a pin is grounded. Both plugs must be removed from their units; if only one plug is removed, a false indication is possible, for a conductor may be grounded through a circuit in the unit.

A short circuit other than a grounded one occurs when two conductors accidentally touch each other directly or through another conducting element. Two conductors with frayed insulation may touch and cause a short. Too much solder on the pin of a connector may short to the adjacent pin. Sufficient current may then flow to blow a fuse. However, it is entirely possible to have a short between two cables carrying signals, such as audio signals to a rear-deck speaker. Such a short will not be indicated by a blown fuse.

As when checking for a ground, the device used for checking for a short is the ohmmeter. A short between two conductors may be detected by a low resistance reading between them. In Fig. 1-16, by removing the jumper and disconnecting both plugs, a short test may be made. This is performed by measuring the resistance between the two suspected conductors.

Shorts are not reserved for cables; they occur in many components, such as coils, motor windings, and capacitors. The best method for testing such components is to make a resistance measurement and compare the results against the manufactured specs given on schematics or in maintenance manuals.

THE ALTERNATOR

Automotive alternators were pioneered in the U.S. by the Chrysler Corporation. Other car makers have long since seen the light, however, and all domestic manufacturers now use this form of dynamo.

Compared to the DC generator, the alternator is lighter, more compact, and less troubleprone. Also, it does a better job of charging the battery, especially at low engine speeds.

Alternators are made in many different sizes, depending on their intended use. For example, any one of the generators at Hoover Dam can produce *millions* of volt-amperes, but generators used on cars produce only a few hundred volt-amperes.

Regardless of size, however, all generators operate on the same basic principle—a magnetic field cutting through conductors, or conductors pas-

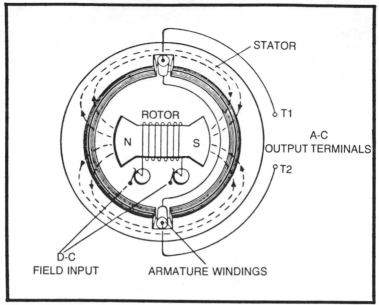

Fig. 1-17. Rotating-field AC generator.

sing through a magnetic field. Thus, all generators have at least two distinct sets of conductors. They are (1) a group of conductors in which the output voltage is generated, and (2) a second group of conductors through which direct current is passed to obtain an electromagnetic field of fixed polarity. The conductors in which the output voltage is generated are always referred to as the armature windings. The conductors in which the electromagnetic field originates are always referred to as the field windings.

In addition to the armature and field, there must also be motion between the two. To provide this, AC generators are built in two major assemblies, the *stator* and the *rotor*. The rotor is so called because it rotates inside the stator.

TYPES OF AC GENERATORS

Thre are various types of alternating-current generators in use today. However, they all perform the same basic function. The revolving-field AC generator (Fig. 1-17) is by far the most widely used and is the type used in cars. In this generator, direct current from a separate source (battery) is passed through windings on the rotor by means of sliprings and brushes. This mechanical arrangement maintains a rotating electromagnetic field of fixed polarity (similar to a rotating bar magnet). The rotating magnetic field, following the rotor, extends outward and cuts through the armature windings embedded in the surrounding stator. As the rotor turns, alternating voltages are induced in the windings, since magnetic fields of first one polarity and then the other cut through them. Since the output power is taken from stationary windings, the output may be connected through fixed terminals (T1 and T2 in Fig. 1-17). This is advantageous in that there are no sliding contacts and the whole output circuit is continuously insulated.

Sliprings and brushes are adequate for the DC field supply because the power level in the field is much smaller than in the armature circuit.

BATTERY PRINCIPLE OF OPERATION

When a cell is fully charged, the negative plate is spongy lead, the positive plate is lead peroxide, and the electrolyte contains a maximum amount of sulfuric acid. Both the negative and positive plates are very porous and are readily acted upon by the acid. A cell in this condition can produce electrical energy through reaction of the chemicals.

Discharge

If the terminals of the battery are connected to a closed circuit, the cell discharges to supply electric current (Fig. 1-18). The chemical process that occurs during discharge changes both the lead (Pb) of the negative plate and the lead peroxide (PbO_2) of the positive plate to lead sulfate ($PbSO_4$) and the sulfuric acid (H_2SO_4) to water (H_2O). Thus, the electrolyte becomes weaker during discharge, since the water increases and the sulfuric acid decreases. As the discharge progresses, the negative and the positive plates finally contain considerable lead sulfate. The discharge should always be stopped before the plates have entirely changed to lead sulfate.

Charge

To charge the cell, an external source of direct current must be connected to the battery terminals. The chemical reaction is then reversed and returns to the positive and negative plates and the electrolyte to their original condition. When all the sulfate (SO_4) on the plates has been returned to the electrolyte to form sulfuric acid (H_2SO_4), the cell is fully recharged and ready to be used for the next discharge. Charging must be started before both plates have become entirely sulfated. If this is not done, the plate surfaces are no longer chemically different and therefore will not respond to the charging current, since two dissimilar plates must be in the electrolyte to produce the action. The chemical processes in the cell during discharge and charge can be followed in Fig. 1-18.

The generator on the vehicle produces current to charge the battery. The voltage in this type of system is usually held constant. With a constant voltage, the charging rate to a low battery will be high. But as the battery approaches a charged condition, the opposing voltage of the battery goes up (in effect) so that it more and more strongly opposes the charging current. We might say that such a battery is becoming "filled up" and thus signals, by its opposition to the charging current, that it needs a smaller charging current. As the battery approaches a charged condition, the charging voltage (which is held constant) is less and less able to maintain a charging current to the battery. As a result, the charging current tapers off to a very low value by the time the battery reaches a fully charged condition.

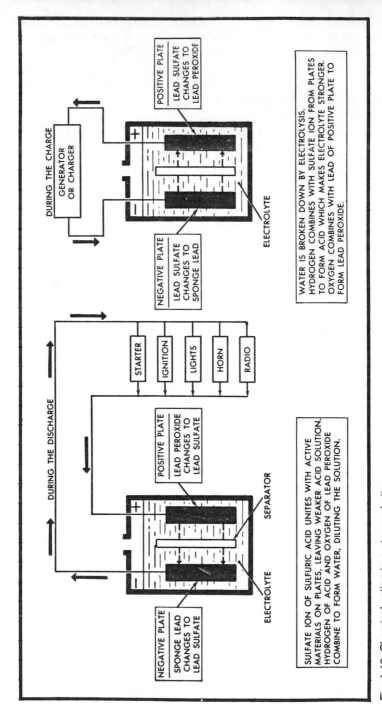

Fig. 1-18. Chemical action in a storage battery.

DURING THE CHARGE

GENERATOR OR CHARGER

POSITIVE PLATE

LEAD SULFATE CHANGES TO LEAD PEROXIDE

NEGATIVE PLATE

LEAD SULFATE CHANGES TO SPONGE LEAD

ELECTROLYTE

WATER IS BROKEN DOWN BY ELECTROLYSIS. HYDROGEN COMBINES WITH SULFATE ION FROM PLATES TO FORM ACID WHICH MAKES ELECTROLYTE STRONGER. OXYGEN COMBINES WITH LEAD OF POSITIVE PLATE TO FORM LEAD PEROXIDE.

DURING THE DISCHARGE

STARTER
IGNITION
LIGHTS
HORN
RADIO

POSITIVE PLATE

LEAD PEROXIDE CHANGES TO LEAD SULFATE

NEGATIVE PLATE

SPONGE LEAD CHANGES TO LEAD SULFATE

SEPARATOR

ELECTROLYTE

SULFATE ION OF SULFURIC ACID UNITES WITH ACTIVE MATERIALS ON PLATES, LEAVING WEAKER ACID SOLUTION. HYDROGEN OF ACID AND OXYGEN OF LEAD PEROXIDE COMBINE TO FORM WATER, DILUTING THE SOLUTION.

30

CHARGING SYSTEM

A complete charging system using the devices already described is depicted by the schematic in Fig. 1-19. Figure 1-19A shows the indicator light ("idiot" light) version and B shows the ammeter version of a late-model Ford charging system.

The alternator produces power in the form of alternating current. The alternating current is rectified to direct current by six diodes (eight diodes in 61-ampere alternators). The alternator regulator automatically adjusts the alternator field current to maintain the alternator output voltage within prescribed limits to correctly charge the battery. The alternator is self-current-limiting.

If a charge-indicator lamp is used in the charging system (Fig. 1-19A), the system operation is as follows: When the ignition switch is turned on, a small current flows through the lamp filament (turning the lamp on) and through the alternator regulator to the alternator field. When the engine is started, the alternator field rotates and produces a voltage in the stator winding. When the voltage at the alternator stator terminal reaches about 3 volts, the regulator field relay closes. This puts the same voltage on both sides of the charge indicator lamp causing it to go out. When the field relay has closed, current passes through the regulator A terminal and is metered to the alternator field.

If an ammeter is used in the charging system (Fig. 1-19), the regulator *I* terminal and the alternator stator terminal are not used. When the ignition switch is turned on, the field relay closes and electrical current passes through the regulator A terminal and is metered to the alternator field. When the engine is started, the alternator field rotates, causing the alternator to operate. The ammeter indicates current flow into (charge) or out of (discharge) the vehicle battery.

Fuse links are included in the charging-system wiring. This is to prevent damage to the wiring harness and alternator if the wiring harness should become grounded or if a booster battery is connected to the charging system with the wrong polarity.

Since the output of an alternator is an alternating one, each stator winding supplies a negative voltage to its associated diodes one moment, and a positive voltage the next. When a stator output is negative, electrons flow out of the stator and through one of the diodes in the bottom row—against the arrowhead. The electrons then flow into the car body (ground), through the body to the ground connection of the battery (and other load devices—lights, etc.), through the battery (and other loads), and back to the top row of diodes. To complete the circuit, the electrons must return to the alternator—not necessarily to the same stator winding that they left, but to any of the windings. As explained earlier, each stator output is positive as often and for as long as it is negative. It is when a stator winding is positive that electrons returing from work in the battery and other devices can return to the winding. Electrons flow against the arrowhead of a diode in the top row and into the stator winding during the time when it is positive.

IGNITION SYSTEM

The battery ignition system is important to the electronics installer for two reasons. For one thing, some of the most beneficial installations that can

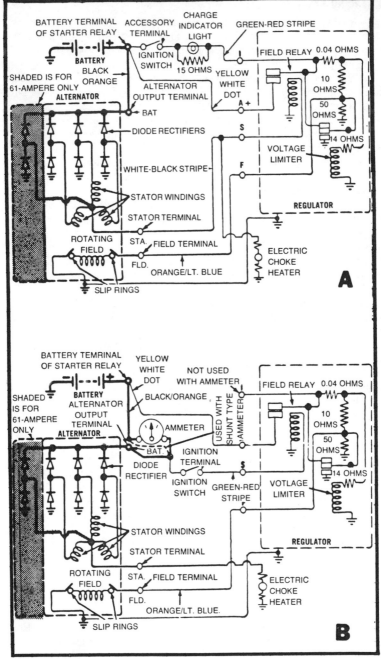

Fig. 1-19. Charging systems; indicator light (A) and ammeter (B) types. (Courtesy Ford Marketing Corp.)

be made in a vehicle involve replacement of old electromechanical parts with purely electronic parts. These installations save energy, reduce toxic emissions, cut maintenance expenses, and improve vehicle performance. Another reason to learn about the ignition system is that it is a prime source of noise and interference in radios and tape players installed in cars.

A schematic diagram of an ignition system is shown in Fig. 1-20, and what the various components in the system do can be noted.

Battery

The battery and generator furnish the source of voltage and current for the ignition system. The battery is required when first starting but, after the vehicle starts moving, the generator takes up the ignition load.

Ammeter

Most electric circuits in the vehicle are connected through the ammeter to the battery. This enables the driver to determine at a glance whether the generator or the battery is carrying the load, that is, whether the battery is being charged or discharged. Many cars now use an indicator light in place of the ammeter.

Ignition Coil

The ignition coil consists of a primary winding of a few hundred turns of relatively heavy wire (No. 18 is a commonly used size) which is about 0.04-inch in diameter, plus a secondary winding of many thousands of turns of a very fine wire (No. 38 is a commonly used size) which is about 0.004-inch in diameter, both assembled around a soft iron core, enclosed by a metal case, and topped with an insulating cap which carries the terminals (Fig. 1-21). Since the countervoltage induced by the collapsing magnetic field is about the same value for each turn, the fact that the secondary has many more turns means that the secondary voltage will go much higher than the primary voltage. With a turn ratio of 100:1 (100 turns in the secondary to 1 turn in the primary), the secondary voltage could go 100 times as high as the primary. Since the countervoltages induced in the primary (by the rapid collapse of the magnetic field brought about by capacitor action) may reach 200 volts or more, the secondary voltage could reach 20,000 volts. This high voltage is carried through the ignition distributor and distributed to the correct spark plug.

Ignition Distributor

The ignition distributor has several jobs to do in the ignition system. First, it must close and open the primary circuit to produce the magnetic buildup and collapse in the ignition coil. Second, it times these actions so the resultant high-voltage surges from the secondary will be produced at the right time. Third, it must direct the high-voltage surges to the proper spark plugs. (See Fig. 1-22 for a view of a typical distributor.) The primary circuit through the distributor consists, essentially, of a set of contacts and a capacitor connected across the contacts. The contacts are closed by spring pressure and opened by a cam driven through the distributor shaft from a

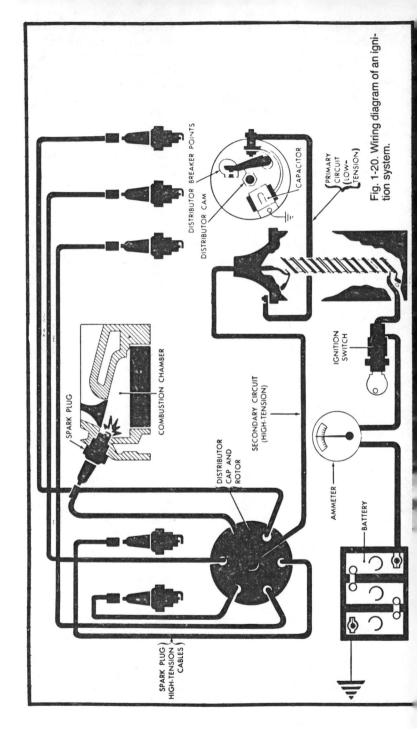

DISTRIBUTOR BREAKER POINTS

DISTRIBUTOR CAM

CAPACITOR

PRIMARY CIRCUIT (LOW-TENSION)

Fig. 1-20. Wiring diagram of an ignition system.

SPARK PLUG

COMBUSTION CHAMBER

IGNITION SWITCH

SECONDARY CIRCUIT (HIGH-TENSION)

DISTRIBUTOR CAP AND ROTOR

AMMETER

BATTERY

SPARK PLUG HIGH-TENSION CABLES

gear on the engine camshaft. Often, the oil pump is driven from the same gear. As the cam rotates, the cam lobes move around under the contact arm, causing the contacts to open and close.

The secondary circuit through the distributor consists of a rotor mounted on top of the cam, and a cap with high-tension terminals. In action, the rotor turns with the cam, connecting (through its metal segment) between the center high-tension terminal and the various outer high-tension terminals. This directs the high-voltage surges from the coil (which enter through the center high-tension terminal) to the various engine spark plugs (which are connected, in firing order, to the outer high-tension terminals).

Spark timing advances are required so that the spark will occur in the combustion chamber at the proper time in the compression stroke. At high speed, the spark must appear earlier so the fuel-air mixture will have ample

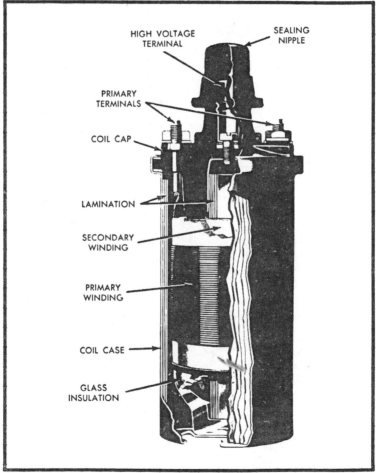

Fig. 1-21. Ignition coil, sectional view.

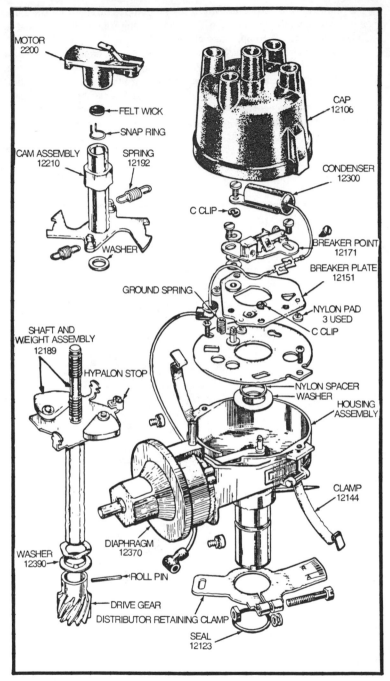

Fig. 1-22. Distributor, disassembled view.

MOTOR
2200

FELT WICK

SNAP RING

CAM ASSEMBLY
12210

SPRING
12192

CAP
12106

CONDENSER
12300

C CLIP

WASHER

BREAKER POINT
12171

BREAKER PLATE
12151

GROUND SPRING

NYLON PAD
3 USED

C CLIP

SHAFT AND
WEIGHT ASSEMBLY
12189

HYPALON STOP

NYLON SPACER

WASHER

HOUSING
ASSEMBLY

CLAMP
12144

WASHER
12390

DIAPHRAGM
12370

ROLL PIN

DRIVE GEAR

DISTRIBUTOR RETAINING CLAMP

SEAL
12123

36

time to burn and give up its energy to the piston. At part throttle, when the fuel-air mixture is less highly compressed, a spark advance is required to ignite the slower burning mixture in ample time for it to burn and deliver its power. Centrifugal and vacuum mechanisms produce these advances.

The *centrifugal advance* mechanism is located in the distributor housing and consists essentially of a pair of weights mounted on pins on a weight base and linked by weight springs to the advance cam (Fig. 1-23). When idling, the springs hold the advance cam in a no-advance position. As speed increases, the centrifugal force on the weights (Fig. 1-24) causes them to move out. This action forces the toggles on the weights to move against the advance cam so the cam is pushed ahead against the spring tension. As the advance cam turns ahead, the breaker cam lobes open and close the contacts earlier in the cycle. This advances the spark.

The *vacuum advance* mechanism makes use of a vacuum chamber connected to the intake manifold and a vacuum diaphragm linked to the breaker plate assembly (Fig. 1-25). The breaker plate is supported so it can turn back and forth a few degrees. When there is a wide-open throttle and little or no vacuum in the intake manifold, a full measure of fuel-air mixture is entering the cylinders and no spark advance is needed. But when the throttle is partially closed, part of the fuel-air mixture is throttled off and the mixture entering the cylinders is less highly compressed. For satisfactory combustion, the spark must be further advanced beyond the advance produced by the centrifugal mechanism. To secure this additional advance, the vacuum line admits manifold vacuum to the vacuum passage, thereby allowing atmospheric pressure to push the diaphragm inward, compressing the return spring. This movement, through the linkage from the diaphragm,

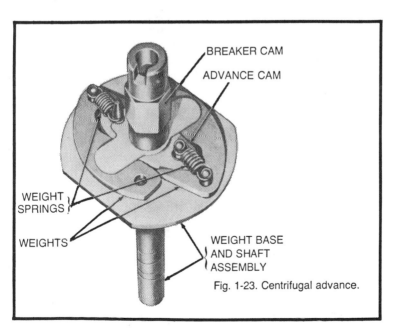

Fig. 1-23. Centrifugal advance.

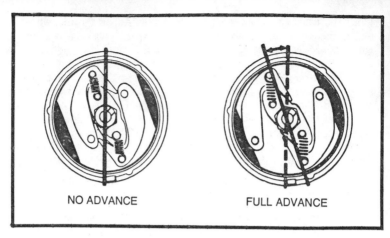

NO ADVANCE   FULL ADVANCE

Fig. 1-24. Action of centrifugal advance.

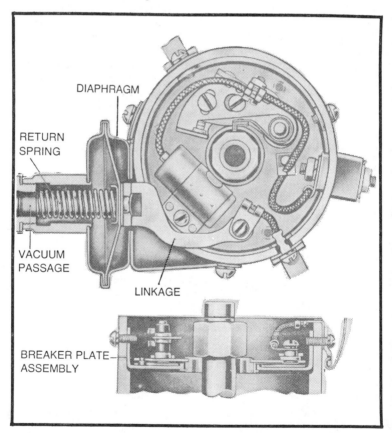

DIAPHRAGM

RETURN
SPRING

VACUUM
PASSAGE

LINKAGE

BREAKER PLATE
ASSEMBLY

Fig. 1-25. Vacuum advance.

causes the breaker plate to be turned ahead so that the contacts are opened and closed earlier in the cycle. This advances the spark. Usually, the vacuum line is tapped into the carburetor just at the upper edge of the throttle valve when it is closed. This permits no advance on idle, but causes a vacuum advance as the throttle valve is opened so its edge moves past the vacuum passage.

SOLID-STATE IGNITION

In this system (Fig. 1-26), two components have been removed, the capacitor and the distributor point set. Yet, both the solid-state and the breaker-type ignition systems retain the distributor rotor, a conventional-type ignition coil, and the distributor. The stoppage of current flow in the ignition coil primary windings causes its magnetic field to collapse. This electrical action induces a surge of high-voltage current in the coil's secondary windings, which in turn is delivered to the spark plugs in the correct order and at the precise time needed for firing the mixture in the combustion chamber most efficiently. Timing circuitry in the electronic module senses when the coil has fired and then redirects electric current to the primary circuit of the coil in order to repeat the firing process. In other words, this action is similar to what happens when the points close and open in the conventional breaker-point type of distributor. The dwell varies with engine speed. This is normal and cannot be altered, thus any measurement is meaningless.

Although the ignition coil for a solid-state system is similar to that of the conventional system, there are two items worth mentioning: The tower terminal is labeled BAT for battery and the other is labeled DEC for distributor electronic control; the use of any other ignition coil with the Ford

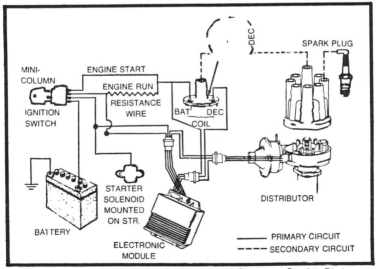

Fig. 1-26. A solid-state ignition. (Courtesy Ford Customer Service Div.)

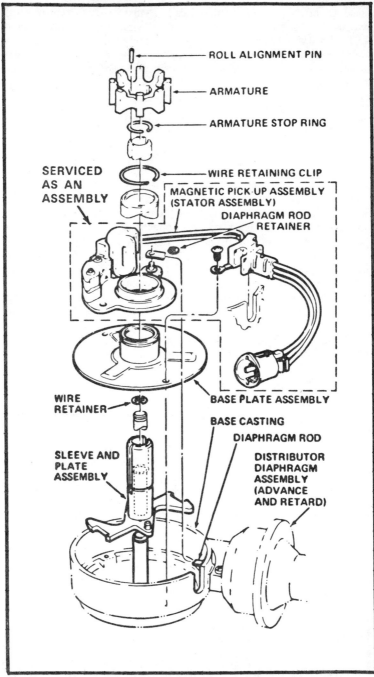

Fig. 1-27. The distributor used in a Ford solid-state ignition.

solid-state ignition system will cause the ignition system to malfunction, and possibly damage the electronic devices.

Solid-State Ignition Parts

Having discussed the basics of the solid-state ignition system and how it works, let's take a closer look at the parts that make up this new system and compare them with a conventional distributor. Note the exploded view in Fig. 1-27.

- Both the solid-state distributor and the breaker-point distributor are mounted and driven in the same way.
- The magnetic pickup (stator) assembly which provides the signal to the control module contains a permanent magnet. Also, part of the stator assembly is a pickup coil with many windings of fine wire.
- The armature is mounted on the sleeve and plate assembly. It has the same number of teeth as there are cylinders in the engine.
- High voltage from the coil to the spark plugs is directed through the distributor in the same way as in a conventional ignition system. Also, automatic advance or retard of the spark is controlled in the same way as in a conventional system. However, instead of moving the breaker-point plate, the plate for the magnetic pickup coil is moved.

Note that there has been no change in the shaft, gear, weights, springs, cap, and rotor. They are the same design for both solid-state and conventional ignition systems.

How the Solid-State Distributor Works

The breaker cam has been replaced with an armature resembling a rimless wheel with spokes or "teeth." As each tooth of the armature nears the permanent magnet, an electrical signal is generated in the pickup coil. Note Fig. 1-28A, which shows a top view of a solid-state distributor for a V-8 engine.

As each tooth of the armature moves away from the permanent magnet, an electrical signal of opposite polarity is generated in the pickup coil. Note in B that the armature tooth has rotated past the permanent magnet. As the armature tooth nears the permanent magnet and moves away (as the distributor shaft rotates), the signals generated go from positive to negative; however, when the armature tooth and the stator tip are in alignment, the signal is zero—between positive and negative. (See Fig. 1-28C.)

Whenever the armature tooth and the stator tip are in alignment, this zero signal tells the control module to turn off, producing the same effect in the coil primary circuit as the opening and closing of contacts in a conventional ignition system; it "breaks" the primary circuit.

The sudden stoppage of current in the ignition coil primary windings causes the magnetic field to collapse, thus inducing a high voltage in the coil secondary windings.

This high-voltage surge is delivered to the correct spark plug (the one ready to fire) by the distributor rotor, cap, and high-tension wiring (exactly as it happens in a distributor using contact points).

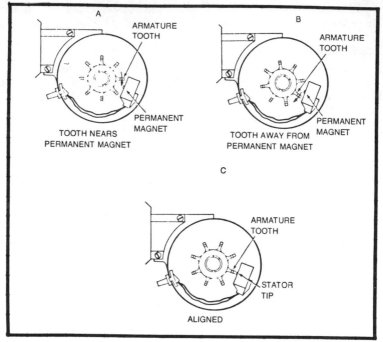

Fig. 1-28. Action of the armature, or reluctor, in a solid-state ingition. (Courtesy Ford Customer Service Div.)

Inside the electronic module is a timing circuit that turns the primary circuit on again to engage the coil for the next spark cycle. This can be compared to "dwell" in a conventional ignition system.

CAPACITIVE DISCHARGE IGNITION

Capacitive discharge (CD) ignitions are somewhat different in theory, and produce different results than magnetically controlled electronic ignitions. Magnetically controlled ignitions produce a long-lasting spark that produces relatively complete combustion and low emissions. The CD ignitions produce a short-lived high-voltage (40,000 volts or more) impulse capable of firing spark plugs under difficult conditions—even when plugs are fouled. Most kit-type electronic ignitions are CD units. An important characteristic of a CD system is that the distributor points are retained to control the ignition. However, since the points carry less current in CD systems, they encounter fewer problems.

These ignitions often employ a kind of electronic switch not discussed so far—the SCR.

The SCR

The SCR, like the transistor, is a solid-state device. It provides a current path that consists of a solid material—silicon. In fact, the full name of this device is *silicon controlled rectifier*. Its schematic symbol is shown in Fig. 1-29A.

SCRs are similar to transistors in that they have three terminals and can act as switches.

The SCR as an element in a simple circuit is shown schematically in Fig. 1-29B. What we have here is actually two circuits in one. There is a high-power circuit, consisting of the source battery and load, plus the anode and cathode of the SCR. There is a low-power control circuit consisting of the switch, gate battery, and the gate and cathode parts of the SCR.

The source battery in Fig. 1-29 is connected in the proper polarity to cause electrons to flow from the cathode to the anode of the SCR and through the complete high-power circuit. (A load is any useful device that consumes power.) However, the battery voltage would have to exceed a certain value—the breakdown voltage of the SCR—for conduction to take place. A battery is chosen with a voltage below this value, and conduction would never exceed a small value except for the action of the SCR gate. When the switch is closed and the gate voltage is applied to the SCR gate, the breakdown voltage of the SCR is lowered. Now, the source voltage is large enough for the SCR to conduct, completing the high-power circuit. Since the gate circuit consumes little power, the SCR permits a low-power circuit to switch on a high-power circuit.

The SCR, once turned on, is hard to turn off. The gate loses control, so that merely opening the switch is not enough to turn off the SCR. The SCR can be turned off if the polarity (direction) of the source voltage is reversed; that is what happens in a CD ignition system.

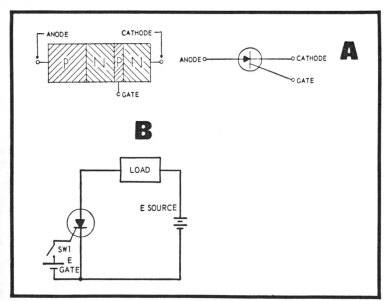

Fig. 1-29. In A, a pictorial and schematic representation of an SCR. In B, an SCR being used to control a high-power circuit.

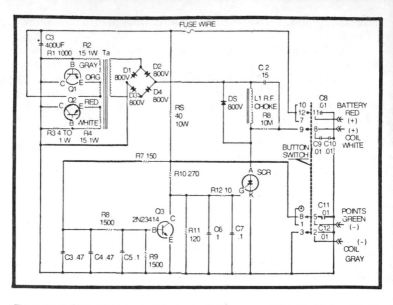

Fig. 1-30. A CD ignition system from Heath Company of Benton Harbor, Michigan.

CD Ignition Kit

The schematic of a Heath CP1060 kit-type ignition system is shown in Fig. 1-30. This circuit exemplifies CD ignitions. When the ignition switch is turned on and the points are closed, the nominal 12 volt DC supplied from the vehicle battery is applied to the converter circuit. This circuit consists of the primary winding of transformer T1 and transistors Q1 and Q2. The battery voltage causes a current flow through two paths of resistance. One path consists of resistors R1 and R2, and the other path consists of resistors R3 and R4. Because the combined resistance of R3 and R4 is less than the combined resistance of R1 and R2, a slightly larger current flows in the lower half of the primary winding of T1 than in its upper half.

Since the lower half of the primary winding carries a slightly higher current than does its upper half, voltages are developed that tend to increase the conduction of transistor Q2, while at the same time decreasing the conduction of transistor Q1. This action tends to reinforce the original current imbalance and results in voltages that further drive Q2 into conduction and Q1 into cutoff.

Transistor Q2 remains in conduction, with transistor Q1 cut off, until current through the lower half of the primary winding can no longer increase. This reduces the voltage supplied to transistor Q2 and causes it to reduce conduction. At the same time, the collapsing magnetic field of the transformer develops voltages that are of opposite polarity to the original voltages. These opposite polarity voltages bring transistor Q1 into conduction and, at the same time, drive transistor Q2 into cutoff. Capacitor C1 is used to filter out noise transients before they reach the converter circuit.

44

The alternate conduction of transistors Q1 and Q2 converts the 12V DC to an alternating signal of approximately 400V at the secondary of transformer T1. The diode bridge (diodes D1 through D4) changes the alternating signal to a DC potential of about 400V, which causes capacitor D2 to charge through the engine's ignition coil. During this same time, battery voltage is applied through resistor R5 to the points. Capacitors C6 and C7, along with resistor R12, serve as a filter to prevent false triggering of the SCR by any random voltage variations.

As the first cylinder comes up on a compression stroke and reaches the position where its spark plug should fire, the points open. At this time, the voltage through R10 and R12 turns the SCR on and short-circuits the power supply. The effect of this short circuit is reflected to the primary of T1, where it removes the drive from transistors Q1 and Q2 and stops the converter operation. The SCR also connects the positive side of capacitor C2 to the negative ignition coil connection and thus forms a closed circuit consisting of C2, the SCR, and the primary winding of the ignition coil. This connection allows capacitor C2 to deliver its stored charge to the ignition coil and causes the voltage in its primary winding to rise from zero to some 400V in approximately 2 microseconds.

In the closed circuit made up of capacitor C2, the SCR, and the primary winding of the ignition coil, a resonant tank circuit is formed between the

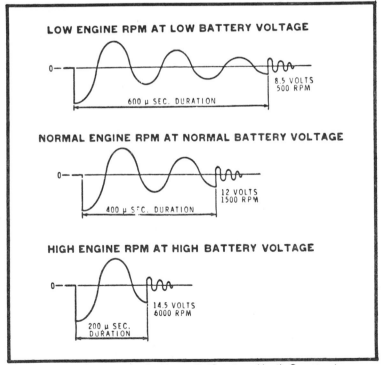

Fig. 1-31. Waveforms at the ignition coil. (Courtesy Heath Company)

primary winding and the capacitor. As capacitor C2 delivers its stored charge through the SCR to winding of the ignition coil, it creates a magnetic field within the coil. This field, representing stored energy, collapses when C2 reaches a zero charge, thus maintaining current through the primary winding of the ignition coil in the same direction as before. This current continues to flow in the circuit until C2 is charged in a reverse direction to approximately 300V. At this point, the current attempts to reverse and causes the SCR to turn off. The reverse voltage causes the diode bridge to conduct as a short circuit and discharges capacitor C2 back to zero from its reverse charge, and continues charging it to near its original voltage. This transfer of energy between the primary winding of the ignition coil and capacitor C2 continues until transistor Q3 is caused to turn on. Diode D5 and the RF choke are used to control the turn on characteristics of the SCR.

The turn on characteristics of transistor Q3 are determined by capacitors C3 and C4. Resistors R7, and R8, and R9 form a voltage divider that allows C3 and C4 to charge to about 6V. At low engine speed, or low battery voltage, these capacitors must charge for a longer period of time before they can reach the voltage necessary to turn on Q3. Under these conditions, Q3 remains cut off to allow capacitor C2 to deliver its full energy to the ignition coil. At high engine speeds, or high battery voltage, these capacitors retain some residual charge that enables them to reach the turn on voltage of Q3 sooner, thus lowering the overall amount of energy delivered to the ignition coil. Figure 1-31 shows a comparison of waveforms at the positive (+) side of the coil for different engine speeds and battery voltages. Capacitor C5 serves to prevent any erratic triggering of transistor Q3.

Chapter 2
CB and Other
Two-Way Radio Systems

A type of radio system with which one can both send and receive messages is a two-way radio system. The most popular form of two-way radio, of course, is CB, or citizens band. Other two-way radio activities—or *services* as the FCC calls them—include the land-mobile (police, fire, and business), marine, aviation, and amateur services. Later chapters in this book show how to install and operate equipment for all of these services.

CITIZENS RADIO SERVICE

Because citizens band (CB) equipment is inexpensive and almost anyone is eligible for a license, there are more licensed stations in the citizens radio service than in any of the other two-way radio services.

The purpose of CB radio is to provide for private short-distance radio communications service for the business or personal activities of licensees, for radio signaling, for the control of remote objects or devices by means of radio—all to the extent that these uses are not specifically prohibited.

Although all CB stations share a common purpose, there are three different classes of CB stations.

1. Class A station: A station in the citizens radio service licensed to be operated on an assigned frequency in the 460-470 MHz band and with input power of 60 watts (60W) or less.

2. Class C station: A station in the citizens radio service licensed to be operated on an authorized frequency in the 26.96-27.23 MHz band for the control of remote objects or devices by radio, or for the remote actuation of devices that are used solely as a means of attracting attention, or on an authorized frequency in the 72-76 MHz band for the radio control of models used for hobby purposes only.

47

3. Class D station: A station in the citizens radio service licensed to be operated on an authorized frequency in the 26.965-27.405 MHz band with output power of 4 W or less, and for radiotelephony only.

Class A stations may be authorized as mobile stations, base stations, fixed stations, or as stations to be operated at unspecified or temporary locations. Class C and D stations are authorized as mobile stations only; however, they may be operated at fixed locations under some circumstances.

Class A stations in this service will normally be authorized to transmit AM or FM telephony only. However, the use of tone signals or signaling devices solely to actuate receiver circuits such as tone-operated squelch or selective-calling circuits, the primary function of which is to establish or establish and maintain voice communications, is permitted. The use of tone signals solely to attract attention is prohibited.

Class C stations in this service are authorized to use amplitude tone modulation or on-off unmodulated carrier only, for the control or remote objects or devices by radio or for the remote actuation of devices that are used solely as a means of attracting attention. The transmission of any form of telegraphy, telephone, or record communications by a Class C station is prohibited. Telemetering, except for the transmission of simple, short-duration signals indicating the presence or absence of a condition or the occurrence of an event, is also prohibited.

Class D stations in the CB service are authorized to use amplitude voice modulation, including single sideband and reduced or suppressed carrier, for radiotelephone communications only. However, the use of tone signals or signaling devices solely to actuate receiver circuits such as tone-operated squelch or selective-calling circuits, the primary function of which is to establish or establish and maintain voice communications, is permitted. The use of tone signals solely to attract attention or for the control of remote objects or devices is prohibited.

Most of the existing CB radio stations are Class D stations. Some rules and other helpful recommendations from the FCC regarding the use of the Class D service (ordinary CB) follow:

- There are a total of 40 channels available to all CB stations on a shared basis.
- Channel 9 may be used only for communications involving immediate or potential emergency situations or assistance to motorists.
- Select any of the remaining 39 channels to conduct normal personal or business radio communications.
- To prevent unintentional "bleedover" interference to channel 9, the FCC recommends that all transmissions involving highway travelers be conducted on a channel other than channel 10, preferably one several channels away from channel 9.
- Nonsubstantive hobby use is permitted on all "free" channels.
- Communications are limited to 5 minutes duration. Waiting time between communications is 1 minute.

- Only your call letters need be broadcast at the beginning and end of each transmission. Handles can be used additionally for identification purposes, but are not ·substitutes for call letters.
- No linear amplifiers can be manufactured, sold or used. The presence of a linear amplifier on the premises will be considered "de facto" evidence of its use.
- No modulation boosting devices—mike amplifiers—can be used if they are capable of driving the transmitter beyond 200% modulation.
- Do not use CB radio in any connection with acts contrary to any Federal or local law or ordinance.
- Never transmit the "mayday" or any other international distress signal unless there is a confirmed, grave, and imminent danger to life or property.
- You should keep the following documents at all times with your CB radio: FCC Rules and Regulations (Part 95) and transmitter identification card, FCC Form 452-c.
- Promote good CB practice. Encourage other CBers to follow the above suggested practices.

10-CODES

Almost everyone knows that "10-4" means "yes" or "acknowledged" or "agreed." There are a good many other 10-codes used on the CB channels, and on the police and fire channels as well. Collectively, these expressions comprise a sort of spoken shorthand that facilitates and speeds up communications on the busy two-way radio channels. About 100 such expressions are given in Table 2-1, but only a handful are in regular use. In general, the 10-codes enhance communications, but overusing them defeats their purpose. If you ask for a 10-81, you may get very tired before you are able to arrange for a hotel room. It is best to stick to the expressions that persons listening are apt to know. The complete list is given in Table 2-1 so that you will have the feeling of possessing a 10-35.

Note that some of the expressions are designated APCO. This stands for Association of Public Safety Communications Officers. APCO originated the 10-code for the police and fire services. CBers adopted the APCO expressions, modified some, and added others of their own. The APCO version is the one you will hear when you are listening to the fire and police frequencies on a scanner.

LAND MOBILE RADIO SERVICES

In 1921 the Detroit police department experimented with radio communications, wryly using the call letters "KOP." Since that time, radio communications has become indispensable to the police and to other agencies engaged in maintaining public safcty, as well as to various industries and land transportation businesses.

Limited-range communications services are used by police, fire, highway, and forestry departments among other branches of state and local

Table 2-1. The 10 Codes Used on the CB and Police and Fire Frequencies.

CB-10 Code

10-1.... Unable to copy
Receiving poorly
Signal weak (APCO)
10-2.... Receiving well
Signal good (APCO)
10-3.... Stop transmitting (APCO)
10-4.... Acknowledge
Affirmative (APCO)
10-5.... Relay this message to (APCO)
10-6.... Busy, stand by (APCO)
10-7.... Leaving the air
Out of service (APCO)
10-8.... Back on the air
In service - subject to call (APCO)
10-9.... Repeat your message
Say again (APCO)
10-10.... Transmission completed
Negative (APCO)
10-11.... Speak slower
On duty (APCO)
10-12.... Stand by (Stop) (APCO)
I have visitors
10-13.... Advise weather and road conditions
Existing conditions (APCO)
10-14.... Message/information (APCO)
10-15.... Message delivered (APCO)
10-16.... Make pickup at
Reply to message (APCO)

10-17.... Urgent business
Enroute (APCO)
10-18.... Anything for us
Urgent (APCO)
10-19.... Return to
(In) contact (APCO)
10-20.... What is your location (APCO)
10-21.... Call   by phone (APCO)
10-22.... Disregard (APCO)
10-23.... Standby
10-24.... Arrived at scene (APCO)
10-25.... Assignment completed
Report to (meet) (APCO)
10-26.... Do you have contact with
Estimated time of arrival (APCO)
10-27.... Disregard last information
I am moving to channel
License/permit information (APCO)
10-28.... Identify your station
Ownership information (APCO)
10-29.... Records check (APCO)
10-30.... Time is up for contact
Illegal use of radio
10-31.... Danger/caution (APCO)
Pick up
10-32.... Units needed - specify (APCO)
10-33.... Emergency-help me quick (APCO)
I'll give you a radio check

10-34.... Trouble at this station
Time (APCO)
10-35.... Confidential information
10-36.... Correct time is
10-37.... Wrecker needed at
10-38.... Ambulance needed at
10-39.... Your message delivered
10-41.... Please tune to channel
10-42.... Traffic accident at
10-43.... Information
Traffic tie-up at
10-44.... I have a message for you
10-45.... All units within this range please report
10-46.... Assist motorist
10-47.... Emergency road repairs needed
10-50.... Accident - F, PI, PD
Break channel
10-51.... Wrecker needed
10-52.... Ambulance needed
10-53.... Road blocked
10-55.... Intoxicated driver
10-56.... Intoxicated pedestrian
10-57.... Hit & run accident-F, PI, PD
10-60.... What is next message number
10-62.... Unable to copy, use phone
10-63.... Prepare to make written copy
10-64.... Message for local delivery
Net directed to
10-65.... Awaiting your next message
Net clear

10-66.... Message cancellation
10-67.... All units comply message
10-70.... Fire alarm
10-71.... Proceed with transmission in sequence
10-73.... Speed trap
10-74.... Negative
10-75.... You are causing interference
10-77.... Negative contact
10-80.... Will meet at
10-81.... Reserve hotel room for
10-82.... Reserve motel room for
10-84.... My phone no. is
10-85.... My address is
10-88.... Advise phone number of
10-89.... Radio repairman needed at
10-90.... I have TVI
10-91.... Talk closer to microphone
10-92.... Your transmitter is out of adjustment
10-93.... Check my frequency this channel
10-94.... Test intermittently with normal modulation (voice)
10-95.... Test with no modulation (no voice) for
10-97.... Check (test) signal
10-99.... Unable to receive your signal
Mission completed - all units secure
10-100.. Nature calls
10-200.. Police needed at

governments. Doctors, hospitals, rescue organizations, and others also use land-mobile radio in providing emergency service to the public.

Industries such as utilities, petroleum, forest products, motion pictures, relay-press, manufacturers, industrial radio location, and small businesses also rely on such communications.

In land transportation, radio facilities are made available to railroads, taxicabs, the trucking industry, buses, and automobile emergency services. Land-mobile radio services have experienced great growth in recent years.

The land-mobile services are covered by Volume V of the FCC Rules and Regulations, which may be obtained for $7 from the Superintendent of Documents, Government Printing Office, Washington, DC 20402. Additions, amendments, and other supplementary material are sent automatically to purchasers of FCC Rules and Regulations.

Public Safety Radio Services

Police Radio Service. Types of stations in the police radio service include base and mobile, mobile relay, control, and zone and interzone stations. In addition, subject to certain limitations, installations may be made in vehicles which, in an emergency, would require the cooperation of the police, such as fire department vehicles, ambulances, emergency units of public utilities, lifeguard emergency units, and rural school buses.

Radio facilities authorized for public safety services must not be used to carry program material of any kind for use in connection with radio broadcasting, and must not be used to render a communications common carrier service except for stations in the special emergency radio service while being used to bridge gaps in common carrier wirelines.

Coordinated service may be rendered without cost to subscribers, or contributions to capital and operating expenses may be accepted by the licensee. Such contributions must be on a cost-sharing basis and prorated on an equitable basis among all persons who are parties to the cooperative arrangement. Records that reflect the cost of the service and its nonprofit, cost-sharing nature shall be maintained by the base station licensee and held available for inspection.

Arrangements may be made between two or more persons for the cooperative use of radio station facilities, provided all persons are eligible to hold licenses to operate the type of station shared.

A *zone* station is a fixed station that communicates with similar stations in the same area by means of AM continuous-wave (unmodulated) telegraphy. An *interzone* station uses AM telegraphy to communicate with interzone stations in other areas, or zones.

The frequency bands used by the police and the types of stations used in each band are given below.

    1.610-7.935 MHz—Base, mobile, zone, and interzone
    37.02-46.02 MHz—Base and mobile
    72.02-75.98 MHz—Operational fixed
    154.65-159.210 MHz—Base and mobile
    453.050-458.950 MHz—Base and mobile
    952-960 MHz—Operational fixed

Fire Radio Service. Fire department base stations are authorized to intercommunicate with mobile units on fire apparatus, with other stations in the public safety services, and with receivers at fixed locations. Relay stations will be authorized only where a showing is made that a fire radio system cannot function satisfactorily over necessary distances, or where, in an integrated system comprising two or more fire licensees, the number of necessary frequencies can be reduced.

Frequencies used fall in the following bands.

1.63 MHz—Base and mobile
33.42-46.5 MHz—Base, mobile, and fixed
72.02-75.98 MHz—Operational fixed
153.77-170.150 MHz—Base, mobile, and fixed
453.050-465.625 MHz—Mobile and base
952-960 MHz—Operational fixed

Forestry-Conservation Radio Service. Forestry-conservation base stations are authorized to intercommunicate with mobile units in the same service, with other stations in the public safety services, and with receivers at fixed locations. Relay stations will be authorized only where a showing is made that a forestry-conservation radio system cannot function satisfactorily over necessary distances, or where, in an integrated system comprising two or more forestry-conservation licensees, the number of necessary frequencies can be reduced.

Highway Maintenance Radio Service. Highway maintenance base stations are authorized to intercommunicate with other fixed and mobile stations in the same service, with other stations in the public safety services, and with receivers at fixed locations. Relay stations will be authorized only where a showing is made that a highway maintenance radio system cannot function satisfactorily over necessary distances, or where, in an integrated system comprising two or more highway maintenance licensees, the number of necessary frequencies can be reduced.

Special Emergency Radio Service. Special emergency stations are intended for use by persons having establishments in remote locations where other communications facilities are not available, relief agencies that have a disaster communications plan, physicians normally practicing in remote areas, ambulance services, beach patrols responsible for lifesaving, rural school buses, and communications common carriers. Special emergency base stations in the same service, with other stations in the public safety services, and with receivers at fixed locations. Transmission of nonemergency communications is strictly prohibited, except that common carriers may use communications temporarily for restoring a normal communications service disrupted as a result of an emergency. Operation of mobile systems in the special emergency service is limited to use of one frequency per system.

Local Government Radio Service. Official activities of cities and other municipalities, other than fire and police protection, may be aided by stations in this service.

Industrial Radio Services

The industrial radio services are used by certain enterprises that require radio communications to function safely or efficiently. Industrial radio services are power, petroleum, forest products, motion picture, relay-press, special industrial, business, industrial radiolocation, manufacturers, and telephone-maintenance radio.

Power Radio Service. Individuals or companies eligible to operate power radio systems are: those engaged in generating, transmitting, collecting, purifying, storing, or distributing—by means of wire or pipeline—electrical energy, artificial or natural gas, water, or steam for use by the public or use by the members of a corporation or organization; or, a nonprofit organization formed for the purpose of furnishing a radio communication service solely to persons who are actually engaged in one or more of those activities. Applicants and licensees must cooperate in the selection and use of assigned frequencies authorized. Each frequency or band is available on a shared basis only, and will not be assigned for the exclusive use of any one applicant. Such use may be restricted as to geographical area.

Mobile system frequencies have been made available on the basis of single-frequency operation. Not more than one frequency or band of frequencies is assigned to a single applicant, normally.

Petroleum Radio Service. Those eligible to operate stations in the petroleum radio service are persons engaged in prospecting for, producing, collecting, refining, or transporting (by means of pipelines) petroleum or petroleum products, including natural gas; or a nonprofit organization formed for the purpose of furnishing a radio communication service solely to persons who are actually engaged in one or more of those activities.

Forest Products Radio Service. Those eligible to operate stations in the forest products radio service are persons engaged in tree logging, tree farming, or related woods operations; or a nonprofit organization formed for the purpose of furnishing a radio communication service solely to persons who are actually engaged in one or more of those activities.

Motion Picture Radio Service. Eligible to operate stations in the motion picture radio service are persons engaged in the production or filming of motion pictures, or a nonprofit organization formed for the purpose of furnishing a radio communication service solely to persons engaged in one of these activities.

Relay-Press Radio Service. Those eligible to operate stations in the relay-press radio service are persons engaged in the publication of a newspaper or in the operation of an established press association; or, a nonprofit organization formed for the purpose of furnishing a radio communication service solely to persons who are actually engaged in one or more of these press-related activities.

Special Industrial Radio Service. Eligibility for special industrial radio service is limited to those engaged in plowing, soil conditioning, seeding, fertilizing, or harvesting for agricultural or forestry activities; spraying or dusting insecticides, herbicides, or fungicides in areas other than enclosed structures; livestock breeding; maintaining, patrolling, and repairing gas or liquid-transmission pipelines, tank cars, water or waste-disposal wells, industrial storage tanks, or distribution systems of public utilities;

acidizing, cementing, logging, perforating, or shooting activities, and similar services incidental to the drilling of new oil or gas wells, or the maintenance of production from established ones; supplying of chemicals, mud, tools, pipe, and other unique materials or equipment to the petroleum production industry as the primary activity of the applicant; delivering ice or fuel to the consumer in solid, liquid, or gaseous form for heating, lighting, refrigerating, or power-generating purposes by means other than pipelines or railroads; or delivering and pouring of ready-mixed concrete or hot asphalt mix.

Business Radio Service. The business radio service is something of a catchall for activities not otherwise encompassed by the industrial radio service, nor included in the public safety or transportation categories. Users of this service are: businesses, schools, charitable organizations, churches, hospitals, clinics, and medical associations, or anyone providing a nonprofit radiocommunications service for any of the above.

Industrial Radiolocation Radio Service. Allocations in this service are made to concerns that must establish a position, distance, or direction by means of radio for purposes besides navigation. Examples of such concerns are those engaged in geographical, geological, or geophysical activities. Frequency allocations for this service are in the LF, MF, VHF, and higher bands. Specific bands used are 1.605 to 1.8 MHz, and 3.23 to 3.4 MHz.

Manufacturers Radio Service. This is a service for factories, shipyards, or mills employing power-driven machinery and material-handling equipment to manufacture or merely assemble some product. Concerns that are primarily wholesalers, retailers, or providers of services are not eligible for licenses in this service, but are eligible for licenses in the business radio service.

Telephone Maintenance Radio Service. Assignments in this service are made to telephone companies and others providing wireline or radio communications services to the public for hire.

Land Transporation Radio Services

The various modes of land transportation—railroads, trucks, buses, and automobiles—are served by land transportation stations. Also, organizations such as the American Automobile Association are eligible for licensing in this service.

Motor-Carrier Radio Service. This service is used by truckers, bus lines, moving and storage companies, or by a nonprofit organization furnishing radio communications to any of these on a shared-cost basis.

The frequencies used in the motor-carrier radio service are in the bands listed below.

> 30.66-44.6 MHz—Base and mobile
> 72.02-75.98 MHz—Operational fixed
> 159.495-160.2 MHz—Base and mobile
> 452.325-457.875 MHz—Base and mobile
> 952-960 MHz—Operational fixed

Railroad Radio Service. Railroads were among the earliest industrial users of two-way radio. Early systems used by the railroads were of the inductive type. Signals were radiated a short distance from a wire running along the track to an antenna on the engine or caboose. Railroads now use modern equipment licensed in the railroad radio service. Amtrak and Auto Train are also eligible for licenses is this service.

72.02-75.98 MHz—Fixed
160.215-161.565 MHz—Base and mobile
452.325-457.95 MHz—Base and mobile

Taxicab Radio Service. Those eligible to operate stations in the taxicab radio service are persons regularly engaged in furnishing to the public a nonscheduled passenger land transportation service not operated over a regular route or between established terminals. An organization may be considered eligible for an authorization, although not directly engaged in the operation of taxicabs, provided that all persons who are members or shareholders would themselves be eligible. The frequencies used in the taxicab radio service are given below.

152.27-157.71 MHz—Base and mobile
452.05-457.5 MHz—Base and mobile

Automobile Emergency Radio Service. Those eligible to operate stations in this service are associations of owners of private automobiles that provide emergency road service, and public garages operating vehicles used in emergency road service. The frequencies of the automobile emergency road service are given below.

150.815-157.5 MHz—Base and mobile
452.925-457.6 MHz—Base and mobile

AVIATION RADIO SERVICES

The aviation radio services cover 17 classifications of aircraft and ground stations—some used for communications, some for navigation, and some for both.

Almost all stations licensed in the aviation radio services use amplitude modulation. There are some FM hand-held, vehicular, and base units, but they are licensed in the business radio service.

Pilots of departing aircraft communicate with the control tower on the appropriate ground control frequency for taxi and clearance information, and remain on that frequency until they are ready to request takeoff clearance. At that time, the pilot switches to the control tower frequency.

The airport ground control frequencies of 121.7 and 121.9 MHz are normally provided to eliminate frequency congestion on the tower frequency. Provision of these frequencies for ground control and their use by aircraft and airport utility vehicles operated on the surface of the airport thus provide a clear VHF channel for arriving and departing aircraft. They are used for issuance of taxi information, clearances, and other necessary contacts between the tower and aircraft or other vehicles operated at the airport. Normally, only one of these ground control frequencies is assigned for use at an airport; however, at locations where the amount of traffic so warrants, both frequencies may be assigned with one or the other designated as a clearance delivery frequency.

In general, control towers operate on different frequencies. The frequency at which a specific control tower operates may be obtained from aeronautical charts published by the U.S. Coast and Geodetic Survey, or from the Airman's Information Manual, published by the Federal Aviation Administration (FAA). There is, however, an additional "standard" frequency for transmission from control towers: 122.5 MHz.

A Flight Service Station (FSS) is a facility operated by the FAA to provide flight assistance to aircraft. Common FSS transmitting frequencies are 122.1, 122.2, 122.3, 122.6, and 123.6 MHz.

Unicom stations are privately owned stations used for communicating with private aircraft. These stations are frequently operated by aircraft sales and service organizations. Unicom stations do not issue clearances to aircraft, but at airports with no FAA control tower they provide an advisory service concerning air traffic, wind, altimeter setting, and so forth. At stations with a control tower, a Unicom station provides communications not related to safety of flight. A pilot might use such a station to order a taxicab before landing, for example. Unicoms operate at 122.8 MHz at airports with no control tower, and at 123.0 MHz at airports that have a control tower.

MARITIME RADIO SERVICE

One of the earliest practical applications of radio was summoning aid for ships in distress. This is, of course, still the most important application of the maritime radio service. Other important applications include: (1) obtaining navigational and weather information, (2) arranging for passage through locks, bridges, and waterways, (3) arranging rendezvous with tugboats and other vessels, and (4) making telephone calls to points on land.

Most ocean-going and Great Lakes vessels are required to have two-way radio facilities on board. Also, any vessel transporting more than six persons for hire and is operated on the open seas or in any U.S. tidewater adjacent to the open seas must have two-way radio. Ocean-going vessels also have radiotelegraph facilities. Many small boats in inland waterways and lakes have two-way radios, even though they are not required by the FCC.

Older marine units operate in the so-called 2-to-3 MHz band, which is actually a band of frequencies between 1.6 and 2.85 MHz. Specific frequencies in this band are reserved for specific purposes. For example, there are a number of frequencies for ship-to-ship communication. On these frequencies, direct communication is allowed between all ships licensed for this band. Other frequencies in the band are reserved for ship-to-shore communication. Communications with shore is restricted to contact with Coast Guard stations, limited private shore stations, and commercial shore stations.

Limited private shore stations may be operated by persons engaged in the operation of commercial vessels, and are used mainly for communicating with the vessels operated by the station owner. However, these stations may also sometimes communicate with the vessels of other licensees.

Commercial shore stations are used to provide telephone service to ships. These stations, concentrated along shorelines and waterways, are linked to the national telephone system. To receive calls, the shipboard receiver is left on, tuned to the frequency of the coastal station from which a call may be expected. (Special devices may be employed to keep the receiver quiet until an incoming call is received.)

Besides the 2-to-3 MHz band, there are other marine bands in the LF, HF, and VHF spectrums. The trend now is toward the use of the VHF band by stations that operate within about 50 miles of shore. This band includes marine channels between 156.3 and 157.4 MHz, and marine telephone channels between 161.9 and 162.0 MHz. Besides the natural advantages of VHF, that band has much less congestion.

Stations in the 2-to-3 MHz band have employed double-sideband AM for telephony, but the FCC has moved to require these stations to convert to single-sideband operation. Stations in the increasingly important VHF band use FM.

AMATEUR RADIO SERVICE

The purposes of the amateur radio service are to: serve the public as a voluntary, noncommercial communication service, particularly with respect to providing emergency communications; contribute to the advancement of the radio art; provide a reservoir of trained radio operators, technicians, and electronics experts; advance the skills of amateurs in both the technical and communication phases of the art; and contribute to international goodwill.

Relatively speaking, the amateur radio service is loosely regulated, and it is a tribute to amateurs that the amateur bands tend to be orderly. Frequencies authorized for amateur use range from 1800 kHz to well beyond 40 GHz. Fifteen different type of emissions are authorized, and just about every conceivable type of emission is actually used. Furthermore, the equipment used by amateurs, unlike the equipment used by other services, need not be approved specifically by the FCC. In fact, a great many amateurs build their own transmitters, antennas, and so on. The equipment used must, however, meet certain technical standards.

Every amateur station must have a fixed transmitter location. Only one fixed transmitter location will be authorized per call sign, but one amatuer may have many call signs. The fixed transmitter location is designated on the license for each amateur station. These are exceptions: When remote control is authorized, the location of the control position as well as the location of the remotely controlled transmitter are considered fixed transmitter locations and are so designated on the station license. Unless remote control of the transmitting apparatus is authorized, such apparatus must be operated only by a duly licensed amateur radio operator present at the location of such apparatus. Besides a fixed transmitter, many amateurs also operate portable (hand-carried) and mobile (vehicular, airborne, or shipboard) transmitters.

In addition to complying with all other applicable rules, an amateur mobile station operated on board a ship or aircraft must comply with all of the following special conditions: (a) The installation and operation of the amateur mobile station shall be approved by the master of the ship or captain of the aircraft; (b) the amateur mobile station shall be separate from and independent of all other radio equipment, if any, installed on board the same ship or aircraft; (c) the electrical installation of the amateur mobile station shal be in accord with the rules applicable to ships or aircraft as promulgated by the appropriate government agency; (d) the operation of the amateur mobile station shall not interfere with the efficient operation of any other radio equipment installed on board the same ship or aircraft; and (e) the amateur mobile station and its associated equipment shall not constitute a hazard to the safety of life or property.

An amateur station may be used to communicate only with other amateur stations, except that in emergencies or for test purposes it may also be used temporarily for communication with other classes of stations licensed by the Commission, and with the United States Government stations. Amateur stations may also be used to communicate with any radio station other than amateur which is authorized by the Commission to communicate with amateur stations. Amateur stations may be used also for transmitting signals or energy to receiving apparatus for the measurement of emissions, temporary observation of transmission phenomena, radio control of remote objects, and for similar experimental purposes.

NOISE REDUCTION AND TROUBLESHOOTING

Radio sets installed in cars, trucks, and RVs present special problems. Frequently trouble appears in the installation only while the vehicle is in motion. This is usually the result of a poor connection which shows up because of the vibration of the radio equipment. To locate the source of the trouble, check all cabling for looseness and improperly tightened plugs and connectors. While the equipment is in operation, the cabling should be wiggled and the basic components of the radio set should be rocked so that any abnormal result may be noted.

Before troubleshooting an installed radio set, you must first be familiar with the location of the basic components of the equipment and the switches, fuses, and circuit breakers. The radio equipment usually requires the same voltage as the electrical system of the vehicle, normally 12 volts.

OPERATING VEHICULAR EQUIPMENT

When operating radio equipment in a vehicle, observe the following cautions:

1. To prevent possible damage to the radio equipment, turn it off while the engine is racing. Turn off all radio equipment to prevent damage from abnormally high voltage.
2. Do not run the vehicle battery down by unnecessary or lengthy use of the radio equipment when the engine is not running. If long periods of testing are required, keep the vehicle engine running at a speed that maintains the battery charge.
3. Be sure to turn off all equipment when not in use. Do not turn off the radio equipment by just turning off the ignition switch; turn off *all* individual switches.

ELECTRICAL NOISE

One of the most difficult troubles to sectionalize in a vehicular installation is noise, especially the noise generated by the vehicle ignition system.

Ordinarily, the vehicle electrical system is adequately shielded and bonded, to effectively eliminate all noise generated in the vehicle, and also to prevent interference with other radio equipment in the immediate vicinity. Sometimes, the bonding breaks loose and causes noise. Before a radio set is removed from a vehicle for repairs because of noise, first eliminate the vehicle itself as a possible source of noise by turning the engine off.

A visual inspection can reveal such obvious faults as loose or broken bonding or shielding, loose plugs, couplings, ground clamps, and loose or disconnected noise bypass capacitors on the generator or voltage regulator. In general, any portion of the shielding on the installation that might permit exposed wiring to radiate noise from ignition or the generator systems should be examined carefully. After one has had experience with a certain vehicle, he may be able to recognize its own peculiar noise characteristics. In some cases, the noise source can be located by performing certain simple tests which are given in the paragraphs that follow.

Sectionalizing Electrical Noise Troubles

When noise interference enters the radio set, the vehicle should be moved to an open space away from high-tension power lines, radio installations, other vehicles, and electrical equipment that could cause noise disturbances.

Interference Present with Vehicle Engine Off. If noise is present in the radio *receiver* output when the engine is turned off and all other electrical accessories are turned off (including any other radio sets), disconnect the antenna and ground the antenna terminal of the set being checked. If the noise continues, the trouble is in the radio set. Reconnect the antenna; if gounding the antenna terminal stops the noise, the noise was coming in on the antenna. If other radio equipment using a similar frequency range is installed in the vehicle, repeat this test to verify that the noise is caused externally. If the noise is external, move the vehicle to a new location, free from electrical noise, before continuing with further tests.

If no noise is present in the receiver with the antenna connected, turn on each of the accessories (including any other radio equipment) one at a time, and note whether any noise appears. Turn off each accessory before turning on the next one so that the vehicle battery is not drained excessively. If noise appears, check any input noise filter capacitors or chokes associated with the accessory producing the noise. With the accessory turned on, disconnect one side of the filter capacitor temporarily; if the noise level rises, the capacitor in question is good.

Interference with Engine Running and Vehicle Stopped. If a rhythmic, periodic popping noise is heard that changes in frequency as the speed of the engine is changed, the disturbance is probably caused by the ignition system. If trouble is traced to the ignition system, check all wiring for proper shielding and bonding. Tighten all cable clamps and connectors and see that all ground wires are securely in place. In general, ignition noise is caused by defective bonding; loose, burned or improperly gapped spark plugs; or burned distributor points.

Run the engine at a fast idle and momentarily turn off the ignition switch. If the noise in the receiver is reduced for the interval that the ignition is off, the trouble is in the ignition system. A typical induction-coil ignition system with noise-reduction components is shown in Fig. 2-1.

Generator Noise. If a whining, squealing sound is heard in the receiver while the engine is running, the cause may be a defective generator. Run the engine at a fast idle speed, then let it slow down. If the interference decreases and goes to a lower pitch as the engine and generator slow down, the generator is probably causing the noise. See that the generator is not loose. Check that the bypass capacitor is properly grounded. See that all leads connected to the generator are tight. A charging system with noise-reduction components appears in Fig. 2-2.

Regulator Noise. If an intermittent clicking sound is heard in the receiver, the interference may be coming from a faulty voltage regulator. The spring that holds the armature open when the solenoid is not energized may have lost some of its tension, and it will cause the armature contact to be intermittent. On certain types of regulators, this spring can be bent back to its normal position. All wiring to and from the regulator should be checked for positive contact, and the bypass capacitors should be bridged with good ones to eliminate them as a possible cause of noise. All shielding and bonding to the regulator should be checked for positive mechanical contact.

Interference Caused by Static Noises. Certain types of interference can occur when the engine is turned off and the vehicle is still in motion, as when going down a grade. If excessive, irregular, cracking noises occur in the receiver only when the vehicle is in motion, the trouble could be caused by a loose connection or static electricity generated by friction. See that all ground straps and lockwashers are secure and making good contact. Any two metal surfaces that are not bonded together and that are scraping or rubbing can cause scratch noises. Correct this by connecting all suspected points with heavy braid shielding.

Unusual Noise Sources

Gauge noise is characterized by a hissing or crackling sound. Tapping the face of each gauge while the engine is running usually reveals which

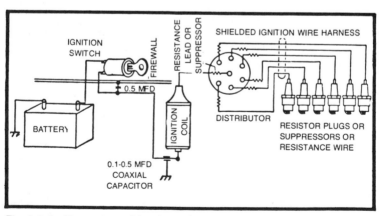

Fig. 2-1. Ignition system with noise-reduction components.

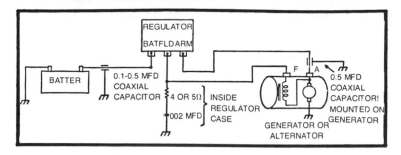

Fig. 2-2. Charging system with noise-reduction components.

gauge is at fault. Bypass the gauge lead to ground with a 0.5 μF capacitor connected close to the sensing element.

Use bonding braid to electrically bond the hood and each corner of the engine block to the vehicle's frame to eliminate static caused by metal-to-metal friction. Treat electrically noisy tires with antistatic powder. Use front-wheel static collectors for irregular popping sounds that disappear when the brakes are applied. Finally, use a heavily graphited penetrating oil on the exhaust pipes and muffler supports if they seem to be producing noise.

Chapter 3
Basic Skills

The efficient and reliable installation of electronic units in cars and other conveyances requires a variety of skills. One must be able to trace wiring diagrams so as to find the proper points to make connections. One must know how to actually make the connections, and this involves soldering and the use of connectors. And one must be able to use tools effectively to accomplish mounting and the other purely mechanical procedures required.

WIRING DIAGRAMS

The wiring diagram presents detailed circuitry information concerning electrical and electronics systems. A master wiring diagram is a single diagram that shows all the wiring in a complete system or in a car. In most cases, this diagram would prove to be too large to be usable; it is normally broken down into logical functional sections, each of which may be further subdivided into circuit diagrams. By breaking a system into individual circuit diagrams, each individual circuit may be presented in greater detail. The increased detail provides for easier circuit tracing, testing, and maintenance.

Wiring diagrams fall into two basic classes—chassis wiring and interconnecting diagrams—each with specific purposes and many variations in appearance (depending on application).

Figure 3-1A is an example of one type chassis wiring diagram commonly used. This drawing shows the physical layout of the electrical or electronic unit, and all component parts and interconnecting tie points. Each indicated part is identified by reference designation number, thus facilitating use of the parts list to determine values and other data. (The values of resistors, capacitors, or other components are normally not indicated on wiring diagrams.) The polarity of semiconductor diodes and of the polarized capacitor is shown. Since this specific diagram shows physical layout and

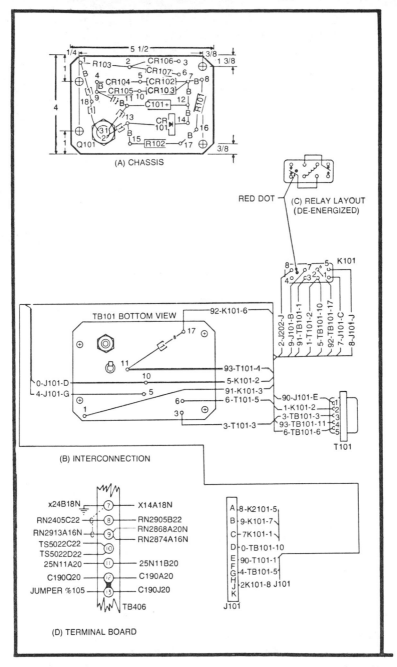

Fig. 3-1. Wiring diagrams. (A) Chassis wiring. (B) Interconnection wiring. (C) Sealed-component (relay) layout. (D) Terminal board.

dimensioning details for mounting holes, it could be used as an assembly drawing and also as an installation drawing.

Figure 3-1B shows the reverse side of the same mounting board, together with the wiring interconnections to other components. Actual positioning of circuit components is not indicated, and wire bundles are represented as single lines with the separate wires entering at an angle. The angle indicates the direction to follow in tracing the circuit to locate the other end of the wire (3-1D).

The wire identification coding on this aircraft diagram consists of a three-part designation. The first part is a number representing the color code of the wire. (Automobile wiring diagrams designate color coding by abbreviations of the actual colors.) The second is the reference part designation number of the item to which the wire is connected. The last is the designation of the specific terminal to which connection is made.

Figure 3-1C, while not a wiring diagram, illustrates a method commonly used to show some functional aspect of sealed or special components.

One way of identifying wires is shown in Fig. 3-2, a diagram of the front-end wiring of a Chrysler Corporation model. The circuit-designation letter identifies the basic function of the unit in accordance with a code. The letter is L, for *lighting*, in this case. There are a number of wires in the lighting system, and the one pointed out is No. 6. Note that this is *not* the gauge of the wire. Wires that are segmented by the use of splices, etc., are given a letter segment designation, A in the present case. Note that after the junction with wire L6B from the left park and turn signal, the wire becomes simply L6 (see Fig. 3-2).

The numbers and letters after the hyphen in the Chrysler system give the wire gauge (18 gauge here) and the wire color (black with a yellow tracer, or stripe). The color code and connector symbols used by Chrylser are shown in Fig. 3-3.

Many of the symbols used in automotive wiring diagrams look much like the parts they represent (consider, for example, the horn symbols in Fig. 3-2). Other symbols are used that are more abstract, and these are discussed along with schematic diagrams in a later section.

A single connector, consisting of a plug and receptable, may connect several wires together. Each of the terminals on the plug is numbered on the wiring diagram to help identify it on the actual connector. For example, the bulkhead connector in Fig. 3-2 bears the numbers 12-16, 11-15, 10-14, and 9-13. The drawing in Fig. 3-4, which represents the actual bulkhead connector (located in the car's firewall, between the engine compartment and dashboard area), is similarly numbered. The numbers also help one to follow wires from one diagram to another—for example, from an engine-compartment diagram to an instrument-panel diagram.

General Motors Corporation identifies wires by a slightly different manner in its diagrams, as the Chevrolet diagram in Fig. 3-5 shows. The numbers and letters along the wires tell the wire size and color. A designation such as 14-3 means that there are three 14-gauge wires running together as a cable. The circuits in the Chevrolet diagram are identified by numbers in boxes at connection points, according to the code in Table 3-1.

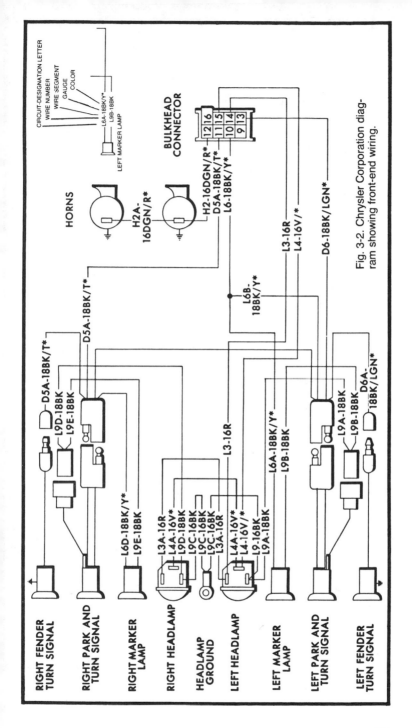

Fig. 3-2. Chrysler Corporation diagram showing front-end wiring.

65

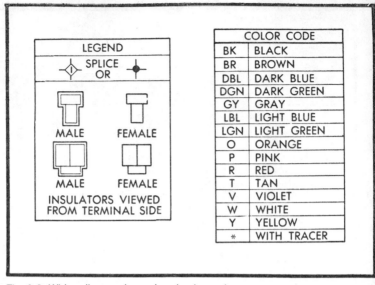

Fig. 3-3. Wiring-diagram legend and color code.

SCHEMATICS

The main purpose of the schematic diagram is to establish the electrical operation of a particular system. It is not drawn to scale, and it shows none of the actual construction details of the system (such as a physical location within a car, physical layout of components, wire routing, or any other physical detail) not essential to understanding circuit operation.

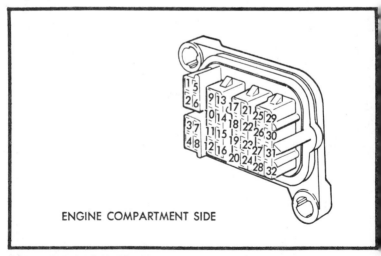

Fig. 3-4. Sketch of a bulkhead connector.

Electromechanical Drawings

Electromechanical devices such as relays, horns, and electric motors are quite common in cars. For a complete understannding of these units, neither an electrical drawing nor a mechanical drawing would be sufficient, and confusion would result from the use of two drawings. Therefore a combination type of drawing, using some aspects of each component type, is used. These drawings are usually simplified both electrically and mechanically, and only those items essential to the operation are indicated on the drawing.

Figures 3-2 and 3-5 both show several types of lamps, or lights. Note that the Chrysler drawing shows the configuration of the connector of a

Table 3-1. Electrical-Circuit Identification for Chevrolet.

Circuit Number	Circuit Color	Circuit Name	Circuit Number	Circuit Color	Circuit Name
2	Red	Feed, Battery – Unfused	40	Orange	Feed, Battery – Fused
3	Pink	Feed, Ign. Sw. "On" Controlled – Unfused	41	Brown–White	Feed, Ign. Sw. Accsy. Controlled – Fused
3	White,–Purple & Orange	Primary Ignition Voltage – Dropping Resistor. .38 ohm/ft.	43	Yellow	Radio Feed
3	White–Red & Black	Primary Ignition Voltage – Dropping Resistor 30 ohm./ft.	44	Dark Green	Instrument and Panel Lights, Feed (Usually Light Switch to Fuse)
4	Brown	Feed, Ign. Sw. Accy. Controlled – Unfused	45	Black	Marker and Clearance Lamps (Trailers – ICC Requirement)
5	Purple	Neutral Safety Switch Feed or Neutral Safety Switch to Relay (Truck) or Relay to Ignition Switch (Truck) (Auto. Trans.)	46	Dark Blue	Rear Seat Speaker Feed from Radio Single or Rt., Stereo
			47	Dark Blue	Auxiliary Circuits (Trailer)
			49	Gray	Mod. Assembly to Control
			50	Brown	Blower Switch – Feed
6	Purple	Starter Solenoid Feed	51	Yellow	Blower Feed – Low
7	Yellow	Primary Ignition Resistance Bypass	52	Orange	Blower Feed – High
8	Gray	Instrument and Panel Lights, (Fused No. 44 Circuit)	55	Orange	Kick-Down on Automatic Transmission
9	Brown	Tail and License Lamp, Forward Side Marker Lamps	56	Tan	Amplifier to Heatsink (Radio)
		Tail, Clearance and Marker Lamps (Trailers)	59	Dark Green	Compressor to Air Conditioning Switch
			60	Orange–Black	Feed, Battery – Circuit Breaker Protected
10	Light Blue	Dimmer Switch Feed	63	Tan	Blower–Switch Control – Low and Feed
11	Light Green	Headlamp, High Beam			
12	Tan	Headlamp, Low Beam	65	Purple	Blower Motor to Relay
13	Purple	Front Parking Lamps	70	Red–White	Feed, Relay Controlled Circuit Breaker Protected
14	Light Blue	L.H. Indicator and Front Direction Light	72	Light Blue	Blower Switch Medium to Blower Resistor
15	Dark Blue	R.H. Indicator and Front Direction Light	75	Dark Green	Back-Up Switch or Parking Brake Alarm Feed
16	Purple	Direction Signal Switch, Feed from Flasher	80	Pink–Black	Feed-Key Warning Buzzer
17	White	Direction Signal Switch, Feed from Stop Switch	90	Pink–Black	Feed, Cutout Sw. Controlled Circuit Breaker Protected
18	Yellow	Stop and Direction Lamp or Direction Lamp Only–Rear L.H.	91	Black	Windshield Wiper – Low
19	Dark Green	Stop and Direction Lamp, or Direction Lamp Only - Rear R.H.	92	Light Blue	Windshield Wiper – High
			93	Yellow	Windshield Wiper Motor Feed
20	Red	Stop Lamp (Trailer)	94	Dark Blue	Windshield Washer Switch to Windshield Washer
22	White	Ground – Direct (Trailer Wiring)			
24	Light Green	Back-Up Lamp	101	Dark Blue	Resistor Output to Blower Relay
25	Brown	Generator or Generator Armature to Voltage Regulator "A" (Includes Generator Telltale Circuit) or Regulator to Ignition Switch (Truck)	102	White	SI Alternator Regulator Sensing Circuit
			105	Black	Ammeter – Generator
			106	Black–White	Ammeter – Battery
26	Dark Blue	Field Circuit (F) (Gen. Reg.)	107	Dark Blue	Over-Speed Warning Light
27	Brown	Traffic Hazard Switch, Feed from Flasher	111	Black	Buzzer to Low Air Pressure or Vacuum Switch
28	Black	Horn Switch	112	Dark Green White	Telltale Temperature Gauge (Hot)
29	Dark Green	Horn Feed			
30	Tan	Fuel Gauge to Tank Unit	119	White	Generator (Alternator) to Regulator
31	Dark Blue	Oil Pressure – Engine	120	Black	Power Trans. Relay to Thermo Switch (Truck)
32	Yellow	Map Light			
33	Tan	Warning Light – Brake Alarm	121	Brown	Tachometer to Coil
34	Purple	Fog or Drive Lamp	124	Black	Switch on Shift Lever to Adapter, or to Motor on Rear Axle (Low), or to Adaptor (Low) (Truck)
35	Dark Green	Telltale Temp. Gauge (Hot), or Std. Temp. – Readable Gauge.			
38	Dark Blue	Flasher, Fuse Feed	125	Light Green	Switch to Diff. Lock-Out Valve (Truck)
39	Pink–Black	Feed, Ign.Sw. "On" Controlled Fused	126	Brown	Diesel Ignition – Buzzer to No. 4 "L" on Voltage Regulator (Truck)

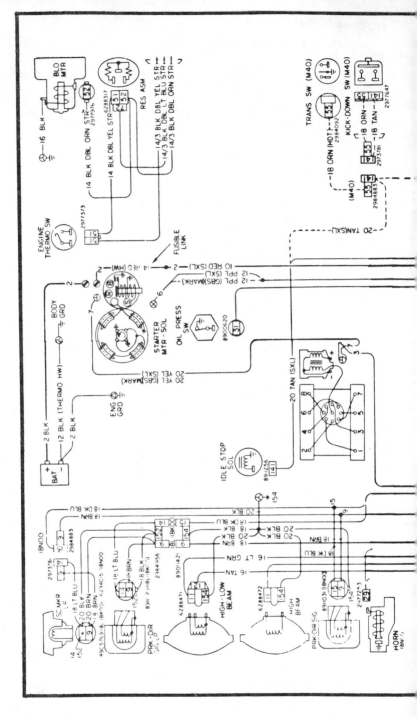

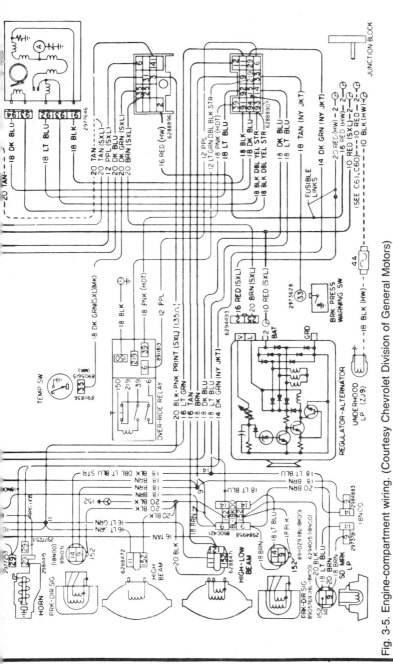

Fig. 3-5. Engine-compartment wiring. (Courtesy Chevrolet Division of General Motors)

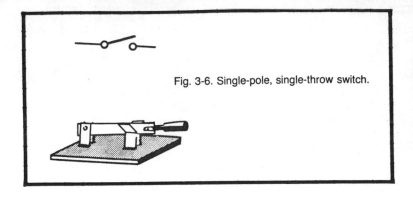

Fig. 3-6. Single-pole, single-throw switch.

headlamp, and the Chevy drawing shows the actual shape of the lamp. The Chevy drawing also shows the filament of the lamp as a coil of wire, which, of course, it is. Also, both drawings show directional-signal lamps and other lamps differently than headlamps. On a schematic, a single general symbol is used for all lamps.

Some other symbols used on wiring diagrams and on schematics for radios and other accessories are shown in Fig. 3-6 through 3-20 along with representations of the items symbolized. The pictures, in some cases, do not represent automotive components, but they illustrate the principles of the items symbolized.

Switches

A simple single-pole, single-throw knife switch is shown in Fig. 3-6. It makes and breaks a connection for one line, and only at one point. The symbol shows two small circles indicating contact points and a straight line indicating the movable throw switch.

Figure 3-7 illustrates a double-pole, double-throw switch. It is similar to the single-throw switch, except that it has two blade switches mechanically connected, and can make and break contact in two different positions.

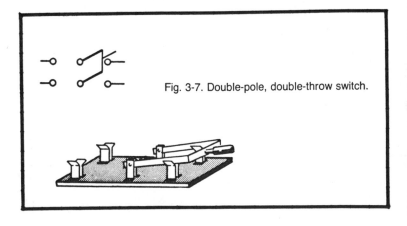

Fig. 3-7. Double-pole, double-throw switch.

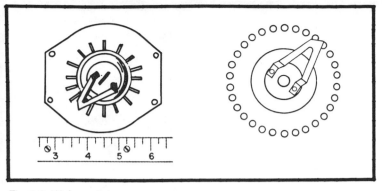

Fig. 3-8. Wafer switch.

A wafer switch is shown in Fig. 3-8. The symbol indicates a 3-pole, 3-circuit switch with two nonshorting and one shorting moving contact.

Fuses

Two types of fuses are illustrated in Fig. 3-9. There are many types of fuses but they all have the same function: to protect a circuit from overloading. The two types of fuses shown are the cartridge type and the screw plug type. When a circuit draws too much current, a metal wire or strip within the fuse melts, interrupting the flow of current. Note that the symbol is the same regardless of fuse type.

Circuit Breakers

Circuit breakers perform the same function as fuses. Instead of melting, however, they merely open the contacts, thereby interrupting the flow of current. Three types of circuit breakers and their symbols are shown in Fig. 3-10.

Resistors

One of the most common electronic components is the resistor. A resistor opposes the flow of electrons. In some substances—such as glass, rubber, and cotton—resistance is great enough to stop the flow completely. Three types of resistors and their symbols are illustrated in Fig. 3-11.

Figure 3-12 illustrates the potentiometer and its symbol. A potentiometer is a variable resistor commonly used as a volume control for radios and televisions.

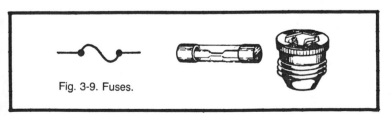

Fig. 3-9. Fuses.

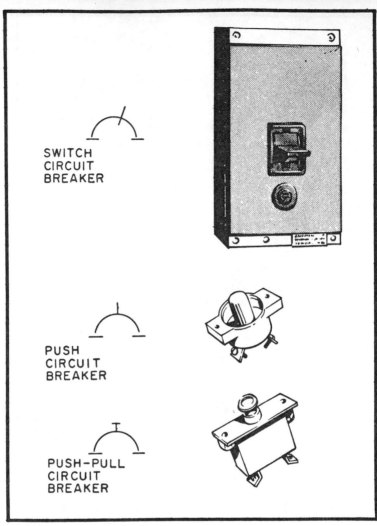

SWITCH
CIRCUIT
BREAKER

PUSH
CIRCUIT
BREAKER

PUSH-PULL
CIRCUIT
BREAKER

Fig. 3-10. Circuit breakers.

A rheostat and its symbol are shown in Fig. 3-13. A rheostat is another form of a variable resistor. It is similar in construction to a potentiometer. A rheostat is almost always wirewound, whereas a potentiometer can be either of wire or carbon. A rheostat normally is used as a resistor in a lighting system to vary the light intensity.

Capacitors

Three types of capacitors and their symbols are illustrated in Fig. 3-14. Capacitors are devices used to store or release electrons as they are needed in the circuit.

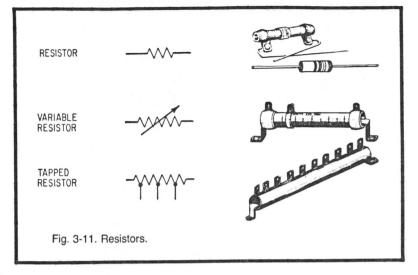

RESISTOR

VARIABLE
RESISTOR

TAPPED
RESISTOR

Fig. 3-11. Resistors.

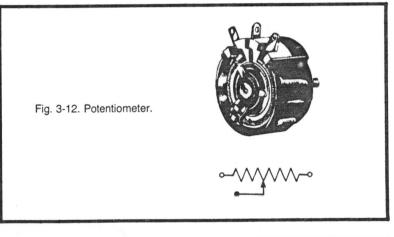

Fig. 3-12. Potentiometer.

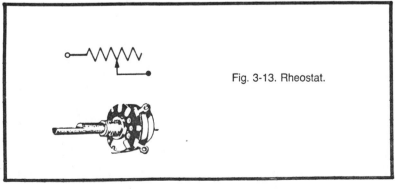

Fig. 3-13. Rheostat.

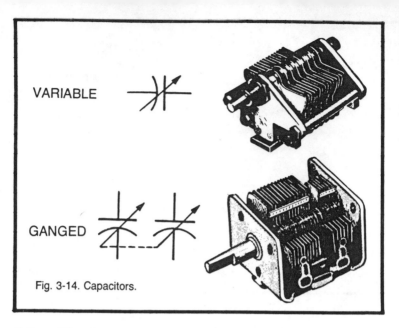

VARIABLE

GANGED

Fig. 3-14. Capacitors.

Coils and Transformers

Figure 3-15 illustrates two types of inductors (coils) and their symbols. One is an air-core coil type, and the other is an iron-core, usually referred to as a "choke." Inductors are used to smooth out variations in current flow.

Two types of transformers and their symbols are shown in Fig. 3-16. Transformers are used to step AC voltage up or down, or to transfer AC voltage from the primary to the secondary.

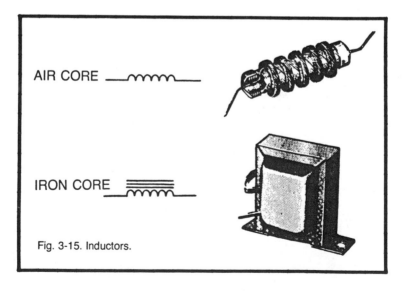

AIR CORE

IRON CORE

Fig. 3-15. Inductors.

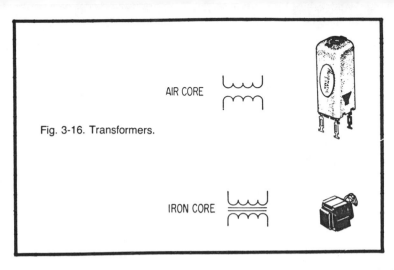

AIR CORE

Fig. 3-16. Transformers.

IRON CORE

Figure 3-17 illustrates a relay coil (with contacts) and its symbol. A relay is an electromagnetic switching device energized by a coil through which an electric current flows, causing its core to act as an electromagnet. A familiar example of an electromagnet is a low voltage wall thermostat for a furnace or heating plant for a home; the thermostat contains a switch that is actuated by a bimetallic element. The bimetallic element is affected by temperature changes within a room. In turn, any change in temperature actuates the relay.

Rectifiers

Figure 3-18 shows a rectifier and its symbol. Rectifiers are used in radio and television to convert AC line voltage to DC voltage, and in alternators to convert the generated AC to the DC needed by the battery and the car's electrical system.

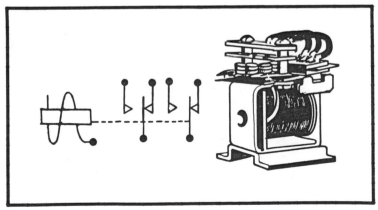

Fig. 3-17. Relay coil with contacts.

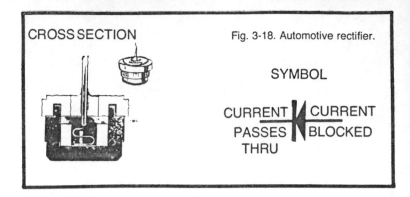

CROSS SECTION

Fig. 3-18. Automotive rectifier.

SYMBOL

CURRENT   CURRENT
PASSES   BLOCKED
THRU

Transistors

Illustrated in Fig. 3-19 are two types of transistors, the PNP and the NPN. Note that the difference in the symbols is the direction in which the arrowhead is pointing.

Miscellaneous

Figure 3-20 illustrates the symbols used for ground and wire connections, and several of the more common types of equipment and their symbols used in communications. You are familiar with headphones, microphones, loudspeakers, and wire and ground connections; they need no explanation.

SOLDERING

Soldering operations are a vital part of electrical installation procedures. Some practice is required to develop proficiency in soldering techniques; however, practice serves no good purpose unless it is founded upon a thorough understanidng of basic principles. This discussion is devoted to providing information regarding some important aspects of soldering operations.

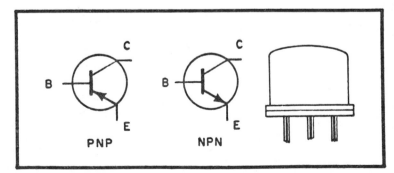

Fig. 3-19. Transistors.

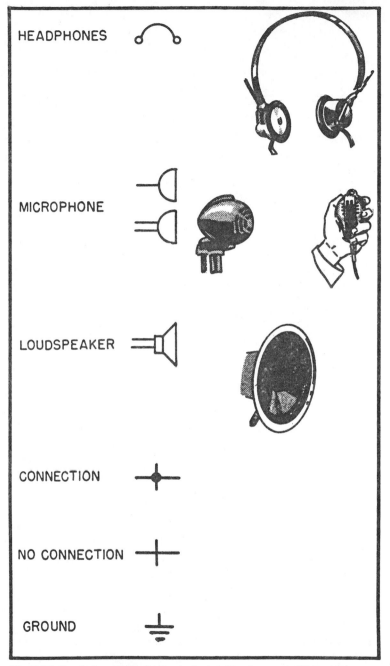

HEADPHONES

MICROPHONE

LOUDSPEAKER

CONNECTION

NO CONNECTION

GROUND

Fig. 3-20. Symbols and illustrations of ground, wire connections, and some common communication accessories.

Soldering Iron

The iron or gun should be selected on the basis of the heat required. A 100-watt gun is satisfactory for splices and terminals; a 30-watt iron should be used for repair of printed circuits.

The tip should be free of oxide, scale, and carbonized flux. Solder dissolves copper gradually, causing pits to develop in the tip. Such pits should be filed smooth and the tip retinned (i.e., coated with solder).

During use, periodically wipe the tip to remove excess solder and flux.

Temperature

Both the solder and the connection must be heated to a high enough temperature for the solder to flow. If either is heated inadequately, "cold" solder joints result. Cold joints are mechanically weak and highly resistive. On the other hand, exceeding the flow point temperature is likely to damage the parts being soldered. Various types of solder flow at different temperatures. When soldering, it is necessary to select a solder that flows at a temperature low enough to avoid damage to the part being soldered, or to any other part or material in the immediate vicinity.

The duration of high-heat conditions is almost as important as the temperature. Insulation and many other materials used in electrical equipment are susceptible to damage from heat. These materials are damaged if exposed to excessively high temperatures, or deteriorate if exposed to less drastically elevated temperatures for prolonged periods. The time and temperature limitations depend on many factors—the kind and amount of metal involved, the degree of cleanliness, the ability of the material to withstand heat, and transfer and dissipation characteristics of the surroundings.

Soldering Process

Cleanliness is a prime prerequisite for efficient, effective soldering. Solder will not adhere to dirty, greasy, or oxidized surfaces. Heated metals oxidize rapidly, and the oxide must be removed prior to soldering. Oxides, scale, and dirt can be removed by mechanical means (such as scraping or cutting with an abrasive) or by chemical means. Grease or oil can be removed by a suitable solvent. Clean the joint immediately prior to the actual soldering operation.

Items to be soldered should normally be tinned before making mechanical connection. When the surface has been properly cleaned, a thin, even coating of flux may be placed over the connection to prevent oxidation while the parts are being heated to soldering temperature. Rosin-core solder is usually preferred for automotive work, but a separate flux may be used instead. Acid-core solder or acid flux should be avoided because of its corrosive action.

The tinning on a wire should extend only far enough to take advantage of the depth of the terminal or receptacle. Tinning or solder on wires subject to flexing causes stiffness and may result in breakage.

The tinned surfaces to be joined should be shaped and fitted, then mechanically joined to make a good mechanical and electrical contact. They must be held still with no relative movement of the parts while being soldered. Any motion between parts will probably result in a poor connection.

Soldered Connections

Frequent arguments occur concerning the proper method of making soldered connections to terminals and binding posts. For many years it was considered necessary to wrap the lead tightly around the terminal, in order to provide maximum mechanical support and strength.

A major testing organizaton tested many standard capacitors and resistors soldered to terminals of various types. The joints were then subjected to vibrations far in excess of those encountered in passenger vehicles. The connections were made with various degrees of wrapping around the terminals, with main reliance for physical strength being placed on the solder. As a result of this test and others conducted by other organizations, the joints illustrated in Fig. 3-21 are recommended. Wrappings of 3/8 to 3/4 inch are recommended so that the joint need not be held during the application and cooling of the solder.

Excessive wrapping of leads results in increased heat requirements, more strain on parts, greater difficulty of inspection, greater difficulty of assembly and disassembly of the joints, and increased danger of breaking the parts or terminals during desoldering operations. Insufficient wrapping may result in poor solder joints due to movement of the lead during soldering.

The areas to be jointed must first be heated to, or slightly above, the flow temperature of the solder. Solder is then applied to the heated area. Only enough solder should be used to make a satisfactory joint. When the joint is adequately heated, the solder will flow evenly. Heavy fillets or beads should be avoided. Excessive temperature tends to carbonize flux, thus

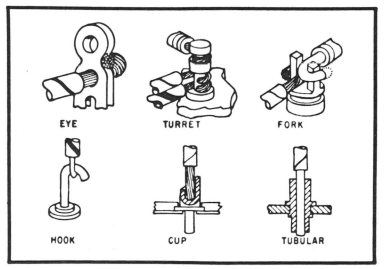

EYE   TURRET   FORK

HOOK   CUP   TUBULAR

Fig. 3-21. Recommended methods of making connections.

hindering the soldering operation. Allow the joint to cool in the air. Do not use a liquid to hasten cooling.

If, for any reason, a satisfactory joint is not initially obtained, the joint must be taken apart, the surfaces cleaned, excess solder removed, and the entire soldering operation (except tinning) repeated.

After the joint has cooled, all flux residues should be removed. Any flux residue remaining on the surface of electrical contacts may collect dirt and promote arcing at a later time. This cleaning is necessary even though rosin-core solder is used.

Connections should never be soldered or desoldered while equipment power is on or while the circuit is under test. Always discharge any capacitors in the circuit prior to any soldering operation.

PRINTED CIRCUITS

Printed circuits—originally used in radios and other electronic devices—are formed by depositing conducting material on the surface of an insulated sheet. A printed method of producing circuits is both cheaper and more accurate than hand wiring.

In automobiles, the instrument cluster on which the various gauges and indicator lights are mounted is something of a nerve center; the circuitry is complex and the connections are many. It is here that printed circuitry is used. Also, many of the accessories discussed in this book are available in kit form. To assemble them, it is necessary to know how to deal with printed circuits.

Printed Circuit Repairs

Although procedures for printed circuits are similar to those for conventional circuits, more skill and care is required. Any defective part should be pinpointed by analysis of the symptoms before attempting to trace trouble on a printed-circuit board.

Breaks in the foil strip can cause either permanent or intermittent trouble. When searching for a break in the foil, first determine whether the strips have a protective coating. If so, it will be necessary to penetrate this film when checking for continuity. A needlepoint test probe works very nicely.

Use a multimeter or an ohmmeter for checking continuity. The meter should pass no more than one milliampere. If the circuit contains diodes or other semiconductors, observe proper biasing conditions.

First check for continuity from one end to the other of each strip (being sure to penetrate the protective coating and, at the same time, careful not to damage the strip). If an open is indicated, move the probes toward each other, one at a time, until continuity is indicated. The break then lies between the last two positions of that probe. Carefully inspect the break to determine its extent and the repair process needed.

If the break is small, carefully scrape away any protective coating, clean the area with a stiff-bristle brush and an approved solvent, and flow solder over the break. If there is any indication that the strip might peel loose from the board, bridge the break with a small section of bare wire. Apply solder along the entire length of the wire to bond it firmly to the conducting strip. Keep the solder within the limits of the strip being repaired, to prevent overflow onto or near an adjacent strip. Be careful not to overheat any part of the area.

If a strip is burned out or fused, cut and remove the damaged strip and replace it with a wire soldered from terminal to terminal on the board.

A printed circuit board can withstand only a limited amount of flexing. Excessive flexing breaks the board, which must then be replaced.

After repairs are completed, thoroughly clean the board, restore the protective coating, and allow to dry thoroughly before reinstalling or applying power to the circuit.

Removal of parts from a printed circuit board often requires the simultaneous movement of several soldered connections. Use the pencil-type soldering iron and special tips whenever possible. Remove excess solder from each connection, using a scribe or needle probe to scrape away the solder. Do not rock or pry the part to loosen the connection—rocking may damage the board. When all connections are free, simply lift the part.

To install the replacement part, solder each connection separately, in turn.

CONDUCTORS AND TERMINALS

Although modern technical literature has been emphasizing the use of printed circuits, conductors are still important as signal- or current-carrying devices. (For the purpose of this discussion the term *conductor* will refer to both wire and cable.) As a significant part of operating equipment, conductors deserve appropriate attention.

Wire

For wire-replacement work, the wiring diagram for the particular car should first be consulted, since it lists the wire type used. When this information cannot be obtained, you must select the correct conductor needed for the job. The three major factors involved in this selection, in descending order of importance, are size, insulation, and the characteristics required to satisfy specific environments in which the wire must function.

Conductor Size

For DC applications, the allowable voltage drop and current-carrying capacity govern the choice of wire size. Wire size is, therefore, basically a function of the current or the allowable resistance, except when this results in a very small conductor size.

Small conductors are difficult to handle and are subject to breakage in soldering or due to vibration. Experience has shown that these difficulties may be avoided by using No. 22 AWG or larger wire for general circuit wiring. Solid wire should be used only for short jumper connections not exceeding 3 inches in length, unless the parts being connected are solidly mounted and not subject to vibration.

Insulation

A wide variety of insulating material is available, which makes its specification particularly important. Since each insulation has its peculiar characteristics, no single type is always suitable for general usage. The major insulation requirements include good dielectric strength; high insulation resistance (internal and surface); wide temperature range (with high softening and low "brittle" points); flexibility; color stability; and resistance to abrasion, crushing, moisture, fungus, burning, oil, and acids.

Some of the insulations used for general hookup wire include butadiene styrene copolymers, Celanese, fiberglass, nylon, vinyl, polyvinyl chloride, cellulose acetate, polystyrene, polyethylene, Teflon, and various silicone-treated materials. An insulation wall thickness of not less than 0.013 inch is recommended for all wiring within the confines of an enclosure or where mechanical protection is provided. Where wiring is exposed or subject to wear or abrasion, heavier insulation is required.

Environmental factors such as temperature, humidity, vibration, contaminants, and corrosive elements must be taken into consideration. These requirements are included as a part of the specification for the equipment where the wire is to be used.

Terminals

Since most automotive wires are stranded, terminal lugs are used to hold the strands together and facilitate fastening the wires to terminal studs. The terminals are either soldered or crimped. Soldered terminals are found most often on foreign cars. Replacement terminals must be of the size and type specified on the electrical wiring diagram for the particular models. Soldered and crimped terminals may be used interchangeably, but both must have the same amperage capacity and the same sized hole in the lug.

The increased use of "crimp on" solderless terminals is based to a large degree upon the limitations of soldered terminals. The quality of soldered connections depends mainly upon the operator's skill. As pointed out previously, temperature, flux, cleanliness, oxides, and insulation damage due to heat also contribute to defective connections.

Solderless terminals require little operator skill. Another advantage is that a crimping tool does not require an external power source. This allows

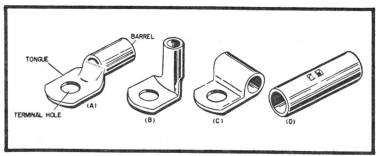

Fig. 3-22. Types of solderless terminals.

Fig. 3-23. Insulation-piercing connector, especially useful for making solderless connections to car wiring.

terminals to be installed at minimum cost. The connections are made more rapidly, are cleaner, and are more uniform.

The basic types of terminals are shown in Fig. 3-22. Part A shows the straight type; B, the right-angle type; C, the flag type; and D, the splice type. There are also variations on these types, such as the use of a slot instead of a terminal hole, 3- and 4-way splice-type connectors, and others.

A further refinement of the solderless terminals is the insulated type; the barrel of the terminal (Fig. 3-22) is enclosed in an insulation. The insulation is compressed along with the terminal barrel when crimping, but is not damaged in the process. This eliminates the necessity of taping or placing an insulating sleeve over the joint.

Splicing

A splice, other than one made with a crimp on splice or connector, is an emergency measure only. Solder may or may not be used, as circumstances warrant, but in any case the splice should provide a solid electrical and mechanical joint. The splice should be taped to give insulation equivalent to the rest of the cable. Make a permanent repair as soon as possible.

A new wire can be permanently spliced to an existing wire, without breaking the existing wire, by using an insulation-piercing connector as shown in Fig. 3-23. The procedure for connecting wire HR in the figure to wire HB, without breaking HB, is as follows:

1. Insert the end of wire HR into hole A of the connector as far as it will go.
2. Insert wire HB into slot B of the connector. Make sure wire HR does not slip out of slot A.
3. Hold the two wires in place and, with a pair of pliers, press the metal tab down into the connector.
4. Fold the flap over the connector and squeeze the flap until it snaps into place.

Terminal Blocks

Terminal blocks are made from an insulating material which supports and insulates a series of terminals from each other as well as from ground. They provide a means of installing connections to various electrical devices.

83

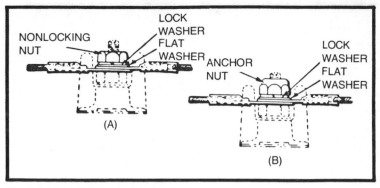

Fig. 3-24. Installation of cable terminals.

Two methods of attaching terminals to terminal blocks are illustrated in Fig. 3-24. In A of the figure, a standard nonlocking nut is used. In this method of installation, the use of a lockwasher is necessary. The preferred method is shown in B of the figure. An anchor, or self-locking nut, is used and the lockwasher is retained for additional insurance. Anchor nuts are especially desirable in areas of high vibration. In both installations, it is required that a flatwasher be employed, as shown in the drawing.

USING TOOLS

Almost any installation of an electronic unit in a vehicle involves the use of tools—screwdrivers, pliers, wrenches, soldering equipment, drills, etc. Most operations with these tools are not difficult to perform safely and successfully. However, there are some purely mechanical procedures that require extra care to produce good results and be accomplished safely. A few such procedures are discussed next.

Metal-cutting operations—such as cutting with a hacksaw or making holes with a twist drill—require a certain amount of care and skill, and they can be dangerous. Such operations are frequently necessary in the course of an installation—in making or modifying mounting brackets for a tape player, for instance. Stripping wires is not as dangerous, but it must be done properly if reliable connections are to be made.

Sawing

The hacksaw is often used improperly. Although it can be used with limited success by an inexperienced person, a little thought and study given to its proper use will result in faster and better work with less dulling and breaking of blades and less risk of injury.

Good work with a hacksaw depends not only upon the proper use of the saw, but also upon the proper selection of the blades for the work to be done. Figure 3-25 will help you select the proper blade to use when sawing metal with a hacksaw. Coarse blades with fewer teeth per inch cut faster and are less liable to choke up with chips. However, finer blades with more teeth per inch are necessary when thin sections are being cut. The selection should be

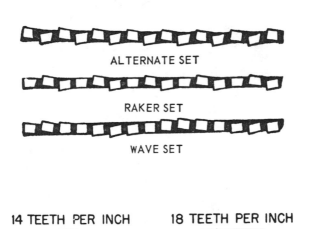

ALTERNATE SET

RAKER SET

WAVE SET

14 TEETH PER INCH

FOR LARGE SECTIONS
OF MILD MATERIAL

18 TEETH PER INCH

FOR LARGE SECTIONS
OF TOUGH STEEL

24 TEETH PER INCH

FOR ANGLE IRON, HEAVY
PIPE, BRASS, COPPER

32 TEETH PER INCH

FOR THIN TUBING

**KEEP AT LEAST TWO TEETH CUTTING
TO AVOID THIS**

Fig. 3-25. Selecting the proper hacksaw blade.

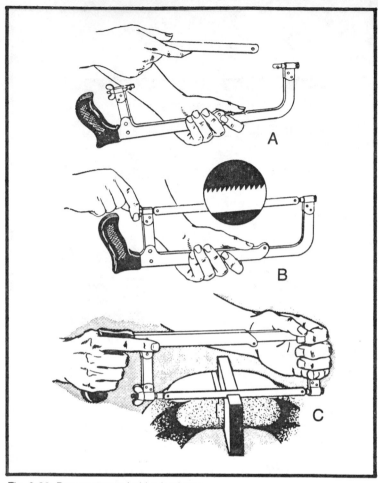

Fig. 3-26. Proper way to hold a hacksaw.

made so that as each tooth starts its cut, the tooth ahead of it will still be cutting.

To make the cut, first install the blade in the hacksaw frame so that the teeth point away from the handle of the hacksaw. (Hand hacksaws cut on the push stroke.) Tighten the wingnut so that the blade is definitely under tension. This helps make straight cuts.

Place the material to be cut in a vise. A minimum of overhang will reduce vibration, give a better cut, and lengthen the life of the blade. Have the layout line outside of the vise jaw so that the line is visible while you work.

The proper method of holding the hacksaw is depicted in Fig. 3-26. See how the index finger of the right hand, pointed forward, aids in guiding the frame.

Fig. 3-27. Making a long cut near the edge of stock.

When cutting, let your body sway ahead and back with each stroke. Apply pressure on the forward stroke, which is the cutting stroke, but not on the return stroke. From 40 to 50 strokes per minute is the usual speed. Long, slow, steady strokes are preferred.

For long cuts (Fig. 3-27), rotate the blade in the frame so that the length of the cut is not limited by the depth of the frame. Hold the work with the layout line close to the vise jaws, raising the work in the vise as the sawing proceeds.

Saw thin metal as shown in Fig. 3-28. Notice the long angle at which the blade enters the saw groove (kerf). This permits several teeth to be cutting at the same time.

Metal which is too thin to be held, as shown in Fig. 3-28, can be placed between blocks of wood, as shown in Fig. 3-29. The wood provides support for several teeth as they are cutting. Without the wood, as shown at B in Fig. 3-29, teeth will be broken due to excessive vibration of the stock and because individual teeth have to absorb the full power of the stroke.

Cut thin metal with layout lines on the face by using a piece of wood behind it (Fig. 3-30). Hold the wood and the metal in the jaws of the vise, using a C-clamp when necessary. The wood block helps support the blade and produces a smoother cut. Using the wood only in back of the metal permits the layout lines to be seen.

Hacksaw Safety. The main danger in using hacksaws is injury to your hand if the blade breaks. The blade will break if too much pressure is applied,

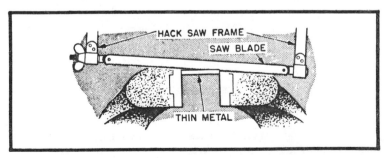

Fig. 3-28. Cutting thin metal with a hacksaw.

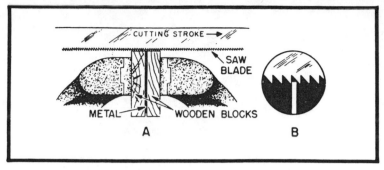

Fig. 3-29. Cutting thin metal between two wooden blocks.

if the saw is twisted, if the cutting speed is too fast, or if the blade becomes loose in the frame. Additionally, if the work is not tight in the vise, it will sometimes slip, twisting the blade enough to break it.

Drilling

In drilling any metal, there are several general steps to be followed. First, mark the exact location of the hole. Second, secure the work properly. Then use the correct cutting speed and appropriate cutting oil or other coolant, where applicable. Finally, apply pressure on the drill properly. It is assumed that you have selected the correct drill size.

Locating the Hole. The exact location of the hole must be marked with a centerpunch. The punch mark forms a seat for the drill point, thus ensuring accuracy. Without the punch mark, the drill may have a tendency to "walk off" before it begins to cut into the metal.

Holding the Work. Most work is held for drilling by some mechanical means such as a vise or clamps. It is *mandatory* that the work be *well secured*. If not, the work or stock may rotate at high speed or fly loose, and become a high-speed projectile, endangering all persons within range. Various securing procedures are discussed in the following paragraphs.

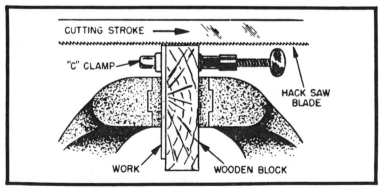

Fig. 3-30. Cutting thin metal using wooden block with layout lines.

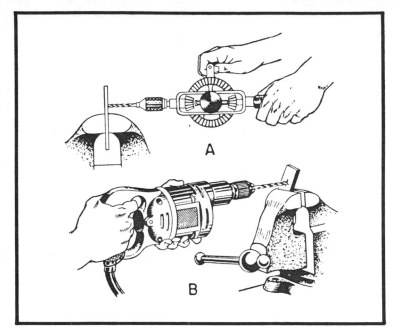

Fig. 3-31. Holding small pieces in a vise for drilling.

When drilling small pieces, such as a mounting bracket with a hand-held drill, it is best to hold the work in a vise so that the axis of the drill is horizontal (Fig. 3-31). This position provides better control of the drilling operation and will tend to ensure a hole which will be square with the surface of the work.

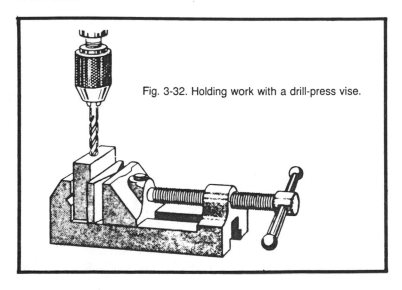

Fig. 3-32. Holding work with a drill-press vise.

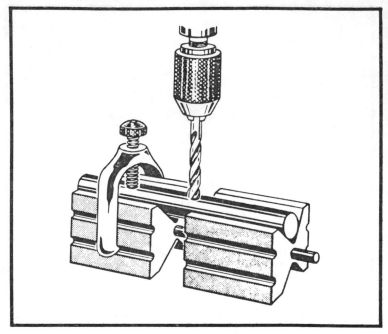

Fig. 3-33. Holding work in V-blocks.

When drilling small pieces with a drill press, hold the work either in a drill press vise (Fig. 3-32), or between V-blocks (Fig. 3-33). CAUTION: Be sure to fasten the drill press vise or V-block to the drill press table.

To hold thin metal, place it on a block of wood to provide support directly beneath the intended hole. This support will also help minimize drill breakage when the feed pressure is applied. Secure the C-clamp as shown in Fig. 3-34 and drill through the metal and into the wood. Stop drilling when wood chips appear, to avoid damage to the drill table.

Drilling Hints. It is necessary to use a cutting oil to lubricate and cool the drill when drilling steel and wrought iron. Cast iron, aluminum, brass and other soft metals may be drilled dry, although at high drilling speeds it is advisable to use some heat conducting medium to cool these metals. Compressed air, water, and lard oil are examples of such cooling media. Be sure to use protective goggles whenever you use compressed air.

Always apply pressure on a line which goes straight through the axis of the drill. (Side pressure will enlarge the hole and can break the drill.)

Keep the drill steady and apply enough pressure to keep it cutting. Too much pressure will overload the motor; too little pressure will merely cause the drill to "polish" instead of cut. This will quickly dull the cutting edges of the drill. You will know the pressure is correct when the drill bites continuously without overloading the drill motor.

When drilling large holes, do it in stages. A pilot hole is a good idea, since it serves as a guide for the larger drill and helps to increase accuracy.

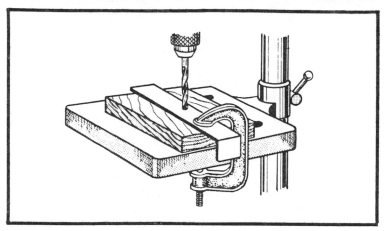

Fig. 3-34. Holding thin metal for drilling.

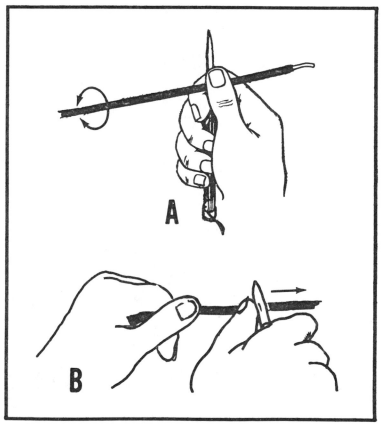

Fig. 3-35. Stripping insulated wire with a pocket knife.

Stripping Insulated Wire

Insulation may be stripped from wire by using one of several tools. However, a pocketknife or side-cutting pliers are generally used for this work.

When using a pocketknife for stripping insulation, hold the wire in one hand and the knife in the other. Use your thumb to roll the wire over the blade of the knife to cut the insulation almost to the wire itself. See Fig. 3-35A. Then pull off or strip the short piece of insulation from the end of the wire. Because any nick in the wire will eventually cause a break, it is important not to cut clear through the insulation. By not cutting completely through the insulation, the blade of the knife never comes into contact with the wire itself, thus preventing any possible injury to the surface of the wire. However, cutting nearly through the insulation weakens it sufficiently so that the insualtion can be stripped from the wire.

Another way to perform this operation is, while holding the wire in one hand and the pocketknife in the other, hold the wire against the knife blade and cut the insulation off with several strokes of the blade, working around the wire with each successive stroke. See Fig. 3-35B. Notice that the blade

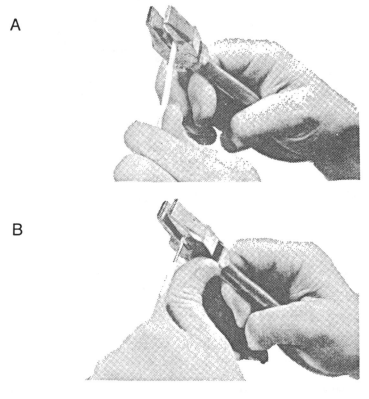

A

B

Fig. 3-36. Stripping insulated wire with side-cutting pliers.

A

B

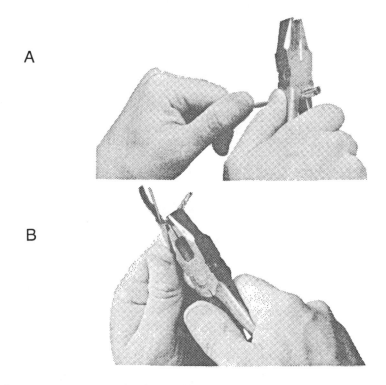

Fig. 3-37. Alternate procedure for stripping insulated wire with side-cutting pliers.

is held almost flat against the insulation. This low angle prevents the blade from cutting into the wire itself.

Insulated wire can be stripped with the side-cutting pliers, as shown in Fig. 3-36, by nicking the insulation all around, being careful not to break through to the wire itself, and stripping the short length of insulation off the end of the wire. Notice that, in Fig. 3-36A, the man's index finger is wedged between the handle of the pliers close to the joint. This affords better control over the cutting edges so that there is less chance that the insulation will be broken completely through. When the nick has been made all around the wire, press your thumb against the side of the pliers to break the insulation at the nick and, without changing the grip of the pliers, strip it off the end. See Fig. 3-36B. Care must be exercised to avoid cutting too far through the insulation and nicking the wire.

Insulated solid wire can also be stripped as shown in Fig. 3-37. Starting at the end of the wire, grip and crush the insulation between the flat places on the inside of the handles close to the hinged joint. In Fig. 3-37A, the insulation has been crushed and the wire exposed. Then, as shown in Fig. 3-37B, grasp the insulation close to the end of the crushed portion and tear it off. Although this method leaves a rather ragged appearing end on the remaining insulation, there is no possibility of damaging the wire.

Chapter 4

Secrets of a Good

Automotive Installation

A large part of any electronics installation in a car is the disassembly of various car structures. For example, before you can install a speaker in a door, you must remove the trim panel of the door. This is not a trivial task. In fact, how to remove most interior parts of a car is not an obvious procedure. The fasteners used by the auto makers are tenacious and often well hidden. It's not that that auto makers are trying to be devious or difficult, it's just that the fasteners must be hidden for appearance's sake and must be tenacious for reliability's sake. Also, when an industry annually makes 10 million units as complicated as a car, the product must be designed for ease of assembly at the factory rather than for the convenience of mechanics or electronics installers.

DOOR TRIM PANELS—FORD

The following door and rear-quarter trim panel removal and installation procedures generally apply to all Ford car lines. If some steps do not apply to the particular vehicle being worked on, proceed to the next step.

Removal

1. Remove the door lock pushbutton control knob and garnish moulding.
2. Remove the window-regulator handle retaining screw access cover and remove the screw and regulator handle (Fig. 4-1).
3. Remove the door latch handle retaining screw access cover (if so equipped) and remove the screw(s) from the door latch handle.
4. Remove the screws from the armrest door pull cup area (if so equipped).
5. Remove the retaining screws from the armrest assembly, disconnect switch wiring (if so equipped) and remove the armrest (Fig. 4-2).

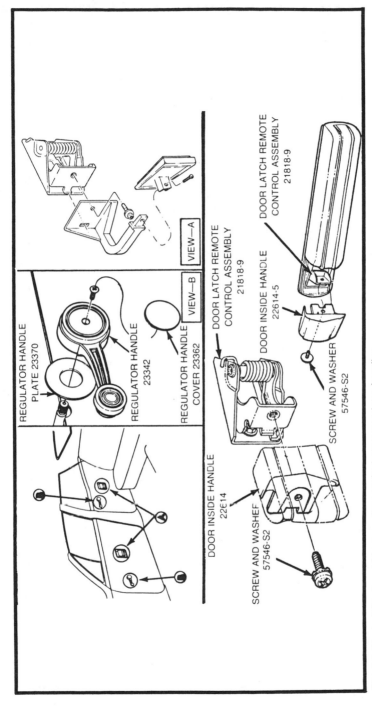

REGULATOR HANDLE PLATE 23370

REGULATOR HANDLE 23342

REGULATOR HANDLE COVER 23362

VIEW—A

VIEW—B

DOOR LATCH REMOTE CONTROL ASSEMBLY 21818-9

DOOR INSIDE HANDLE 22614

SCREW AND WASHER 57546-S2

DOOR LATCH REMOTE CONTROL ASSEMBLY 21818-9

DOOR INSIDE HANDLE 22614-5

SCREW AND WASHER 57546-S2

Fig. 4-1. Typical Ford and Mercury door and window-regulator handles

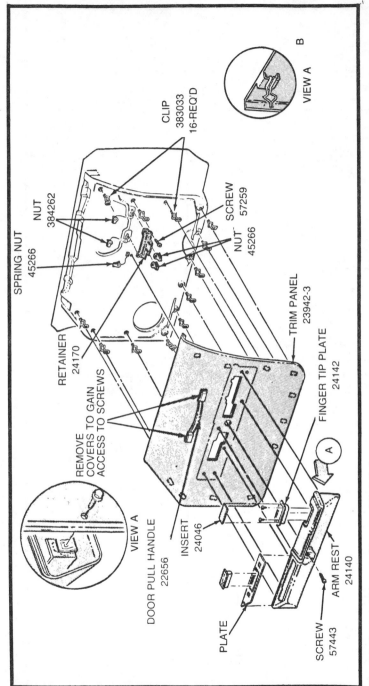

Fig. 4-2. Ford and Mercury trim-panel installations.

CLIP
383033
16-REQ'D

NUT
384262

SCREW
57259

SPRING NUT

NUT
45266

RETAINER
24170

REMOVE
COVERS TO GAIN
ACCESS TO SCREWS

TRIM PANEL
23942-3

FINGER TIP PLATE
24142

VIEW A

DOOR PULL HANDLE
22656

INSERT
24046

A

ARM REST
24140

PLATE

SCREW
57443

VIEW A

B

6. Remove the mirror remote control bezel nut.

7. Remove the door trim panel retaining screws.

8. With a putty knife or similar tool, pry the trim panel retaining clips (inset) from the door inner panel and disengage the panel.

9. Disconnect all wiring (if so equipped) and remove the trim panel.

Installation

1. When the trim panel is to be replaced, if the watershield has been removed, be sure to position it correctly in place before installing the trim panel. Be sure that the armrest retaining clips are properly positioned on the door inner panel. If they have been dislodged, they must be reinstalled before installing the watershield.

2. Position the trim panel to the door inner panel and connect the wiring (if so equipped) and route the mirror control cable through the hole.

3. Push the trim panel and retaining clips into the inner door panel holes and install the retaining screws.

4. Install the remote control mirror bezel nut.

5. Position the armrest to the trim panel, connect the wiring (if so equipped) and install the retaining screws.

6. Install the armrest finish panel (if so equipped).

7. Position the door latch and window regulator handles and install the retaining screw(s).

8. Clean old cement from the handle access covers with naphtha. Use a 1-3/4 × 3/8 inch tape such as 3M No. Y9122 and cement the cover(s) back in place.

9. Install the garnish moulding and door lock pushbutton control knob.

QUARTER TRIM PANELS—FORD

Basically, all quarter trim panels are retained in the same manner. In view of this, one removal and installation procedure will cover all models.

Removal

1. Remove the rear seat cushion and back assemblies.

2. Remove the window regulator handle, if so equipped. Pry the handle retaining screw access cover from the handle and remove the retaining screw (Fig. 4-1).

3. Remove any screws retaining the trim panel to the inner panel, armrest retaining screws, garnish moulding retaining screws and the rear step plate screw.

4. Then, unclip the trim panel retaining clips and pull the trim panel from the quarter panel (Fig. 4-3). Disconnect the power window switch wires (if so equipped) from the switch.

Installation

1. Position the trim panel to the quarter panel and connect the power window wires, if so equipped. Then, snap the retaining clips in the holes.

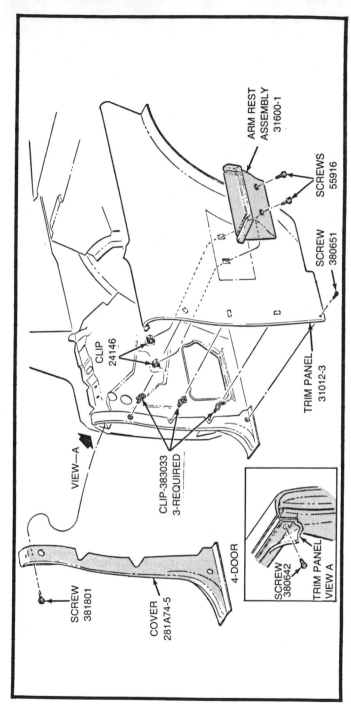

ARM REST ASSEMBLY 31600-1

SCREWS 55916

SCREW 380651

CLIP 24146

VIEW—A

CLIP-383033 3-REQUIRED

TRIM PANEL 31012-3

4-DOOR

SCREW 381801

COVER 281A74-5

SCREW 380642

TRIM PANEL VIEW A

Fig. 4-3. Typical quarter-trim-panel installation for Ford and Mercury.

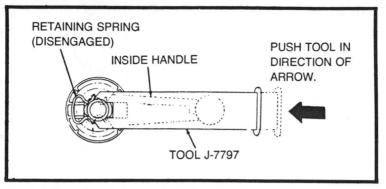

RETAINING SPRING
(DISENGAGED)

INSIDE HANDLE

PUSH TOOL IN
DIRECTION OF
ARROW.

TOOL J-7797

Fig. 4-4. Removing window crank of Chevrolet with special tool.

2. Install the trim panel attaching screw(s).
3. Install the armrest and window regulator handle, if so equipped
4. Install the rear seat cushion and back assemblies.

DOOR TRIM PANELS—CHEVROLET

1. Using tool J-7797 (available at dealers and auto-parts stores, or use two small screwdrivers), remove clips retaining window crank and lock control (Fig. 4-4).
2. Remove four screws securing trim panel located at inside corners of inner door panel (Fig. 4-5).
3. Remove trim panel by carefully prying out at plastic fastener clips located around perimeter of panel.

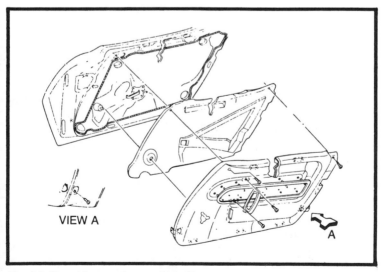

VIEW A

A

Fig. 4-5. Door-trim-panel assembly—Chevrolet.

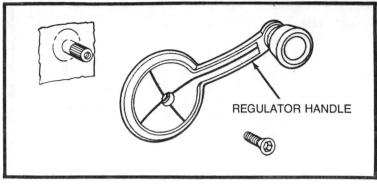

Fig. 4-6. Window-regulator handle—Chrysler Corporation.

4. Remove door lock handle by removing one screw and sliding handle forward.
5. Remove formed plastic cover by peeling along edge at adhesive bead.
6. For installation, follow above steps in reverse order, making sure trim panel is properly aligned.

DOOR TRIM PANELS—CHRYSLER CORPORATION

The following instructions will work for most late-model Chrysler Corporation products.

1. Remove inside handles and armrests (Fig. 4-6). The window regulator handles are retained on the shaft with an Allen setscrew. The handles should be placed in approximately a horizontal position with the knobs facing forward on the doors and rearward on the quarter panel.
2. Remove screws attaching trim panel to door inner panel.
3. Insert a wide-blade screwdriver next to the retaining clips between trim panel and door frame. Snap retaining clips out of door panel and remove panel.
4. Before installing trim panel, inspect condition of watershield (Fig. 4-7).
5. Align trim panel retaining clips with holes of door frame and bump into place with heel of hand.
6. Install trim panel to door screws, escutcheon washer, handles, and armrest.

REAR SEATS—CONVENTIONAL

Routing cables to the trunk or installing speakers in the package shelf often involves removal and replacement of the rear seat back and cushion. The steps immediately following will facilitate the procedures for most American cars. The alternate procedure, given in the next section, will work for other cars.

Removal

1. Apply knee pressure to the lower portion of the rear seat cushion; then push rearward to disengage the seat cushion from the retainer brackets (Fig. 4-8).
2. Remove one of the rear quarter armrests (if so equipped), to remove the seat back assembly.
3. Remove the seat back lower retaining screw (Fig. 4-9).
4. Grasp the seat back assembly at the bottom and lift up to disengage the hanger wire from the retainer brackets.
5. Remove the seat back assembly from the vehicle.

Installation

1. Position the seat back assembly into the vehicle so that the hanger wire is engaged with the retaining brackets (Fig. 4-9).

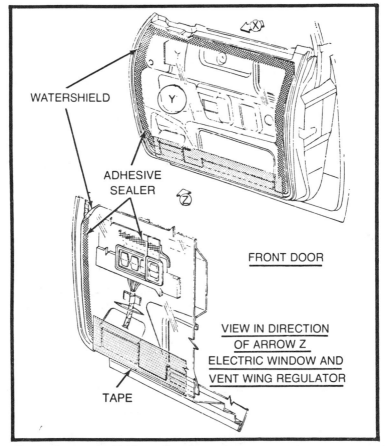

WATERSHIELD

ADHESIVE
SEALER

FRONT DOOR

VIEW IN DIRECTION
OF ARROW Z
ELECTRIC WINDOW AND
VENT WING REGULATOR

TAPE

Fig. 4-7. Door watershields on Chrysler products.

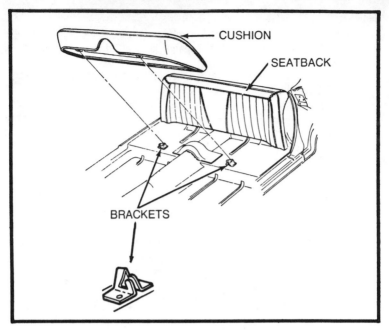

Fig. 4-8. Detachment and removal of rear seat cushion.

2. Install the seat back lower retaining screws and tighten securely.
3. Position the seat cushion assembly into the vehicle.
4. Apply knee pressure to the lower portion of the seat cushion assembly and push rearward and down to lock the seat cushion into position (Fig. 4-8).
5. Install the rear quarter armrest (if removed).

REAR SEATS—ALTERNATE PLAN

Removal

1. Remove the two lower retaining screws securing the rear seat cushion (Fig. 4-10) and remove the seat cushion from the vehicle.
2. Remove the two lower retaining screws securing the rear seat back.
3. Remove the flap from the retainer at the top of the package tray.
4. Then, grasp the seat back assembly at the bottom and lift up to disengage it from the retainer.
5. Remove the rear seat back assembly from the vehicle.

Installation

1. Position the rear seat back assembly to the retainer and install the two lower retaining screws. Tighten securely.

2. Position the flap to the retainer at the top of the package retainer.
3. Position the rear seat cushion into the vehicle and install the two lower retaining screws. Tighten securely.

CONSOLES

Consoles (Fig. 4-11) are typically attached to welded brackets on the floor pan tunnel with screws and bolts. To loosen the rear mountings, raise the carpet lower edges to expose the screw and bolt. All other attaching screws are accessible from within the console. A Chrysler model is illustrated in Fig. 4-11.

A different type of console is represented by the Corvette installation in Fig. 4-12. This installation consists of a front console and a rear console.

PACKAGE SHELF

The package shelf, located between the rear seat back and rear window, is a common place for mounting speakers. Often, there are holes in the sheet-metal panel beneath the shelf for accepting speakers (Fig. 4-13). If the car was purchased with rear-deck speakers already installed, there are holes in the fiberboard shelf itself. These are usually cut to accept 6-× 9-inch oval speakers—a common size. Even when speakers are not already installed, the shelf is scored or the holes partially cut in most cars to accept standard 6-× 9-inch speakers. This assures you of being able to cut the holes quickly and neatly.

Replacing and removing the Chrysler package shelf in Fig. 4-13 are typical of such operations for other makes. The replacement procedure follows (the removal procedure is the reverse of this procedure).

1. Place shelf trim panel face down on bench.
2. Remove gated section of silencer for rear window defroster or speaker, or both.
3. Insert fastener into retainer on shelf trim panel.

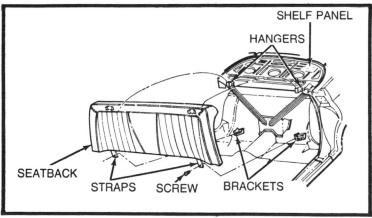

Fig. 4-9. Rear seat back (typical).

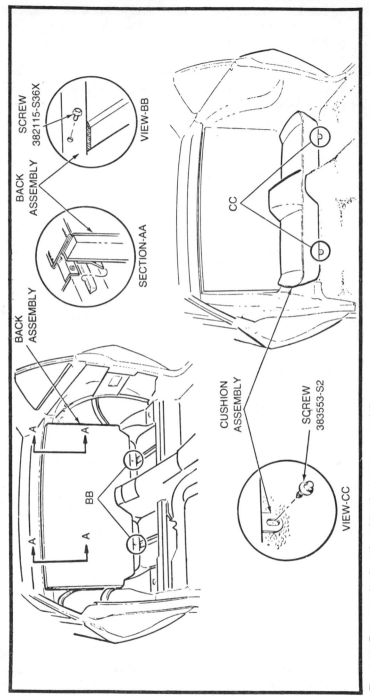

SCREW
382115-S36X

VIEW-BB

BACK
ASSEMBLY

SECTION-AA

BACK
ASSEMBLY

CC

A

A

BB

A

A

CUSHION
ASSEMBLY

SCREW
383553-S2

VIEW-CC

Fig. 4-10. Rear seat back and cushion (subcompact model).

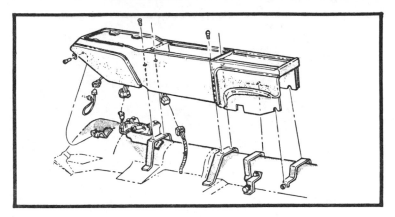

Fig. 4-11. Console attachment (typical).

4. Position and align shelf trim panel to metal shelf panel and snap in place.

SCUFF PLATE

A metal scuff plate is mounted on the door sill of most cars (Fig. 4-14). When running wires from the dash to the rear of the car, through the

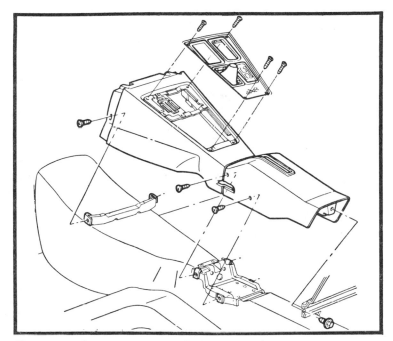

Fig. 4-12. Front and rear sections of 2-piece console.

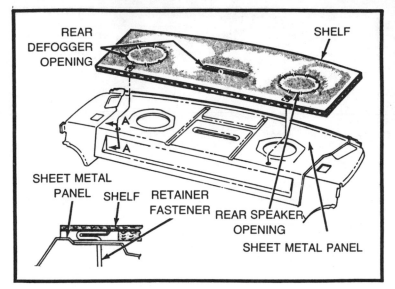

REAR DEFOGGER OPENING

SHELF

SHELF

SHEET METAL PANEL

SHELF

RETAINER FASTENER

REAR SPEAKER OPENING

SHEET METAL PANEL

Fig. 4-13. Shelf trim panel.

passenger compartment, it is often desirable to remove the scuff plate. The wires can sometimes be run under the scuff plate itself, or once the plate is removed, the carpet can be lifted and the wires can be run under the carpet.

The scuff plate is installed as follows:

1. Assemble the spring nut to the rear-quarter trim panel.
2. Position the scuff plate to the body side sill and secure it with screws.

REMOVING THE ORIGINAL RADIO

In upgrading your car's audio system it may be necessary to remove the radio. Figure 4-15 and the steps given next show how to remove the radio of one popular model.

NOTE: On some cars there is a separate convector assembly, which contains the radio's output transistors. Figure 4-15 shows how this unit and other accessories are connected to the radio.

To remove the radio:

1. Disconnect the battery ground cable.
2. On air-conditioned vehicles, remove the left lap cooler duct.
3. Pull off radio control knobs and bezels. For some radios it will be necessary to turn the knob until the slot in the base of the knob is visible and to depress the metal retainer thus exposed with a small screwdriver.
4. Using a deep-well socket, remove the control shaft nuts and then the washers.
5. Disconnect the antenna lead-in cable, speaker, and power feed wiring harness.

6. Remove the radio-to-support-bracket stud nut.
7. Push the radio forward until the control shafts clear the instrument panel and then lower the assembly from the vehicle.
8. To install a radio, reverse the above steps.

CAUTION: Always attach the speaker wiring harness before applying power to the radio.

SPEAKERS

Removing the original-equipment speakers is not a task to be taken lightly. The speakers are about the most inaccessible parts on a car. Figure 4-16 shows how Chevy hides them. The following procedures apply specifically to full-size Chevys, but with the aid of the illustrations, you should be able to adapt the procedures to most other cars.

Chevrolet (Nonstereo) Replacement
1. Disconnect the battery ground cable.
2. Remove screws attaching glove box and remove glove box for access to panel pad.
3. Remove instrument panel pad.
4. Remove speaker wires and three nuts mounting speaker assembly to underside of instrument panel pad.
5. Remove nuts retaining old speakers to bracket.
6. Attach new speakers to mounting bracket with nuts.
7. Install speaker wire, attach speaker assembly to underside of instrument panel pad or top of instrument panel.
   CAUTION: Always attach speaker wiring harness before applying power to the radio.

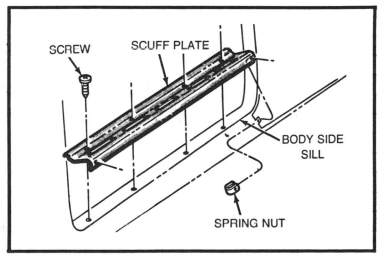

Fig. 4-14. Scuff plate.

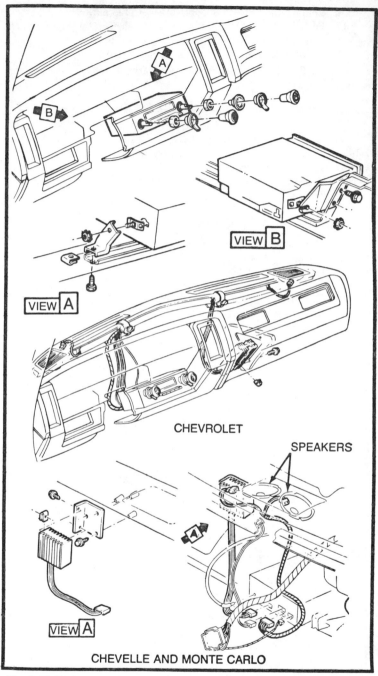

VIEW B

VIEW A

CHEVROLET

SPEAKERS

VIEW A

CHEVELLE AND MONTE CARLO

Fig. 4-15. Typical radio installation (top) and convector installations (bottom).

108

8. Reinstall instrument panel pad, glove box and ground cable to battery.
9. Check speaker operation.

Chevrolet (Stereo) Replacement

1. Disconnect the battery ground cable.
2. Right speaker: Remove the glove box.
3. Air conditioning equipped vehicles: Remove the lap cooler duct for access to left speaker; the flexible hose for access to right speaker.
4. Remove the speaker wire.
5. Remove the speaker mounting nuts and remove the speaker.
6. Install the new speaker to the instrument panel.
7. Attach the speaker wiring harness.
   CAUTION: Always attach speaker wiring harness before applying power to the radio.
8. Reverse steps 1—3 above.

INSTRUMENT PANEL PAD

Figure 4-17 shows how to remove this item from a recent full-sized Chevrolet.

1. Remove glove box for access to lower nuts on studs.
2. Open right and left front doors for access to hidden screws securing pad.
3. Remove screws around perimeter of pad and lift pad carefully. The monaural radio speaker is attached to the bottom of pad.
   NOTE: There are two screws driven into the top of the defroster duct outlet area.
4. Reverse steps 1—3 for installation of pad. Do not overtighten screws, as pad material will puncture.

GARNISH MOULDINGS

When removing a garnish moulding that is overlapped by an adjoining moulding, loosen the end attaching screw to prevent possible damage to both mouldings.

To assure correct alignment when installing the mouldings, install the screw finger tight, align moulding at each end and tighten screws. Use care not to draw screws down too much or the moulding will be damaged at the screw holes.

FLOOR COVERING

To remove the rear floor covering it is necessary to remove the front seat assembly and the rear seat cushion. The front seat mounting brackets are positioned on top of both front and rear floor covers. The rear floor covering is positioned under the front covering.

On units equipped with consoles, the carpet must be assembled over the floor pan mounting brackets or shifting lever. The body wiring is

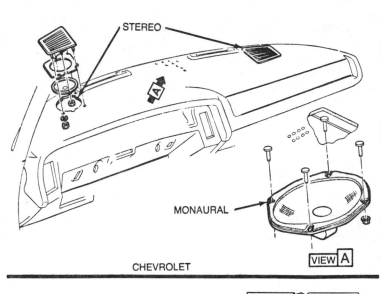

STEREO

VIEW A

MONAURAL

CHEVROLET

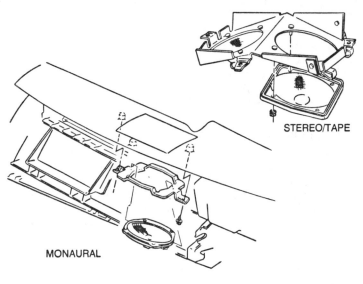

STEREO/TAPE

MONAURAL

CHEVELLE AND MONTE CARLO

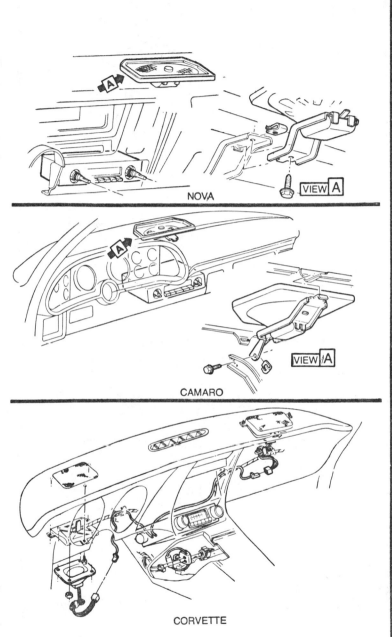

NOVA

VIEW A

CAMARO

VIEW A

CORVETTE

Fig. 4-16. Typical speaker installations, original equipment.

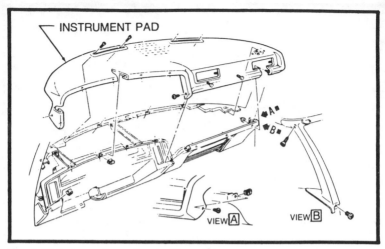

Fig. 4-17. Instrument-panel pad—Chevrolet.

positioned through the holes in the carpet. The front edge of carpet is positioned under the rubber flap on the cowl trim panel. With air conditioning, the carpet front edge must be positioned on front of the air conditioning housing flange and secured with the floor air outlet retainer bracket.

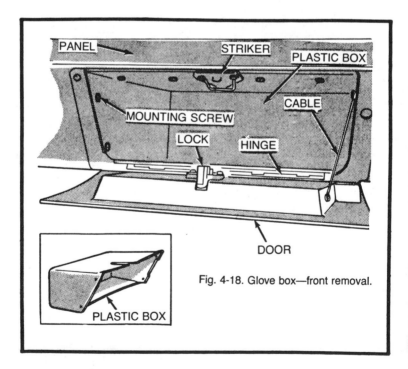

Fig. 4-18. Glove box—front removal.

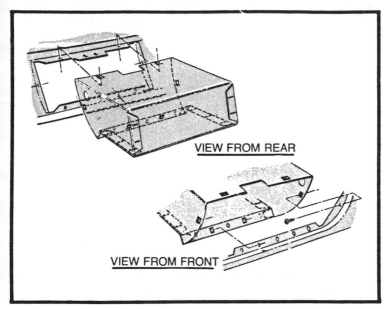

VIEW FROM REAR

VIEW FROM FRONT

Fig. 4-19. Glove box—rear removal.

GLOVE BOXES

The glove box is made in various manners depending on the car line. Some are solid moulded and are removed from the front of the instrument panel (Fig. 4-18). There is also a two piece box with a plastic moulded upper half and a fiber board lower half, attached to each other with screws. When the screws are removed, the two sections would be removed from the front of the instrument panel (lower half first, and upper half last).

Some boxes are one piece fiber board and are removed from the rear and under the instrument panel (Fig. 4-19).

113

Chapter 5
Boat and
Aircraft Installations

The extensive information in earlier chapters on electrical principles, alternators and generators, two-way radio, noise suppression, ignition in internal-combustion engines, wiring, and the use of tools, applies to boats and planes as well as to land vehicles. But the operating environments of boats and planes—water and air—involve many special considerations. The environment of boats, for example, demands resistance to corrosion in most electrical equipment, and the environment of planes demands a streamlined, vibration-resistant design in antennas. Furthermore, there are many electronic products designed specifically to enhance the safety, performance, or utility of boats or aircraft. The special products and problems encountered in these conveyances are treated in a general way in this chapter. Later chapters, in Part 2, describe specific installations of electronic devices in just about every mode of transport, including boats and planes.

CORROSION IN MARINE INSTALLATIONS

The corrosion encountered in marine installations is of two types: galvanic and electrolytic. Both are caused by an electrical current passing from one metal surface to another through water. In the process, the metal is dissolved in the water.

In *electrolytic* corrosion the current that causes corrosion is produced by a battery or generator. *Galvanic* corrosion results from a current generated when two objects made of dissimilar metals are placed near each other in a solution such as sea water.

Galvanic Corrosion

For galvanic corrosion to occur, two dissimilar metals must be in contact with the water, and the metals must be electrically connected over some other path in addition to the water. Unfortunately these conditions are

114

the rule rather than the exception on boats, but there are a number of things you can do to minimize galvanic corrosion in shipboard installations.

One of the most obvious ways to combat corrosion is to protect underwater metals and fittings. Some outboard-engine manufacturers include a sacrificial zinc plate on the lower unit. Zinc, being a *base* metal, is very subject to galvanic activity. The idea of the sacrificial zinc plate is that the zinc, rather than the metal to be protected, will supply the metal to be dissolved by galvanic action. Zinc plates are also available separately to protect small boats.

Painting is one good way of reducing corrosion, but don't rely on painting alone—and don't paint over the zinc plates and defeat their purpose.

If your corrosion problem is really severe, you may want to purchase a special anticorrosion unit such as *Inter-Zinc* (made by Intercontinental Factors of Los Angeles). The Inter-Zinc unit controls galvanic and electrolytic corrosion by means of a renewable zinc unit that is sealed within a copper tube filled with an electrolyte solution.

The galvanic-corrosion problem can be skirted by using metals of the same type whenever possible, since galvanic action depends on dissimilar metals. If you must use dissimilar metals, try insulating them with plastic, rubber, or some other waterproof material. Without a second conducting path in addition to the water, there will be no galvanic action.

For screws and other fasteners try to use those made of a metal more corrosion resistant—that is, more *noble*—than the metal to be fastened. That way, if corrosion occurs it will erode the larger surface rather than the screw or fastener.

Where possible, try to use noble (corrosion resistant) rather than base metals and avoid alloys that contain base metals. Since alloys are made of dissimilar metals, an alloy containing a base metal has a corrosive situation built in. Brass, which consists of zinc and copper, is often used for topside fittings, but it is a poor choice for an underwater metal because the zinc is quickly corroded. Here, in order of galvanic activity (most noble first), is a list of metals commonly used on boats: stainless steel, monel, bronze, copper, brass, lead, steel, iron, aluminum, galvanized steel, galvanized iron, zinc, and magnesium.

Electrolytic Corrosion

In this type of corrosion, metal underwater fittings connected to the positive terminal of a battery or other power source are decomposed in the water. For it to occur, there must be a difference of potential (a voltage) between two metals in the water. Such a voltage can result from the improper installation of electrical equipment on a boat and can occur in the water around a boat, in the bilge, in water-soaked wood, and wherever there is water.

From a study of basic electricity we know that a current in a wire causes a voltage drop from one end of the wire to the other. That is, the voltage is greater at one end than at the other. If both ends are immersed in water, a current will flow in the water from the end with the higher voltage to the other end. This electrical current is in addition to the one in the wire that causes the voltage drop in the wire. The electrical current in the water causes electrolytic corrosion.

The best way to eliminate electrolytic corrosion is to minimize or eliminate the source of the problem, which is the electrical current in water. To do this you must minimize the voltage drop that causes the current. One way is to use heavy-gauge wire for all power leads. Another way is to bond the frames of all electrical units together with large wire or heavy bonding straps. The current that would otherwise flow in the water will then flow through the bonding conductors.

Sometimes it is impossible to eliminate the source of electrolytic corrosion as, for example, when currents flow to or from nearby boats as a result of defective or improperly installed electrical equipment. Then, sacrificial lead plates or some system such as Inter-Zinc may be used.

SOUND WAVES ON THE WATER WAVES

The installation of a car stereo in a boat is as simple and straightforward as in a car. There are a few special considerations, however, and many of them apply to units other than stereos as well.

If you have a power boat, you should consider the purchase of a power amplifier for your stereo to overcome the noise inherent in the operation of such boats. Otherwise your stereo may not have enough volume to overcome the noise, particularly at top speeds or on choppy waters. Ignition noise may be a problem on some older boats, but it is susceptible to the same cures as ignition noise in cars (see the discussion of noise suppression).

If you have a sailboat, ambient noise and ignition interference will not be any problem, and you can forgo the power amplifier and noise-suppression measures. If your sailboat uses an automobile battery for electrical power, current drain should not be any problem either since the typical radio-tape combination draws only about 0.5 ampere at normal volume, which translates to 6 watts at 12 volts DC.

A stereo unit can often be mounted in the dash of a boat more easily than in the dash of a car since the underdash area of boats is not cluttered with the ducts, wiring, and supports found in cars. With some racing sailboats you may wish to avoid any cutting of panels, since in some of these craft all of the panels are structural. You may opt instead for an underdash installation. Such installations are easy to do but, unfortunately, easy for thieves to undo, so it's a good idea to use a quick-release mounting bracket if you are mounting a stereo under the dash of one of the smaller boats with a cabin that can't be locked.

The first step in installing a stero is picking your work area. Working with the boat in the water is not always a good idea. First, small boats at moor pitch and roll as you walk around on them. Then, too, the power tools needed for the installation can present a shock hazard on the water. It is best to take the boat inside for this work if you can.

A good place for installing speakers on some boats is in the compartments under the rear seats. The confined airspace in these compartments enhances the bass response of the speakers. Try to mount the speakers as high as practical up from the floor to preclude possible flooding damage.

The compartments are typically made of vinyl-covered plywood. In cutting holes for the speakers, first cut the vinyl with a razor knife. Often you can use the cutout in the speaker's cardboard box as a template for this. Then drill a starting hole and cut the plywood with a saber saw or keyhole saw. Use the speaker as a template to drill the mounting holes. Fasten the speaker to the compartment, then drill a small hole in the bottom of the compartment and pull the speaker leads through it.

If you decide to mount the stereo itself in the dash, draw the outline of the unit's nosepiece (rectangular projection that will protrude from the dash and that holds the tuning dial and tape-loading slot) and control shafts. Use the stereo's faceplate as a template. Then drill the holes for the control shaft and a starting hole for the saw you will use to cut a hole for the nosepiece. Usually the dash is made of thin fiberglass and can be cut with a keyhole saw. Finally, fit the unit through the opening you have cut and secure it according to the instructions that came with it. If you do not have the instructions, you should be able to adapt the instructions for the stereo installation given in a later chapter.

Before doing any wiring, you may wish to install the power amplifier, if used. Try to find a location that will protect the amp from water spray. A wooden structural member behind the dash often provides a handy, solid, and dry mounting location. Next run the wires from the power amp to the stereo and speakers. Connect the amplifier's power lead to a source of 12 volts DC. The ignition switch is a likely place to make this connection. If you do not have the owner's manual for the units you are installing, refer to Part 2 of this book for the wiring instructions.

Locate the antenna for the radio-tape unit where it will not be kicked or stepped on as people walk around the boat. A few inches in front of the windshield center post is usually a good choice. If you are using an electronic antenna—a good idea if you are plying the waters in an FM fringe area— connect the antenna's power lead to the ignition switch and connect the antenna lead-in wire to the antenna input on the radio-tape unit.

If you wish to avoid any cutting of your boat in making your installation, you can use the mounting brackets and other hardware supplied with an automotive stereo. Surface-mount speakers, such as are often used in cars, will also work well in this situation. Be sure, however, that the screws that come with the stereo or speakers are not so long as to protrude through the hull or ledge area you are using for mounting. If they are too long, procure some corrosion-resistant screws of the proper length.

COMMUNICATIONS ON THE WATER

Before CB sets were in common use, boaters on the inland waters could not use CB effectively for communication and navigation because usually there was no one to talk with. Now hundreds of thousands of boats carry CB radios, and CB radio is a very practical way of talking with other boats or even your home while you are on the water. The availability of CB to obtain weather and navigation information and to summon aid is a great boon to safety on the water.

Fig. 5-1. Grounding tube for small boat. (Courtesy Heath Company)

Expensive mobile-radio transceivers operating in the VHF marine band are also available and provide even more communication possibilities. With this type of radio, which uses frequency modulation and operates in the 156-to-162 MHz band, one can communicate directly with the Coast Guard, other boats, locks, dams, waterway control points, yacht clubs, and marinas.

Marine Antennas

An automotive-type steel whip antenna cannot be used on a boat without special grounding provisions. An ordinary whip antenna requires an earth ground (connection to the earth) or a ground substitute known as a *ground plane*. A ground plane is a conducting surface at the base of an antenna. The metal body of an automobile makes an excellent ground plane, but a wood or fiberglass boat does not. To use an automotive type of antenna on a boat, the boat must have a metal deck or a metal screen or plate acting as a ground plane.

A metal grounding plane should have an area of at least 12 square feet. It should be below the waterline but does not have to contact the water; it can be mounted inside the hull. The thickness of the plate is not important. If it is impractical to install a plate of 12 square-foot area, you can substitute a 6-inch wide (or greater) copper strap around the perimeter of the area, which may be, say, 3 feet by 4 feet. Ground the strap to the motor and connect it to the radio with a short length of strap.

Grounding tubes, such as the one in Fig. 5-1, are available commercially. Both the inner and outer surfaces of the tube contact the water, and the tube is made of a porous metal; therefore the tube presents a large surface area to the water, making an excellent ground.

In some cases the motor will work as a ground, but usually special grounding provisions are required with a simple whip. An alternative is a coaxial antenna (Fig. 5-2A), which requires no ground plane. Coaxial antennas are made for both the VHF and citizens bands.

At VHF wavelengths it is possible to make antennas a full wavelength long. This makes possible a signal gain in the antenna itself. The Phelps Dodge 438-509 antenna, shown in Fig. 5-2B, has a gain of 3 decibels, which effectively doubles the power of any transmitter it is used with. The antenna has a sparkling white fiberglass element housing and polished-chrome base

118

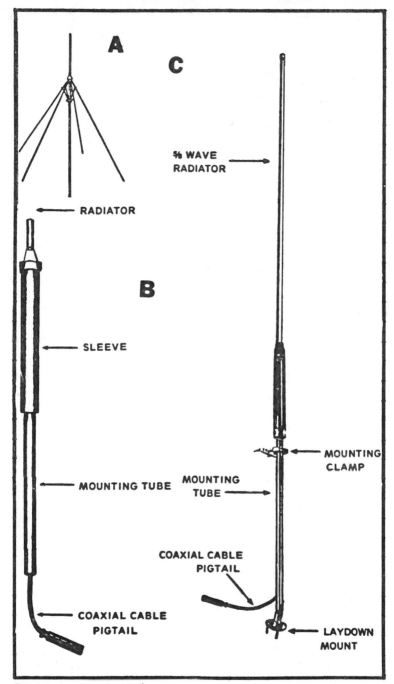

Fig. 5-2. Antennas for VHF marine radios.

119

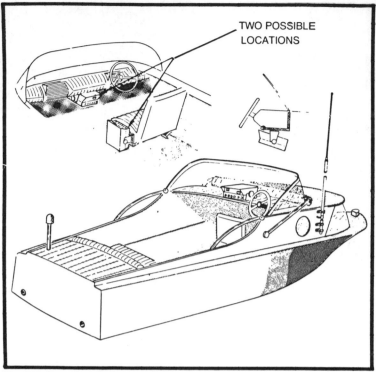

TWO POSSIBLE
LOCATIONS

Fig. 5-3. Some installation possibilities for a small boat. (Courtesy Heath Company)

assembly. It provides a highly efficient antenna for any VHF marine radio system and even enhances the beauty of any craft on which it is installed.

As mentioned earlier, an excellent location for an antenna is in front of the windshield. Figure 5-3 shows another likely location for the antenna as well as some handy sites for the transceiver.

VHF Marine Band

If you decide to install a VHF marine transceiver, Table 5-1 will help you decide what channels to provide crystals for. It will also assist in operating a marine radio system by showing what channel to use in a particular situation—in communicating with other recreational vessels, for example. All ship radios in the VHF band must be capable of transmitting on 156.3 and 156.8 MHz plus at least one additional working frequency.

Even if you decide that you do not need communication capability on the VHF band, you may wish to monitor weather frequencies, marine emergency channels, harbor instructions, fishing reports, ship-to-ship communications, and ship-to-shore communications on VHF. A marine scanner receiver will enable you to monitor several VHF channels without twisting any knobs or turning any controls. The installation of such a unit is described in Part 2 of this book.

Table 5-1. VHF Marine Channels.

CHANNEL	AUTHORIZED COMMUNICATIONS	RECEIVER FREQUENCY (MHz)	POINTS OF COMMUNICATIONS
65	Port Operations	156.275	Intership and ship to coast
6	Safety	156.300	Intership
66	Port Operations	156.375	Intership and ship to coast
7	Commercial	156.350	Intership and ship to coast
67	Commercial	156.375	Intership
8	Commercial	156.400	Intership
68	Noncommercial	156.425	Intership and ship to coast
9	Noncommercial	156.450	Ship to coast
69	Noncommercial	156.475	Ship to coast
10	Commercial	156.500	Intership and ship to coast
70	Noncommercial	156.525	Intership
11	Commercial	156.550	Intership and ship to coast
71	Noncommercial	156.575	Ship to coast
12	Port Operations	156.600	Intership and ship to coast
72	Noncommercial	156.625	Intership
13	Navigational	156.650	Intership and ship to coast
73	Port Operations	156.675	Intership and ship to coast
14	Port Operations	156.700	Intership and ship to coast
74	Port Operations	156.725	Intership and ship to coast
15	Environmental	156.750	Coast to ship
16	Distress, Safety, and Calling	156.800	Intership and ship to coast
17	Communications with the U.S. Coast Guard	156.850	Ship to coast
77	Commercial	156.875	Intership
18	Commercial	156.900	Intership and ship to coast
78	Noncommercial	156.925	Ship to coast
19	Commercial	156.950	Intership and ship to coast
79	Commercial	156.975	Intership and ship to coast
20	Port Operations	161.600	Intership and ship to coast
80	Commercial	157.025	Intership and ship to coast
21	Coast Guard	157.050	Ship to coast
81	Coast Guard	157.075	Ship to coast
22	Coast Guard	157.100	Ship to coast
82	Coast Guard	157.125	Ship to coast
23	Coast Guard	157.150	Ship to coast
83	Coast Guard	157.175	Ship to coast
24	Public Correspondence	161.800	Ship to public coast
84	Public Correspondence	161.825	Ship to public coast
25	Public Correspondence	161.825	Ship to public coast
85	Public Correspondence	161.850	Ship to public coast
26	Public Correspondence	161.875	Ship to public coast
86	Public Correspondence	161.900	Ship to public coast
27	Public Correspondence	161.925	Ship to public coast
87	Public Correspondence	161.950	Ship to public coast
28	Public Correspondence	161.975	Ship to public coast
88	Public Correspondence	162.000	Ship to public coast
WX	Weather	162.400	
WX	Weather	162.550	

RADIO DIRECTION FINDER

A radio direction finder is an excellent navigational aid for any pleasure craft, fishing craft, or any other private or commercial vessel that navigates at night or out of sight of land. Figure 5-4 shows the construction and controls of a direction finder. Shown is Heath's *Mariner II,* which tunes in both the long-wave band, where various marine services can be found, and the broadcast band. As a radio compass, the direction finder can be used to obtain a bearing to any station by turning the directional antenna for the proper reading on the null meter. You can then plot the bearing from the compass rose, a disc at the base of the antenna that is calibrated in 2-degree divisions. A special sensing circuit enables you to eliminate 180-degree ambiguity when you want to home on a station.

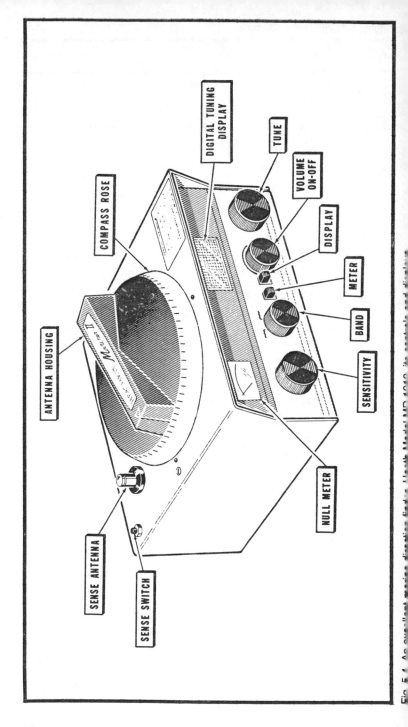

Fig. 5-1. An excellent marine direction finder. Heath Model MR-1010, its controls and displays.

The ferrite antenna of a direction finder is quite directional. If you point either end of it toward a radio station, it will pick up very little signal from that station. If either *side* of it is toward the station, the antenna will receive maximum available signals from that station, as is shown in Fig. 5-5.

The front-panel null meter shows whether a larger or smaller signal is being received from the station you have tuned in. Therefore, if you turn the antenna housing until the meter shows the smallest amount of signal (this is called the *null* point), one end of the antenna will be pointing directly toward the station (Fig. 5-5B). Then, if you set the compass rose to agree with the ship's compass, you can read the direction to the station, in degrees, below the pointer at the end of the antenna housing.

If you tune in a station and turn the antenna housing in a complete circle, you will find that there are two nulls, one for each end of the antenna. The sensing circuits resolve this 180-degree ambiguity by showing you which end of the antenna actually points toward the station.

When the sensing circuits are in use and the whip antenna is raised, the antenna pattern (Fig. 5-5A) is altered. By connecting the two antennas into the circuit at once, the receiving pattern for the combination becomes as shown in solid lines in Fig. 5-6. Now, 180-degree ambiguity can be resolved since the meter will indicate a larger signal as you turn the ferrite antenna clockwise.

Accurate bearings can *not* be taken while the sensing circuits are connected and the whip antenna is raised. The purpose of the sensing circuit

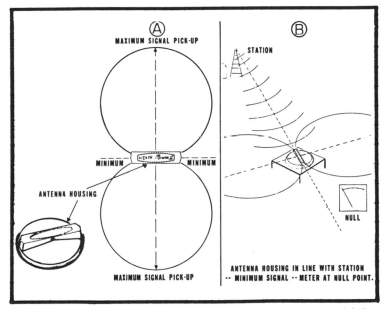

Fig. 5-5. In A, the maximum signal is picked up. This orientation is used during tuning of the radio. In B, the minimum signal is picked up since the null is a narrowly defined position; the null is used for the actual navigation. (Courtesy Heath Company)

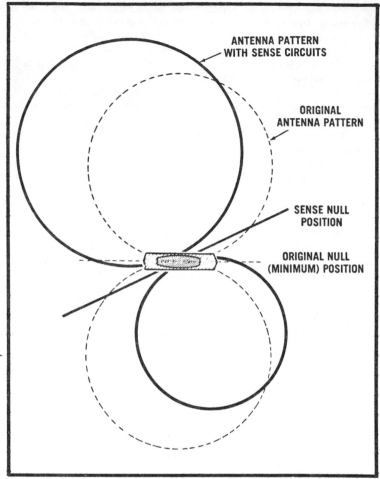

Fig. 5-6. In the sensing mode the receiver has an unbalanced reception that aids in resolving 180-degree ambiguity. (Courtesy Heath Company)

is only to determine a general direction, that is, to resolve 180-degree ambiguity.

The controls of the typical direction finder are as described in the following:

Digital Tuning Display. Indicates the frequency of each station you tune in.

Tune Control. Tunes in the frequency of the desired stations.

Volume Control. Increases or decreases the sound to a comfortable listening level.

Display Switch. For internal battery operation, the tuning display of the Heath *Mariner II* lights up for 20 seconds after you depress and release this switch. For external battery operation, the tuning display comes on when you depress and release this switch, and the display turns off the next time you depress and release the switch.

Meter Switch. Turns the meter lamp on and off.

Band Switch. Selects either the broadcast or long-wave (marine) band.

Sensitivity Control. Adjusts the amount of RF signal that is coupled through the receiver circuits. It is turned clockwise for weak signals and counterclockwise for strong signals to get a good, usable indication on the meter.

Null Meter. Gives a relative indication of the signal strength for each signal you tune in. Tune for a null (low reading) on this meter to get a bearing on a station. It is normal for the meter needle to deflect all the way to the right (to peg) on strong stations.

Sense Switch. Connects the sensing antenna into the circuit so you can resolve 180-degree ambiguity.

When you take a bearing, make sure that you know the exact location of the transmitting station. It should be situated on or very near the coastline. Bearings taken on inland stations, especially in mountainous terrain, are often erroneous due to refraction or reflection of radio waves. Such bearings should be used cautiously.

Use great care when taking bearings on stations that are 50 or more miles away. Sky waves—radio waves that are reflected off the ionosphere—will often cause erroneous readings. The sky waves are usually accompanied by fluctuations in signal strength. The errors caused by sky waves are sometimes called *night effect* because sky waves are usually evident only at night. Beacon stations will give the least trouble from night effect and will *always* give the most reliable bearings.

Bearings taken just before or after sunrise or sunset are often erroneous because of night effect. A noticeable broadening of null areas and even apparent directional shifts may be observed. If it is necessary to take bearings under these conditions, take several bearings and use their average for plotting.

DEPTH SOUNDER

Many boaters believe this is the most useful electronic device that can be installed in a boat. As a safety device, it continuously monitors water depth and indicates the presence of shallow areas and submerged objects. As a fisherman's friend, it helps to locate schools of fish. And as a navigational aid, it enables you to compare the depths beneath your boat with the depth markings on navigational charts.

A depth sounder has an ultrasonic transducer that is capable of transmitting and receiving ultrasonic pulses. Figure 5-7 shows what happens when these pulses are applied to the transducer (transmitted or received).

A piezoelectric ceramic element inside the transducer oscillates (vibrates) at a frequency of approximately 50 kHz. This vibration introduces a motion, or signal, into the water that is directed toward the bottom of the body of water in a relatively wide beam. Because this signal is not audible, it may be considered as a "silent sound" traveling at an average rate of 4800 feet per second in water, or 0.0002083 seconds per foot. As the signal

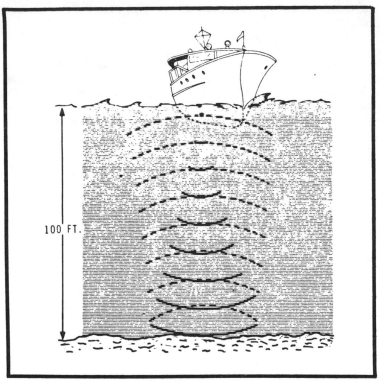

Fig. 5-7. Incident (solid lines) and reflected (dashed lines) waves processed by a depth sounder. (Courtesy Heath Company)

leaves the transducer it causes markings to appear at the zero mark on the chart paper of a recording-type depth sounder.

The time required for the signal to travel from the transducer to the bottom is the product of the water depth (in feet) times the speed of sound in water (seconds per foot). For example, if your boat is in water 100 feet deep, then 100 feet times 0.0002083 seconds per foot gives 0.02083 seconds of sound travel time from the transducer to the bottom.

As the signal strikes the bottom, it is bounced (reflected) back up to the transducer at the same speed. Since the bottom seldom has a smooth, flat surface, the reflected signal is widely scattered. Therefore, only a small amount of the reflected signal actually strikes the transducer directly. The return time for the reflected (echo) signal is another 0.02083 seconds in the example, making a total travel time of 0.04166 seconds.

When it reaches the transducer, this echo signal causes the ceramic element to vibrate at the same 50 kHz frequency that was originally transmitted. This echo signal is amplified in the receiver circuits of the depth sounder and applied to an indicating device. In the case of a recording-type depth sounder, the signal is applied to a stylus that produces a mark on the chart paper. If, for example, the belt speed is 150 rpm and the belt has a circumference of 16 1/2 inches, the speed represents a time of 0.4 second for each revolution. Therefore, the belt would have moved 1.72 inches during a signal travel time of 0.04166 second. This would cause the stylus to mark the paper 1.72 inches below the zero mark, which corresponds to the 100-foot line on the paper.

Since the transmit-receive cycle is repeated 2 1/2 times per second, the overall effect is that of a continuous sounding. Therefore, even relatively small variations of the bottom contour can be observed while the boat is in motion.

Figure 5-8 shows the indication that would be obtained for our example. Note the second echo pulse. The air-water interface forms a good reflecting surface. This causes the first echo signal to be reflected back to the bottom,

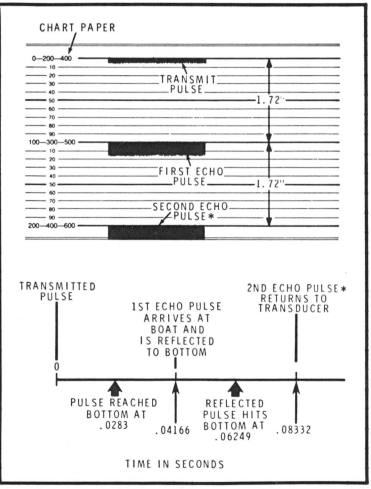

Fig. 5-8. Readout obtained with Heath Company's Model MI-2910 depth sounder and recorder.

127

which in turn reflects this signal back up to the transducer. The signal is then detected by the transducer and is called a second echo. This causes a mark to appear on the chart paper at twice the actual depth, as shown. In shallow water it is common to record third and even fourth echoes.

There are several other types of depth sounders. Instead of employing a chart recorder, these may indicate depth with a flashing light, a television-type screen, or a meter. Only the flashing-light type has enjoyed much popularity with small-boat skippers. The indicator consists of a neon lamp that is mounted on an arm and driven in a circle on the indicator's face by an electric motor. The circular face is calibrated in feet or fathoms, or both, around its circumference. Each time the lamp passes the zero point on the face, the transmitter sends out a pulse in the water. As the neon lamp continues to rotate, it flashes each time an echo is returned. The depth is read at the position where the flash occurs.

The oscilloscope-type sounder indicates depth on a television-like screen and is expensive. The meter indicator gives depths on a meter similar to an ammeter or electrical gauge. This type of sounder is easy to read but gives less information on bottom countour than the other types.

AIRCRAFT INSTALLATIONS

Most installations of electronic equipment aboard aircraft are done by professional technicians employed by the airport FBOs (fixed-base operators). The most common installations done by others are installations of CB radios and antennas. There are a few other accessories, such as clocks and timers, that are available for do-it-yourself installation.

FAA Approval

If you build an electronic unit for an aircraft from a kit, after you complete the assembly you will be required to return the unit to the manufacturer of the kit for inspection of the unit and issuance of an FAA-PMA tag. The inspection will be made by a manufacturing inspection representative designated by the FAA. The final installation of the unit in an aircraft must be inspected by an FAA representative, who will want to see the FAA-PMA tag.

Any permanent aircraft installation must have installation approval on an individual basis by a licensed FAA airframe-and-powerplant (A&P) mechanic or an authorized aircraft repair station. Check with an authorized mechanic or repair station before you begin the installation. The necessary documentation (FAA Form 337 or STC data) also must be completed and filed with the local or regional FAA office (all of this is per FAA Advisory Circular 43.13-1 & 2, *Aircraft Alterations*).

If you plan to install a unit in an IFR-certificated aircraft, the unit cannot be connected to the same fuse or circuit breaker with any IFR-required equipment as defined in Federal Air Regulation 91.33. Furthermore, FAR 23.1357 requires that no protective device may protect more than one circuit essential to flight safety.

COMMUNICATION IN THE AIR ENVIRONMENT

As with boats, there are two types of communication gear that are commonly installed in planes: professional-quality navigation/communication units, operating in the VHF aviation band, and CB radios. The NAV/COMM systems are installed by aircraft sales-and-service organizations and provide the primary means of communication in aircraft. Although installing these units is not a do-it-yourself project, some information about the operation and selection of these units will be helpful. You may be in a position to install a CB set in a plane, but check with an FAA inspector first and try to get the inspector to supervise the installation from start to finish.

CB Installations in Planes

Be very careful in making any alteration to an airplane. Drilling or cutting a hole in a structural member may seriously weaken the member with disastrous results. Often the structural metal appears in the most unlikely-looking places, so check with an A&P mechanic before you do any drilling or cutting. Unauthorized alterations to an aircraft may create legal as well as safety problems.

Some requirements that an FAA inspector may make regarding an installation include mounting the unit in the main panel of the plane, running the power and antenna cables a certain way, substituting a circuit breaker for an inline fuseholder, and using special wire for the power leads.

Figure 5-9 shows an aircraft CB antenna, the Antenna Specialists Model AV-568. The sturdy fiberglass antenna is built to match standard VHF aircraft antennas. Its low profile and aerodynamic design mean low air resistance. The antenna can be mounted either above or below the cabin. Despite its short length (18 inches), the antenna has a good working range from the air. Unfortunately the short length means that tuning is very critical. The antenna is tuned by cutting the wire inside the fiberglass shell in only 1/8-inch increments.

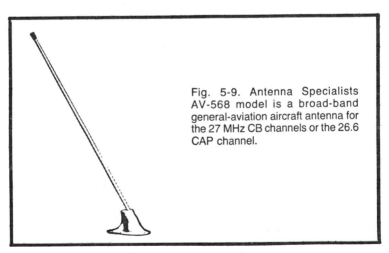

Fig. 5-9. Antenna Specialists AV-568 model is a broad-band general-aviation aircraft antenna for the 27 MHz CB channels or the 26.6 CAP channel.

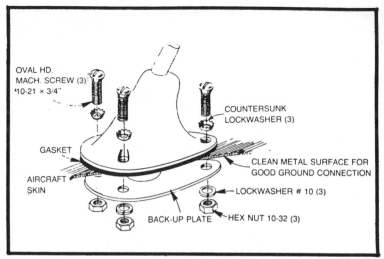

Fig. 5-10. Details of the mount of the AV-568. (Courtesy Antenna Specialists)

A good electrical connection must exist between the mounting bolts (Fig. 5-10) and the metallic frame or skin of the airplane. Good mechanical support must also be present at this location. Aircraft with a nonmetallic outer surface should be provided with a ground plane of at least 24 × 24 inches. This may be a thin metal sheet on the outside, or immediately under the surface on the inside. Metal foil, securely fastened in place, may be used on the inside surface. The ground plane must extend under the vertical portion of the antenna. The ground plane, in any case, must be well bonded electrically to the metal frame of the aircraft to prevent erratic electrical noise in the receiver.

Use a template, if one is provided, or use the antenna base as a template, and drill the required mounting hole plus one for the connector. In mounting the antenna, place the rubber pad between the antenna's base and the aircraft's skin. Place the backup plate inside the aircraft. It is important that the antenna base be properly grounded. In the antenna shown, this is accomplished by the countersunk lockwashers biting through the painted surface under the screw heads.

A piece of RG-58/U or similar coax cable is used to connect the antenna to the radio. One end is terminated in a type BNC connector, and the other end must match the connector on the radio. The cable and connector may not be supplied, as the requirements for these will depend on the aircraft and the particular installation.

For tuning an aircraft antenna, connect an inline wattmeter (or SWR meter) between the transmitter and antenna. Remove the rubber tip of the antenna. Key the transmitter and very carefully trim off wire at the top of the antenna, 1/8 inch at a time, until the wattmeter reads 4% of forward power (1.5:1 VSWR) or less on channel 18, or 150 kHz above the center transmitter frequency to be used. Reattach the tip to the antenna rod to complete the installation.

AVIONICS

The aviation-electronics equipment discussed in the rest of the chapter is not normally user installed. However, no book about mobile electronic equipment would be complete without a discussion of avionics. Furthermore, one of the most important parts of any installation of avionics is the planning of the system. Whether you are qualified to install your own avionics or not, any pilot needs to know what equipment is available and a little about how it works.

NAV/COMM System

The first requirement for any avionics system is NAV/COMM, a dual-purpose navigation/communication system. Shown in Fig. 5-11 is the *Silver Crown* Model KX-175, manufactured by King Radio Corporation, Olathe, Kansas. The NAV and COMM sections have separate ON/OFF switches. Since NAV and COMM are completely isolated from each other, you must turn on both. *Be sure all radios are off before starting the aircraft engine.*

To communicate, you select the COMM frequency with the two knobs on the left. The larger one controls megahertz, from 118 to 135 MHz. The smaller inner knob controls kilohertz, from 0.000 to 0.975 kHz. The selected frequency number appears in the window. The independent volume control, VOL, may be left at a selected level even when the set is off. Automatic squelch is a convenience that eliminates the conventional SQUELCH control. However, when an extremely weak signal is encountered, manual override of the automatic squelch can be accomplished by setting the ON/OFF switch to the TEST position. For testing purposes, manual override will permit noise to come through to indicate that the COMM receiver is working.

To navigate, you select the VOR/LOC/ILS frequency desired with the two knobs on the right. The larger one controls megahertz, from 108 to 117 MHz. The smaller knob controls kilohertz, from 0.00 to 0.95 kHz. The 200 channels required by the FAA are conveniently available. The selected frequency appears in the window at the right. Navigation stations transmit advisories periodically, and these can be heard by setting the switch at the

Fig. 5-11. A modern NAV/COMM unit, manufactured by King Radio Corporation of Olathe, Kansas.

Fig. 5-12. Navigational indicator for a NAV receiver. (Courtesy King Radio Corporation)

right to VOICE. This also removes the coded identification signal sent out by the navigation stations. To hear the identification, set the switch to IDENT. The VOL control is an independent volume control that can be set and left at any convenient level. Note that the units shown are designated NAV 1 and COMM 1. Sometimes, for greater operating convenience and utility, two NAV/COMMs are installed. The second units would be identified as NAV 2 or COMM 2 in the same space.

The indicator for a NAV receiver is a separate unit. One such unit is King Radio's Model KI-201C VOR/LOC indicator, shown in Fig. 5-12. After you set the desired course on the indicator, a left-right course deviation is displayed. The OFF flag disappears when a valid signal is received. The TO/FROM flag shows the position of the VOR navigation station relative to the aircraft.

In buying avionics equipment, you will frequently run into the term *TSOed*. A TSO is a Technical Standard Order issued by the FAA that sets stringent performance and environmental standards for avionics equipment. These standards often go far beyond the minimum standards that must be met, and the TSO specifications are found mainly in high-performance models such as the King Model KX-175 NAV/COMM. A companion model to the KX-175 is the Model KX-170, which also meets FAA standards, though less stringent ones than the TSOs met by the KX-175. The advantage of a unit that is not TSOed is, of course, a lower price.

Fig. 5-13. King Radio Corporation KI-265 indicator for DME.

The avionics units discussed so far are the basic necessities. For operations of aircraft to, from, or on airports with FAA control towers, a two-way radio for communication (COMM unit) is required by the FAA. For cross-country flights, even under visual flight rules (VFR), a NAV unit is a tremendous convenience and a great boon to safety. As a pilot gains more experience, he usually wishes to upgrade his avionics capabilities beyond the basic NAV/COMM, following the advice of King Radio to "Add a skill, add a unit." Regarding an avionics installation, it pays to plan ahead. If you trade up in aircraft in 5 years or less, will the avionics you install today provide for operational capabilities required by the FAA for the next 5 or 10 years? If so, the trade-in value of your aircraft is sure to be higher than otherwise.

One of the first units you may wish to add to the basic installation is a DME (distance-measuring equipment) system. The indicator of a DME system, shown in Fig. 5-13, is panel mounted. The main unit, which computes groundspeed and time to station, is remotely mounted. The DME electronically converts to distance the elapsed time required for a transmitted signal to travel from the DME to a ground station and back. The distance is then indicated in nautical miles on the indicator. This distance, the *slant range* distance, is not exactly the same as the along-the-ground distance, but if the range is at least 3 times the altitude, the error is negligible. Readouts of distance (up to 200 miles) and groundpsccd (up to 400 knots) are continuous with the indicator shown. When you want to read time to station, just switch to the TTS position and up to 40 minutes time to station is displayed.

AREA NAVIGATION (RNAV)

Once you have DME you may wish to go a step further and obtain RNAV capability. To do this, you will need an RNAV computer, such as King

Fig. 5-14. The King KN-74TSO RNAV computer and waypoint selector provides a new and better way to fly.

Fig. 5-15. This VOR/LOC/glideslope indicator features a rectilinear movement for both the vertical and horizontal bars, as opposed to windshield-wiper action in less profession models.

Radio Corporation's KN-74 (Fig. 5-14), and a more sophisticated navigation indicator, such as King's KNI-520 (Fig. 5-15). Using VOR input from your NAV unit and DME input from your DME, you can "move" any receivable VORTAC station to a waypoint of your choice. Then you can fly directly to or from the waypoint. You'll have course-deviation information from your navigation indicator and a distance reading to the waypoint on your DME display.

With RNAV you can "move" a VORTAC station to anywhere within 150 miles of its actual location. The waypoint may be at an airport without radio-navigation facilities, at the end of a runway (for an approved instrument approach), or at a checkpoint of your own choosing for straight-line cross-country navigation. You can fly directly to or from a waypoint as far as 250 miles away as long as your aircraft stays within range of a VORTAC.

You center the needle on your course-deviation indicator to fly directly to or from a waypoint, just as in VOR flying. But with RNAV, course deviation is shown in nautical miles off the centerline, not degrees off course. You can precisely fly the center of a constant-width course 10 nautical miles wide from takeoff to landing. This reduces the "needle chasing" that tends to occur when you cross a VOR station. Clearly, RNAV is a better way to fly.

Chapter 6
Truck and
Recreational
Vehicle Installations

Many of the same electronic products that are installed in cars can also be installed in such other automotive products as diesel trucks, pickups, vans, trailers, motor homes, and campers. In many respects the installations are similar to installations in cars. But, the construction features of many big trucks affect most installations in them. The presence of West Coast style mirrors on many trucks and recreational vehicles, and the size and construction of these vehicles, make antenna installations somewhat special. Finally, there are multifarious electronic gadgets of special or unique interest to owners of recreational vehicles. These general matters are the focus of this chapter. Specific installation instructions for electronic units commonly installed in trucks and recreational vehicles are given in Part 2 of this book.

PUTTING CB IN AN 18-WHEELER

The construction of truck tractors varies considerably. First of all, there are cab-over-engine tractors, such as Peterbilt and BMC Astro, and engine-in-front models, such as Reo and Kenworth. Then, in either type, there are variations in design that depend on the make and model. Unless you are very familiar with the truck in which you wish to install a CB or other unit, it will pay to visit the service department of a dealer for that make of truck. There you can obtain helpful advice and service literature.

In many trucks you can hang the CB transceiver under the dash just as in a car. In the cab-over models you may be able to hang the set from the crossbeam over the windshield. The crossbeam is hollow and has access panels, making it a perfect duct for antenna cable. Often, however, the crossbeam access panels are obstructed by sun visors and padding.

Another possibility for the cab-over models is to mount the CB in the kneehole beside the steering column. Many truckers, especially tall ones, will find this objectionable because of the possibility of bumping a knee on the

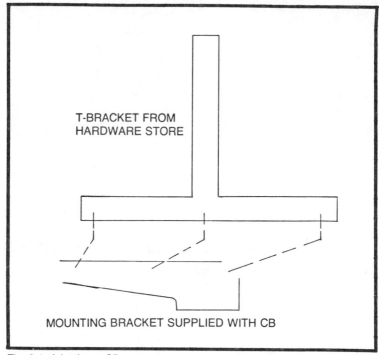

T-BRACKET FROM
HARDWARE STORE

MOUNTING BRACKET SUPPLIED WITH CB

Fig. 6-1. Adapting a CB transceiver mount for use on top of a truck console.

CB. It may be possible to suspend the transceiver from the air-conditioning housing on the ceiling. If the housing is plastic, install a metal plate inside the housing for reinforcement.

Probably the best place to mount a transceiver in a cab-over-engine tractor is on the console. Unfortunately, many transceiver brackets are not drilled in such a way that they can be mounted underneath a transceiver. Even if a bracket could be so used, the speaker, which is normally on the bottom of the transceiver, would be so close to the console that the sound would be muffled. The muffling problem could be solved by mounting a remote speaker on the console or behind the driver, but both the mounting and speaker problems can be solved by adding extra T-shaped brackets to the bracket that comes with the CB set (see Fig. 6-1). This provides convenient mounting holes for the transceiver and gets the speaker off the console.

One far-out possibility is to attach the bracket to the CB as intended by the manufacturer (over the top of the set) and mount the CB upside down on the console. However, you wouldn't mount a unit upside down in a $35,000 car, and it's not a good idea to try it in a $35,000 tractor either.

Proper power connection may be a problem in some large trucks. Unlike all modern American cars, some trucks have a positive-ground electrical system. You can check this with a voltmeter or VOM by taking a reading between ground and the "hot" power bus in the truck's power panel.

With the black, NEG, or − meter lead connected to a negative point and the red, POS, or + meter lead connected to a positive point, the meter needle will deflect upscale (rather than trying to go backwards). In supplying power to the transceiver, it is important to be sure to connect its leads in the proper polarity—negative to negative, positive to positive.

Some radios have only one power lead—the hot one—the ground connection being made through the CB chassis, mounting bracket and the vehicle. Of course, these won't work at all if the CB is mounted on a nonconductive surface and no provision is made for a ground lead. Usually the single power wire or the CB set bears a label telling whether the wire is to be connected to positive or negative.

Some sets have two leads so that they can be used in either positive- or negative-ground systems. In connecting these, just remember to connect the red wire to positive and the black wire to negative. Don't worry about whether the inline fuse is in the hot lead or not.

Truck electrical systems differ somewhat from automobile electrical systems. The starting system is 24 volts, but the battery system is tapped to provide 12 volts for the lights, accessories, and power panel.

Radios and other accessories should be connected directly to the power panel. To gain access to the panel, remove either the console cover or the separate cover over the power panel. The console cover is fastened with self-tapping screws. To remove it completely for easy routing of wires, you may have to unclip the air-conditioning vents. The power-panel consists of rows of circuit breakers and a series of 12-volt buses. Some of these are switched by the ignition switch, some are not. If the CB is to be used even when the switch is off, select one of the unswitched buses for connecting the hot wire. Note that the existing wires are connected with spade lugs installed on the wires with a crimping tool (available at auto, electrical, and hardware stores). Use spade lugs for the CB power connection to ensure reliable connection.

If you mount the radio on the console, drill a 1/2-inch hole near it for the wiring. Always try to keep the wires out of sight as much as possible. You may be able to run the antenna cable through the same hole as the power wire. If dual antennas are to be installed and there are two antenna leads to the transceiver, you will need two holes. Install rubber grommets (bushings) with a 1/4-inch inside diameter hole in any hole through which you plan to run a wire. On each mounting bolt, use two flat washers, one on each side of the console, and a lockwasher next to the nut. The flat washers will prevent the plastic console material from cracking.

If the radio has only one power lead, the metal case must be grounded. Even if the radio has both hot and ground leads, the case should be grounded to reduce ignition noise. If you mount the transceiver to a metal surface, the grounding will probably occur automatically. If you mount it on a plastic console, run a metallic-braid bonding strap from one mounting bolt to some metal structure under the console cover. Then check the grounding by measuring with an ohmmeter for zero ohms between the mounting bracket and the cab's sheet metal. Or, with a voltmeter, measure for 12 − 14 volts between the bracket and the power bus.

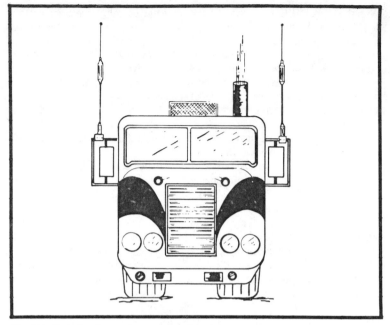

Fig. 6-2. Twin-trucker antennas on a big rig.

For 2-wire radios with a plastic case, don't worry about grounding; the power lead and antenna-cable shield will take care of it. For single-wire radios, however, do not rely on the antenna-cable shield for grounding.

Plan the routing of the power leads. If it will be necessary to add extra wire to them, solder the splices and wrap them with electrical tape. Keep the inline fuse outside the hole in the console and near the transceiver for easy access.

For overhead-mounted units, there are two ways to go with the power wires. One is to drill a hole and install a grommet in the hollow crossbeam and run the wire through the grommet and crossbeam and down the windshield center post. Another way is to run the wires to the side of the cab, down the doorpost, and behind the dashboard to the power panel.

ANTENNA MIRROR MOUNTS

West Coast style sideview mirrors (Fig. 6-2) are popular with truckers and owners of pickups and recreational vehicles. The mirrors are also popular and handy for mounting antennas. Either one or two such antennas may be used. "Twin trucker" antennas are available as a system, complete with a dual phasing harness necessary to connect them properly. Or, the antennas and phasing harness may be purchased separately. If you install two antennas—what is called a *cophase* system—everything must be balanced. That is, each mounting should be in exactly the same location on each side of the cab. Specific instructions for installing single and dual mirror-mount antennas are given in the chapter on antennas, in Part 2 of this book.

INSTALLATIONS IN VANS AND RECREATIONAL VEHICLES

Figure 6-3 shows a typical van installation of a CB system. The location of the various components is typical. Often, in these installations, it is possible to provide additional bracing as shown in Fig. 6-4. Note the side-mounted antenna in Fig. 6-3. These are available in heavy-duty models with stainless-steel shock springs for rugged applications on trucks, mobile homes, boats, sports equipment, and recreational vehicles. The universal mount is adjustable from 0 to 180° for vertical or horizontal mounting or anything in between. The Antenna Specialists Company's Model M-1D (Fig. 6-5) is an excellent example.

Mobile Antenna with Camper Bracket

The Antenna Specialists Model MR-247 camper-mount antenna (Fig. 6-6) solves the problem of where to put the antenna on metal campers and "poptops." The unique mount attaches to any flat surface and adjusts through 90°. It comes with a base-loaded, precision-tuned coil, stainless-steel shock spring and whip, 20 feet of coaxial cable, and a connector for the radio. The same company's Model M-210 is similar, but has a mount designed for each installation on luggage racks, sideview mirrors, ski racks, or any round or square tubing up to 3/4 inch across (Fig. 6-7).

Centered rooftop mounting with the antenna vertical is recommended for this antenna (Fig. 6-8). The antenna bracket also permits mounting the antenna vertically on the side of the vehicle (as close to the top as possible) or on angled surfaces.

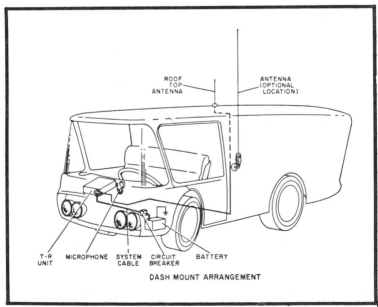

Fig. 6-3. A complete two-way-radio system installed in a van. (Courtesy RCA Corporation)

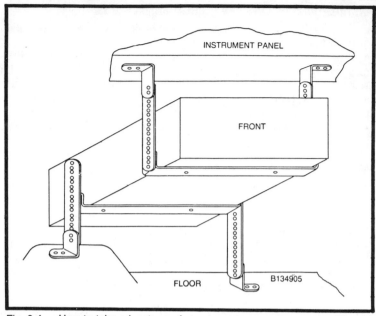

Fig. 6-4. How to take advantage of structures in a van to mount a CB set.

A ground plane is essential for the operation of this antenna. On some vehicles with nonmetallic bodies, it will be necessary to install a ground plane. Check with your RV dealer to determine the exact construction of your vehicle. Some RVs have an extensive aluminum frame under the

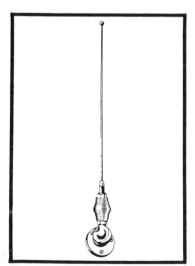

Fig. 6-5. Antenna Specialists antenna with a universal mount.

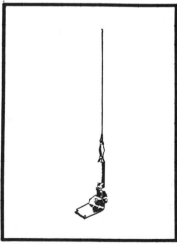

Fig. 6-6. A camper-mount antenna for any flat surface. (Courtesy Antenna Specialists Company)

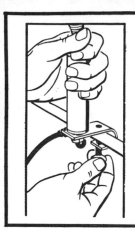

Fig. 6-7. Antenna mount for round or square tubing of mirrors and racks. (Courtesy Antenna Specialists Company)

fiberglass roof that will act as a ground plane, but the spacing between the roof-frame members must be 18 inches or less. If you choose a mounting location where the camper-bracket screws will attach to such a frame, you will not need to install a ground plane.

Before you assemble the antenna, apply some silicone grease on the threaded portions. This will protect them from the weather and make it easier to take the antenna apart. When routing the coaxial cable, choose a path that will conceal and protect it. Avoid any pinching, strain, or abrasion to the cable. Damaged cable is a common cause of poor antenna performance.

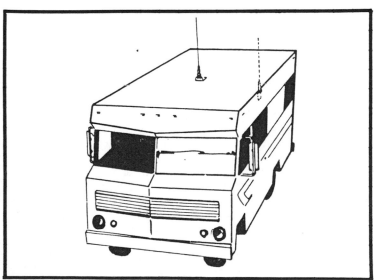

Fig. 6-8. Centered rooftop mounting is recommended for a camper antenna. (Courtesy Antenna Specialists Company)

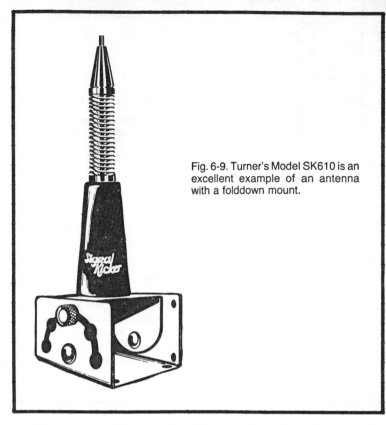

Fig. 6-9. Turner's Model SK610 is an excellent example of an antenna with a folddown mount.

Use a sealant at the mounting holes and where the cable enters the body. This will prevent water from getting inside—a disastrous thing to befall the deluxe interiors found in many vans and campers.

Folddown Mounts

The extra height of RVs and occasional operation off the road under low-hanging branches of trees make it very desirable to have an antenna that you can fold down out of harm's way when necessary. Turner's Model SK610 *Signal Kicker* antenna has a versatile folddown assembly (Fig. 6-9) that can be mounted on horizontal or vertical surfaces. An adapter plate is available to permit mounting the antenna on luggage-rack rails running in either direction. The folddown mechanism swings 180° and has several intermediate positions. A tapered locking bolt avoids rattle and holds the antenna in the desired position as you drive over bumpy roads or rough terrain.

Another folddown mount is Turner's Model SK411 gutter mount, shown in Fig. 6-10. Two bolts clamp the bracket to the rain gutter of almost any vehicle. A third bolt in the center of the mount adjusts the roof standoff. The standoff has a protective cover to prevent marring the vehicle's finish. A

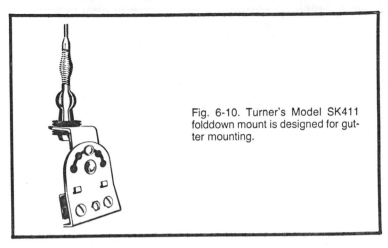

Fig. 6-10. Turner's Model SK411 folddown mount is designed for gutter mounting.

spring-loaded catch holds the antenna in the desired position. The mount folds over a 180° arc with intermediate detents.

Intercom for Recreational Vehicles

A mobile intercom is useful for communicating between the cab and camper of a mobile camper unit. It can also be used in any vehicle (camper, travel trailer, boat, etc.) where communication between two remote locations is desired. The intercom is an ideal baby sitter. It will continuously monitor all activities taking place in the camper while it's traveling down the highway. Music and news from the vehicle's radio can be switched to the camper and provide entertainment to anyone riding in the camper.

One such intercom is Heath's GD-160 *Mobilink*, shown in Fig. 6-11. When the master-unit switch is in the STD BY (stand by) position and the

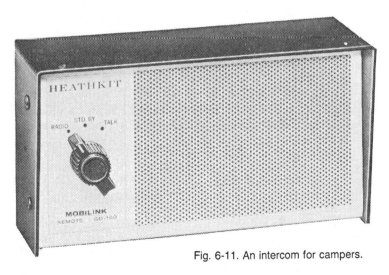

Fig. 6-11. An intercom for campers.

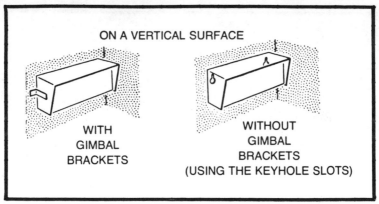

ON A VERTICAL SURFACE

WITH
GIMBAL
BRACKETS

WITHOUT
GIMBAL
BRACKETS
(USING THE KEYHOLE SLOTS)

Fig. 6-12. Mounting an intercom on a vertical surface.

remote-unit switch is in the RADIO or STD BY position, no battery power is drawn by the intercom. The solid-state amplifier circuit provides instant operation when the master-unit switch is in the MONITOR or TALK position, or when the remote-unit switch is in the TALK position.

Both units of the intercom are ruggedly built to withstand the vibration and adverse conditions normally encountered in over-the-road vehicles. The electronic circuits are in the master unit. They operate from the vehicle battery and, therefore, need no auxiliary power supply. A 15-foot, 5-conductor cable is supplied for connecting the master unit in the cab to the remote unit in the camper.

The master unit of an intercom may be mounted in any location in the truck cab that will allow the wires to be connected to the proper points. The remote unit can be mounted in any convenient location in the camper. In mounting an intercom, consider the following points:

- *Accessibility.* Each unit should be mounted in a handy location that will be easy to reach.
- *Available Space.* Be sure the proper amount of space is available at the locations you select.
- *Cable Routing.* Plan how you will route the cable between the master and remote units, including the locations of the holes where the cable will pass through the walls of the cab and camper body.

Some typical intercom mounting arrangements are shown in Fig. 6-12. Using brackets, a unit can be mounted above or below a horizontal surface as well as on a vertical surface, of course.

Refer to Fig. 6-13 to help you understand the operation of a typical intercom. Once you have your intercom installed (refer to installation instructions of manufacturer or instructions in Part 2 of this book), turn the vehicle's ignition switch to the ACC (accessory) position. Turn the master-unit FUNCTION switch to the MONITOR position. Have someone enter the camper and speak in a normal tone of voice. You should hear the person speaking and any other sounds that occur within the pickup range of the remote unit. Adjust the GAIN (volume) control to the desired level.

144

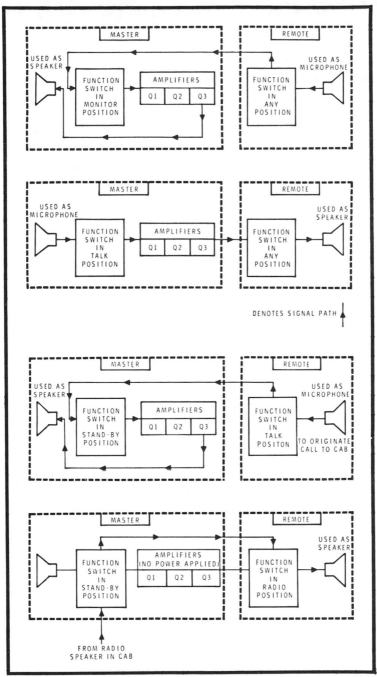

Fig. 6-13. Operation of the Heath intercom.

To check for two-way communication, turn the master-unit FUNC-TION switch to the TALK position and at the same time speak in a normal manner. Your voice should be heard anywhere in the camper.

Next, turn the master-unit FUNCTION switch to the STD BY position. Have the person in the camper turn the remote-unit function switch to TALK and speak in a normal manner. The person's voice should be heard in the cab. This is a call-origination feature from the remote to the master unit.

Turn the remote-unit FUNCTION switch to the RADIO position and the master-unit FUNCTION switch to the STD BY position. Turn on the radio in the cab. The program material should now come from the speaker in the remote unit as well as the regular radio speaker in the cab. The radio's volume control will determine the volume of the program material.

This illustrates most of the features to be found in camper intercoms. Not all intercoms have all of these features, however.

PA SYSTEM FOR RECREATIONAL VEHICLES

A PA amplifier is a handy accessory for any recreational vehicle. An excellent example is Radio Shack's *Realistic* MPA-10 model, a 10-watt public-address amplifier. The PA is designed specifically for use in mobile applications. You can use it in your camper, on picnics, for outdoor events, on a bus or truck, on your boat, at parades—anywhere you'd have a difficult time obtaining 120-volt AC power but can use a 12-volt battery.

The connection of a mobile PA is quick and simple. (Part 2 of this book gives complete instructions.) You can install the PA in almost any location, it takes so little room—in or under a dashboard, in a glove compartment, under a seat, against the roof of a vehicle, or in any convenient place.

Before you drill any holes to install a PA, consider the following:

1. Will other wires be in the way? (Don't drill into them.)
2. Can you route the power and speaker wires easily?
3. How about convenience of use?

If universal mounting brackets are provided with the PA, use them to mount the PA either above or under a solid horizontal surface. Drill holes as appropriate, taking care not to drill into existing wires or trim, and fasten the brackets with hardware (normally provided with the unit). Mount the microphone clip to either side of the PA amplifier, depending on which side is more convenient. If no microphone mounting clip is provided, you can obtain one at any store that sells CB radios. Some of these clips are mounted with hardware, some with magnets, and some with an adhesive surface.

INVERTERS

Inverters are used to supplement the battery as a source of power in cars and other conveyances. A *power* inverter, such as the Heath Model MP-10 (Fig. 6-14), converts the 6- or 12-volt direct current of an automobile-type battery to the 120-volt 60-hertz alternating current required by most electrical devices used in the home. It makes it possible for you to use your AC-powered phonograph in your camper, or to use your electric razor in your car, for example.

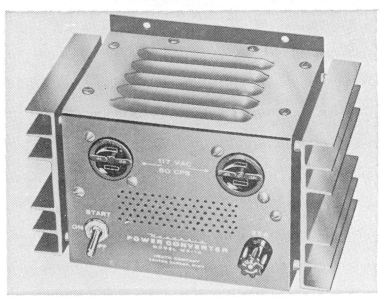

Fig. 6-14. A power inverter converts battery voltage to house-current voltage to power household appliances in a recreational vehicle.

A *voltage* inverter, as exemplified by the Archer Model 22-129 (Fig. 6-15), is a DC-to-DC converter. It makes possible the operation of standard automobile accessories, which are designed for the 12-volt negative-ground electrical systems in modern American cars, with those foreign cars that have a positive-ground system, and with the few vehicles (including old domestic cars) that have a 6-volt electrical system.

Power Inverter

The Heath Model MP-10 power inverter changes direct current (DC) into 60 Hz alternating current (AC). In other words, the MP-10 makes the equivalent of electric house power available from a 6- or 12-volt storage battery.

The electrical operation of the MP-10 involves no moving parts. This results in a long service life. Also, the MP-10 will handle almost any type of electrical load, within its rated power-output capabilities, in a satisfactory manner.

With the introduction of transistors it became possible to create a new type of DC-to-AC power inverter. Older types of power inverters use rotating machines and mechanical vibrators to perform the switching function. The transistorized power inverter closely resembles the vibrator-type converter, but the transistors do the work of the vibrator. Transistors are much more reliable than vibrators. Transistorized power inverters increase conversion efficiency about 20% over the older types.

The DC-to-AC power inverter can be operated from a 6-volt or 12-volt storage battery. The output-voltage waveform is the same in magnitude and

Fig. 6-15. The Archer 22-129A converts a 6-volt negative-ground or a 12-volt positive-ground electrical system to a conventional 12-volt negative-ground system as required by many automotive accessories. (Courtesy Radio Shack)

frequency in either case. However, the inverter is capable of delivering twice as much output power from a 12-volt source as from a 6-volt source.

For example, the Heath MP-10 will take up to 25 amperes of input current in either 6- or 12-volt operation; however, since power equals current times voltage, 12-volt operation will provide twice as much power as 6-volt operation.

For 12-volt operation there is a maximum power rating as well as a continuous power rating. The reason for this is that the transformer will not continuously handle 25 amperes of current. Excessive heating will result, and the transformer may be damaged if this continues too long. If the MP-10 is started "cold" at 77°, it can deliver up to 240 watts continuously for approximately 25 minutes, at which time the load should be reduced.

A power inverter is derated as air temperature is increased. The inverter has internal heat losses, and this heat must be given off to the surrounding air so that electrical components in the unit do not attain temperatures above their ratings and burn up.

If the air around the inverter is warm, the continuous-output power must be reduced, thus reducing the internal heat losses. The warm air can then adequately cool the inverter and keep the component temperature at a safe level. For example, the transformer in Heath's MP-10 is rated at 130°C (266°F). The internal parts of the transistors can operate up to 95°C (203°F). At room temperatures the transformer will be the limiting component. At higher temperatures—say, 50°C (122°F)—the transistors will limit the output power. The inverter will become very hot to the touch when it is operating under maximum continuous-output power. This is normal.

Output Voltage. The output-voltage waveform of the inverter also needs some explanation. It has a different shape than that of standard home power systems, but it will do essentially the same job. The MP-10 has an essentially square waveform, whereas the home usually has a sine waveform.

In Fig. 6-16, notice the difference between the two waveforms, which have identical RMS values (117 volts). The RMS value of a waveform is equal to the DC value required to produce an equal amount of heat in the same resistance. In the case above, the two waveforms will produce the same amount of heat in the same resistance. Usually the most important factor of a waveform is its RMS value, but occasionally the frequency and peak values are also important. For example, a radio designed for home use derives its tube voltage from the peak value of the sine wave. An equivalent square wave powering the same radio will produce somewhat lower tube voltages. The radio will operate adequately from the square wave, but will probably require a slightly higher volume-control setting. Other similar types of equipment will also operate adequately when powered from a square wave, but may also require different control settings.

Equipment Powered by Inverters. It is possible that some equipment, when powered by an inverter, will exhibit peculiar characteristics. Following are some typical examples and possible remedies for when the effect is not tolerable.

Radio receivers, audio amplifiers, and other equipment using a speaker or headphone to produce sound may have a slight 120-hertz buzz. This is

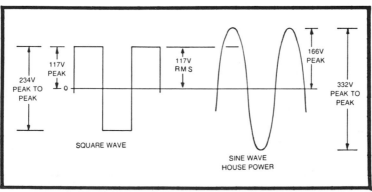

Fig. 6-16. Waveforms of the power converter discussed in the text versus waveforms of house power.

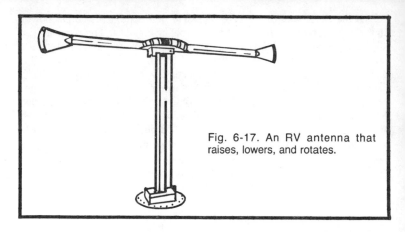

Fig. 6-17. An RV antenna that raises, lowers, and rotates.

caused by the steep slopes of the square wave. The buzz can enter the equipment through its own power supply. It might also enter through the filament wiring for the tubes, but this is less likely. If the power supply in the equipment is in good working order, the buzz will probably not be injected at this point. The most likely place is in the switch circuit. The switch is usually associated with the volume control, where a small amount of energy is radiated from the switch to the volume control, thus injecting the 120-hertz buzz into the audio circuit. A possible cure is to place a 1 or 2 μF, 200-volt capacitor directly across the output of the inverter. This reduces the slope of the square wave, but the inverter may run slightly hotter.

The frequency of the inverter may not be exactly 60 hertz, since the frequency is directly proportional to the input voltage. Also, frequency will change slightly with the load. Motor speed is not critical for most applications; however, record players and tape recorders require a fairly critical speed. Some motors have a speed control. For those that do not, a little experimentation with the battery voltage should provide satisfactory operation. If the voltage is high (motor running too fast), a series dropping resistor in the battery wires may help. For example, if the voltage is 1 volt too high and the current is 5 amps, a 0.2-ohm 7-watt resistor would drop the voltage to produce a good motor speed. Usually this problem is not serious enough to warrant extensive experimentation to obtain acceptable hi-fi performance.

The inverter *cannot* be used backwards to charge a battery. The DC current will not reverse, and transistor damage will result. Always turn the inverter off when it is not in use. This will save unnecessary drain on the battery.

OTHER PRODUCTS FOR VANS, CAMPERS, AND RECREATIONAL VEHICLES

There are quite a number of products for vans, campers, and recreational vehicles that are similar to home and automotive products but specially adapted for use in these vehicles. The installation of a number of such products is described in Part 2 of this book. The following devices are available from recreational-vehicle dealers or from J.C. Whitney & Co., P.O. Box 8410, Chicago, IL 60680.

RV Antenna

Figure 6-17 shows an RV antenna for AM and FM radio, color and black-and-white TV (both VHF and UHF) that rises, lowers, and rotates. The antenna is operated by a crank from inside the RV and can fold flat for traveling. A separate VHF-UHF signal amplifier is available to boost reception in fringe areas and works off the 12-volt power supply of the RV.

The antenna in Fig. 6-17 rises up to 35 inches off the roof, rotates 360° in a turning radius of 31 inches, and folds flush to the roof. Universal shafts adapt to all roofs. The base itself remains stationary, so there are no problems with movement, wear, or leaks. The easy-to-install antenna requires only two 3/8-inch holes in the roof.

Folding All-Directions Antenna

The TV antenna in Fig. 6-18 receives signals from all directions and folds compactly for traveling. The arms fold into a 24-inch tube with a rain cap for protection during travel. The two dipole elements mounted at right angles give nearly uniform reception from all directions, but the antenna is rotatable for peaking the signal and getting the best reception available from the antenna. This antenna uses a 70-ohm coaxial cable for the lead-in wire, which is supplied. Installation is a simple matter of connecting the antenna leads to the back of your TV.

Printed-Circuit Indoor TV Antenna

If keeping the antenna out of sight part of the time by folding it up isn't good enough and you wish to keep it out of sight all the time, there's a printed-circuit antenna (Fig. 6-19) that works indoors. The antenna element

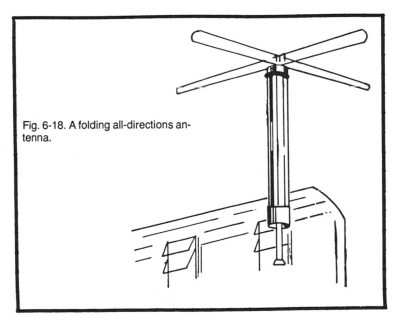

Fig. 6-18. A folding all-directions antenna.

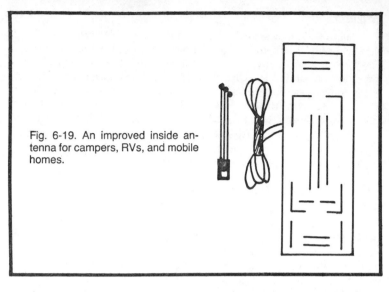

Fig. 6-19. An improved inside antenna for campers, RVs, and mobile homes.

consists of a copper pattern attached to a flat plastic board and has 3 times the area of conventional "rabbit ears" antennas. The improved "capture area" is said to reduce ghosting, snow, and interference in the received picture and produce a good picture even in a metal-walled mobile home. The antenna is good for reception up to 35 miles, in its deluxe version, of VHF, UHF, and FM. THe flat design lets you mount the antenna behind drapes, under carpets, under shelves—or most anywhere.

TV Shelf

Not an electronic product itself, the TV shelf (Fig. 6-20) is an invaluable accessory to the TV in a van, mobile home, camper, or recreational vehicle. The shelf swivels left and right and locks in one of five positions for easy viewing of the TV at any angle. Invaluable in the RV since it saves valuable counterspace, the TV shelf is also applicable to the rec room or kitchen. The die-cast aluminum shelf is light itself, but it can safely hold a TV set weighing up to 50 pounds. The arm extends 16 inches, including the base. The installation consists of simply turning three screws into the wall.

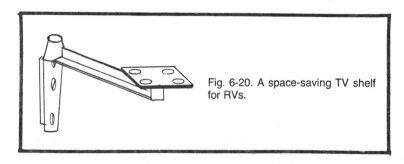

Fig. 6-20. A space-saving TV shelf for RVs.

Fig. 6-21. A stereo entertainment console complete with speakers, into which you tuck your favorite tape player or radio.

Stereo Entertainment Console

One more entertainment product specially made for RVs, vans, and trucks is the roof-mounted stereo entertainment console pictured in Fig. 6-21. The space-saving console provides a neat and handy means of mounting tape players and radios, or any combination of them. It comes complete with 5-inch speakers under padded grilles; you supply your favorite tape player or radio, which will fit neatly between the speakers. This is definitely the way to go if you want your roof-mount installation to look like a factory job.

Dual-Battery Charging System

Figure 6-22 shows a solid-state electronic system that automatically protects and charges the dual-battery system of a boat, camper, or trailer from the vehicle's alternator or generator during operation of the vehicle. When the vehicle is stationary, current is drawn from the auxiliary battery only, so the starting battery always stays fully charged. The automatic control switch is rated at 120 amperes. This valuable aid to mobile living is easily affordable (about 10 dollars) and easily installed.

Fluorescent Lights

Built-in electronic circuitry makes it possible for these lights (Fig. 6-23) to work off a vehicle's 12-volt battery. The installation is a simple 2-wire hookup, just as with regular incandescent lights; but the electronic fluorescent lights produce more light from less current because less energy is wasted as heat. The reduced heating can itself be an advantage, especially in

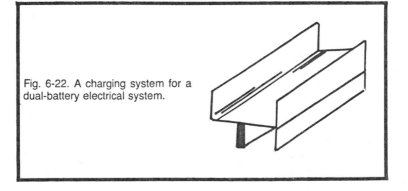

Fig. 6-22. A charging system for a dual-battery electrical system.

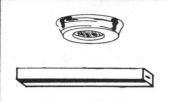

Fig. 6-23. Fluorescent lights with built-in electronic circuits that permit operation from a battery.

hot weather. The lights use standard tubes available anywhere. A built-in input filter prevents interference to radio or TV reception, and a built-in ON/OFF switch provides convenient installation and operation. A circular light with a 22-watt tube draws only about 1.4 amperes. A rectangular light with two 15-watt tubes draws about 1.7 amperes.

Smoke-and-Gas Alarm for Vehicles

Certainly not the least among the electronic products you should consider for your TV, van, bus, boat, truck, or even your car, is a smoke-and-gas detector that can operate off the vehicle's 12-volt battery. Detectors have become very popular with homeowners lately, and in some areas they are being required by law in mobile homes. Like mobile homes, recreational vehicles often have limited egress and a potentially dangerous supply of propane or other gas, so smoke detectors are very desirable for these vehicles. The one shown in Fig. 6-24 is specially designed for vehicles. It is easy to wire in any 12-volt circuit—just hook up the two wires. To complete the installation, simply mount the unit to a wall, ceiling, or dash with the adhesive mounting strips supplied.

Fig. 6-24. A smoke, gas, and fire detector designed to operate from a vehicle's electrical system.

The smoke detector detects fire before visible smoke appears. It detects propane and other flammable gases before they reach explosive concentrations. It also detects carbon monoxide (as well as other poisonous gases) before they reach dangerous levels—reason enough to install it in any vehicle. A piercing 85-decibel alarm shouts warning. A reassuring LED power-on light tells when the unit is on guard. The unit uses only about as much electricity as a single Christmas-tree light. There are no batteries to replace, and no maintenance is required. If you install only one electronic accessory in your recreational vehicle or truck, this is the one to get.

Part 2
Index of
Electronic Installations

Part 2 of this book is concerned with installations of specific accessories in just about every kind of conveyance—including bicycles. Part 1 provides the necessary background for making these installations; it is concerned with matters of general interest—the electrical systems and mechanical designs of various conveyances, the principles of the most popular electronic accessories, and how to work with tools. For your convenience in looking up an installation of interest at any given time, the installations in Part 2 appear in alphabetical order, from *Aircraft Timepiece* to *Windshield Wipers*. As a further aid to information retrieval in this part, a separate mini-index of various categories of installations appears at the end of this introduction.

To provide detailed instructions of dependable accuracy, the following chapters describe the installation of specific makes and models of accessories, often in specific vehicles. In many cases the instructions are directly transferrable to other makes and models. In other cases, the instructions are applicable by extrapolation. In all cases they should be very useful. Even if you are only contemplating an installation, the instructions for a similar installation will show you what is involved and help you to make your purchasing and installation decisions. The installation instructions provided by manufacturers are of widely varying quality, but I hope that you will find the instructions included here to be of uniformly good quality. They cover as wide a range of products and as many contingencies as space permits.

Besides detailed and specific installation instructions, Part 2 provides much information of a more general nature. Where is the best location for my antenna? What do the technical terms used in an antenna manufacturer's literature mean? How does single-sideband work? How do you use a single-sideband CB? What types of signals can you monitor with a scanner? What do you need to know before you install a CD ignition? These are examples of the questions that are answered in the following chapters. I hope this information will help you to decide which accessories to install and help you to get the most out of the ones you decide on.

AUDIO/ENTERTAINMENT INSTALLATIONS

AM Radios *See* RADIOS
Bicycle Radio
FM Radios *See* RADIOS
FM Radio Converter
FM Signal Booster
PA Amplifier
Radios
Speakers
Speaker-Selector Switch
Tape Players

BOAT INSTALLATIONS

Antennas
CB Units
Depth Sounder/Recorder
Direction Finder
Fathometer *See* DEPTH SOUNDER/RECORDER
Foghorn
Hailer *See* FOGHORN
Ignitions
Marine Scanner
Vapor Detector

MOTOR VEHICLE INSTALLATIONS

Burglar Alarms
Digital Clock
Ignitions
Intercom for Recreational Vehicles
Inverters
MPG/MPH Meter
Radar Detector
Siren
Tachometers
Windshield-Wiper Delay

RADIO-COMMUNICATION INSTALLATIONS

Amateur-Radio Installation
Antennas
CB Units
Marine Scanner
Microphone with Built-In Amplifier
Mobile Radio
Police and Fire Scanner
Power Supply (High Voltage)
Two-Way Radio *See* MOBILE RADIO
VHF Scanner *See* POLICE AND FIRE SCANNER

Chapter 7
Aircraft Timepiece

Heath's Model OI-1154 aircraft clock/timer is essentially five instruments in one. The top 4-digit display (Fig. 7-1) always shows Zulu (Greenwich Mean) time in 24-hour format. Four switch-selected functions share the bottom 4-digit display. These functions are as follows: 24-hour local time, 24-minute timer, 24-hour total trip time, and 24-hour trip time, and 24-hour total trip time alarm.

The clock/timer will keep very accurate time once it is installed and correctly set. If the clock/timer is ever momentarily disconnected, or if power is interrupted for more than one-third second, the left digit in both displays will blink to indicate that power has been off and that the clock/timer must be reset.

The entire display of your clock/timer will automatically blank under low-voltage, engine-cranking conditions. This is to conserve power, and preserve memory when the unit is used on a 14-volt system.

SWITCH FUNCTIONS AND DISPLAY MODES

The following paragraphs describe the operation of each of the five Clock/Timer functions (refer to Fig. 7-1).

Function 1...Zulu Time—Local Time

With the function switch turned fully counterclockwise, the indicator dot appears above the Z on the display window. In this switch position, the pushbuttons program only the Zulu clock function. Zulu time, in 24-hour format, will appear on the top display. Local time, also in 24-hour format, will appear on the bottom display. Note that only hours and minutes are displayed in this switch position.

Fig. 7-1. The Heath OI-1154 combination clock and timer.

Function 2...Zulu Time—Local Time

With the function switch turned one step in a clockwise direction, the indicator dot appears below the L on the display window. In this switch position, the pushbuttons program only the local clock function. Local time, in 24-hour format, will appear on the bottom display. Zulu time, also in 24-hour format, will appear on the top display. Note that only hours and minutes are displayed in this switch position.

Function 3...Zulu Time—24-Minute Timer

With the function switch in the center position, the indicator dot appears below the 24 on the display window. In this switch position, the pushbuttons program only the 24-minute timer function. The elapsed time, in minutes and seconds, will appear on the bottom display. Zulu time, in hours and minutes, will appear on the top display. The 24-minute timer will only run with the function switch in the center position.

Function 4...Zulu Time—Total Trip Timer

With the function switch turned one step clockwise from the center position, the indicator dot appears below the TT on the display window. In this switch position, the pushbuttons program only the total trip-timer function. Total trip time, in 24-hour format, will appear on the bottom display. Zulu time, also in 24-hour format, will appear on the top display. The total trip timer automatically counts time, and the display comes on only when the master power switch is on (closed). Turning the master power switch off inhibits the display and the trip-time counter. Total trip time, however, remains in the clock memory with the master switch off.

Function 5...Zulu Time—Total Trip Time Alarm

With the function switch turned fully clockwise, the indicator dot appears below the A on the display window. In this switch position, the pushbuttons program only the total trip timer alarm function. Total trip time alarm, in 24-hour format, will appear on the bottom display. Zulu time, also in 24-hour format, will appear on the top display. The total-trip timer alarm automatically counts time, and the display comes on only when the master power switch is on (closed). Turning the master power switch off inhibits the display and the trip time alarm counter. Total trip time alarm, however, remains in the clock memory with the master switch off.

Refer to Fig. 7-1 for the location of the pushbutton switches referred to in the following paragraphs.

The three secondary pushbuttons on the clock/timer are recessed to prevent accidentally pushing them during operation. Use a pointed instrument to push these buttons.

ZERO—When pushed, sets the entire register for the function in use to zero.

HOLD—When pushed, displays unit minutes and seconds without advancing the time.

RESET—When pushed, resets the total trip timer alarm. The total trip timer alarm may be reset with the FUNCTION switch in any position.

SLOW—When pushed, advances time at 1 minute per second.

FAST—When pushed, advances time at 1 hour per second.

SETTING ZULU TIME

Determine how far off the displayed Zulu time is from the actual Zulu time. Then, correct the displayed time by using the appropriate method listed below.

Zulu Clock Far Off

1. Turn the FUNCTION switch fully counterclockwise. The indicator dot, appearing above the Z on the display window, will be lit. In this switch position, the pushbuttons program only the Zulu clock function.
2. Push the ZERO pushbutton to reset the top display to 00:00.
3. Push the FAST pushbutton until the display indicates about 5 minutes slow as compared with the actual Zulu time. Then release the FAST pushbutton.
4. Push the SLOW pushbutton to slowly advance the Zulu clock until the display indicates the correct time. Then release the SLOW pushbutton.

Zulu Clock Slow (Less Than 2 Minutes)

Push the SLOW pushbutton to slowly advance the Zulu clock until the display indicates the correct time. Then release the SLOW pushbutton.

Zulu Clock Fast (Less Than 2 Minutes)

Push the HOLD pushbutton until Zulu time catches up with the Zulu time display on your Clock/Timer. Then release the HOLD pushbutton. NOTE: While you push the HOLD pushbutton, the Zulu clock display indicates minutes and seconds, but the clock does not advance.

The Zulu clock can be synchronized to a time standard by making it run a maximum of 1 minute fast. Then push the HOLD pushbutton until the standard catches up with your clock/timer display. Quickly release the HOLD button.

SETTING LOCAL TIME

Determine how far off the displayed time is from the actual local time. Then, correct the displayed time by using the appropriate method listed below.

Local Clock Far Off

1. Turn the FUNCTION switch fully counterclockwise, then one step clockwise. The indicator dot, appearing below the L on the display window, will be lit. In this switch position, the pushbuttons program only the local clock function.
2. Push the ZERO pushbutton to reset the bottom display to 00:00.
3. Push the FAST pushbutton until the display indicates about 5 minutes slow as compared with the actual local time. Then release the FAST pushbutton.
4. Push the SLOW pushbutton to slowly advance the local clock until the display indicates the correct time. Then release the SLOW pushbutton.

Local Clock Slow (Less Than 2 Minutes)

Push the SLOW pushbutton to slowly advance the local clock until the display indicates the correct time. Then release the SLOW pushbutton.

Local Clock Fast (Less Than 2 Minutes)

Push the HOLD pushbutton until local time catches up with the local time display on the clock/timer. Then release the HOLD pushbutton. While you push the HOLD pushbutton, the local clock display indicates minutes and seconds, but the clock does not advance.

The local clock can be synchronized to a time standard by making it run a maximum of 1 minute fast. Then, push the HOLD pushbutton until the standard catches up with the clock/timer display. Quickly release the HOLD button.

TYPICAL INSTALLATION

1. Select a convenient mounting location for your clock/timer. The Heath model requires a 3-1/8 inch diameter mounting hole. This location should be readily viewable and within easy reach of the pilot. Make sure the location is not in direct sunlight much of the

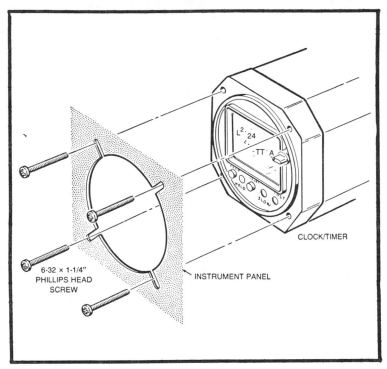

Fig. 7-2. How a clock is mounted in the instrument panel of an aircraft. (Courtesy Heath Company)

time. Also make sure there is at least a 7-inch clearance directly behind the instrument panel for easy installation.

2. Prepare the selected instrument-panel opening, as necessary.
3. Remove and save the four 6-32 × 1-1/4 inch Phillips screws that secure the bezel to the clock/timer cabinet.
4. Refer to Fig. 7-2 and install the clock/timer at the selected location on the instrument panel. Use the four screws removed in the previous step.
5. Identify the three clock/timer power wires (#20 A.W.G.) as follows:

    Black wire—negative ground.

    Red wire—unswitched 14/28 volts DC, fused at 1 ampere.

    White wire—switched 14/28 volts DC, fused at 1 ampere.

NOTE: Use slow-blow fuses.

6. Cut each of the power wires to the proper length, then connect each wire to the proper circuit-protection terminal in the aircraft.
7. Remove the fuse from the fuseholder. Save the fuse for use as a spare.
8. Use cable ties to tie the clock/timer power wires to existing cables.

Chapter 8

Amateur
Radio Installation

This chapter will discuss the installation and operation of an FM transceiver for the radio-amateur 2-meter band. The chapter will discuss the installation of the transceiver in an automobile, but the same principles apply to installations in other types of conveyances, such as a boat, an airplane, or even a snowmobile. For specificity and clarity, the instructions are given with reference to a particular transceiver—Heath Company's Model HW-2036 (Fig. 8-1); however, the instructions apply as well to other similar units. Also covered is a linear amplifier for boosting the power of a 5-to-15 watt transceiver to an output of between 20 and 50 watts.

Make sure that the voltage output of your battery charging system is at least 12.6 volts and that it does not exceed 16 volts under any circumstances. If the votlage is not within these limits, have the system adjusted.

HEATH HW-2036 2-METER TRANSCEIVER

Refer to Fig. 8-2 for a suggested arrangement of components and their interconnections. Then decide where and how you will mount your transceiver. Look at Fig. 8-3 for some under-the-dash mounting suggestions. A home-brew adapter could be made for the driveshaft hump, and the gimbal plate (or gimbal bracket) could be mounted on the adapter.

Figure 8-3 shows the gimbal plate, which can be permanently mounted in the automobile. This gives you the option of removing the gimbal bracket from the passenger compartment when the transceiver is not mounted there. Figure 8-4 shows how the gimbal bracket, gimbal plate, and transceiver fit together. You can remove the transceiver by loosening the thumbnuts (and pulling apart the power wire connector), and you can remove the gimbal bracket by removing the thumbscrews. Of course, you can attach the gimbal bracket permanently to the automobile and not use the gimbal plate. However, it is often convenient to be able to remove the gimbal bracket.

Decide upon the power wire routing path. You can run the red power wire through an existing opening in the firewall direct to the battery. Alternately, there may be an unused circuit available on the accessory fuse block of your automobile, and the power can be taken from this source. The ignition switch will usually control the accessory circuit. Also determine where you will connect the black (ground) power wire.

NOTE: If you prefer, you can install an additional fuse in the red power wire near the battery. The inline fuse already installed will protect the transceiver in either fixed or mobile installations, but will not, for example, protect the battery should the power wire short-circuit to the firewall.

Finally, determine the routing of the antenna transmission line.

Mounting Hardware

If you are going to use the gimbal plate, use the gimbal plate as a template to drill two mounting holes in the lower lip of the dash. Use a 5/32-inch or a #25 drill bit.

Secure the gimbal plate to the dash with two #10 × 1/2-inch sheet-metal screws. Use either pair of slots to position the plate as desired. Extra screws may be needed in some installations.

Refer to Fig. 8-4 and secure the gimbal bracket to the gimbal plate. Use #10 flatwashers and 10-32 thumbscrews. The slots in the gimbal bracket may be toward the rear of the vehicle, if you prefer.

The transceiver has an internal speaker. If you prefer, you can connect an external 8-ohm speaker to the transceiver. If you are going to use the transceiver's internal speaker, push the rear-panel slide switch to INT.

If you are going to use an external speaker, refer to Fig. 8-5 and install a phono plug on the speaker leads. Connect the plug to the SPKR socket on

Fig. 8-1. A synthesized 2-meter FM transceiver. (Courtesy Heath Company)

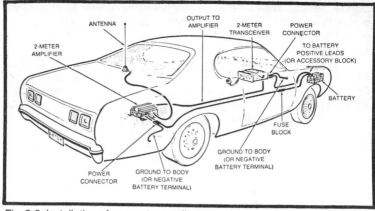

Fig. 8-2. Installation of an amateur-radio transceiver and linear amplifier. (Courtesy Heath Company)

the rear panel, and push the rear-panel slide switch to EXT. Refer to Fig. 8-4, loosen the two thumbnuts, insert the studs on the sides of the transceiver into the slots in the gimbal bracket, and tighten the thumbnuts.

Power Wiring

You can connect the power wire directly to the battery, although it is possible there is an unused terminal available on the accessory fuse block of your vehicle. In this case, connect the red power wire to the unused terminal. A 1/4-inch push-on connector can be used. The ignition switch will usually control this circuit in the same manner as the other accessory circuits. To make sure the circuit is suitable, connect a voltmeter between the terminal and the automobile body and turn the ignition key to either ON or to ACCESSORY. If there is no voltage reading, check to make sure a fuse is actually installed.

On some automobiles, the starter-relay terminal is a convenient place to obtain battery voltage. If you decide to use this connection, buy a solder lug which will fit the relay terminal.

Installation

1. Remove and set aside the fuse from the transceiver's fuseholder.
2. Temporarily place the transceiver in its permanent position.
3. Plug the male connector on the power wires into the female connector on the transceiver.
4. Route the red wire to your battery (or the accessory fuse block). Allow a little extra length for strain relief and cut the wire to length.
5. Install the required type of connector on the red wire and connect it to your battery or the fuse block.
6. Route the black wire from the power connector to the ground point you have selected. Allow a little extra length for strain relief and cut the wire to length.

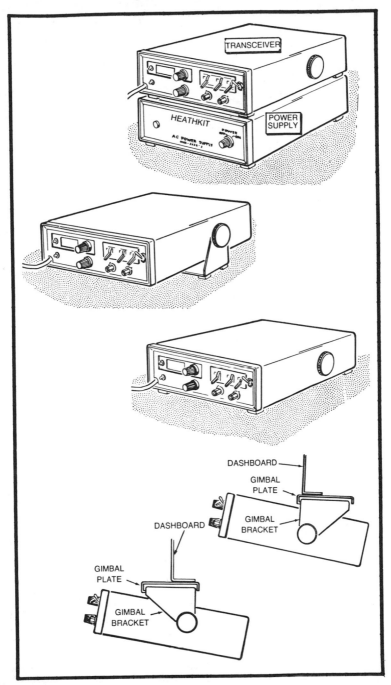

Fig. 8-3. Underdash mounting possibilities for an amateur transceiver.

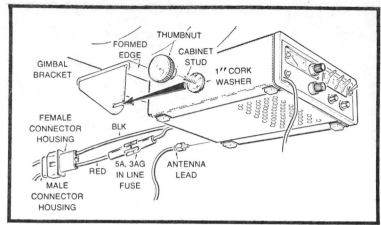

Fig. 8-4. Mounting the transceiver in the gimbal bracket.

7. Install a spade lug on the end of the black wire and secure the lug to the ground point with a #6 sheet-metal screw.
8. Turn the volume control counterclockwise until it clicks and then replace the fuse in the fuseholder.
9. Turn the volume control clockwise until it clicks. The meter face should light, indicating that you have correctly made your power connection.
10. Start your automobile (boat, aircraft) engine.
11. Check for alternator "whine" in the receiver and transmitter.

NOTE: If alternator whine exists, refer to the appropriate section of this handbook or your local automotive garage for assistance in locating the problem.

Operation of 2-Meter Transceiver

Refer to Fig. 8-6 for the location of controls, connections, and adjustment points. Switch positions and control settings are normally as follows:

Speaker. If you use an external 8-ohm speaker, connect it to the rear-panel SPKR socket and push the rear-panel speaker switch to EXT. If

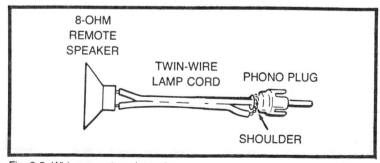

Fig. 8-5. Wiring an external speaker.

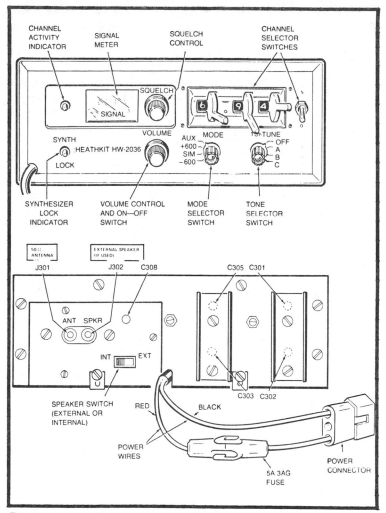

Fig. 8-6. Controls, connections, and adjustment points for a 2-meter amateur transceiver. (Courtesy Heath Company)

you use the built-in speaker, make sure the rear-panel speaker switch is at INT.

Microphone. Use the microphone supplied with the transceiver. Depress the microphone switch to activate the transmit circuits; release the switch to receive.

Signal Meter. The front-panel meter shows both relative transmitter output and relative received signal strength.

Squelch. To adjust the squelch control, first turn it fully counterclockwise. Turn the transceiver on and set the volume control so you hear background noise at average volume. Then turn the squelch-control knob clockwise until the noise just disappears. Setting the squelch control further clockwise requires a stronger received signal to "break" the squelch.

Channel/Activity Indicator. The amber LED (to the left of the meter) lights whenever the receiver is unsquelched.

SYNTH LOCK Indicator. The red LED lights whenever the synthesizer is unlocked. It will normally light briefly when you change frequency, switch from transmit to receive, or switch from receive to transmit.

Mode Switch. The SIM (simplex) position provides transmitter and receiver operation on the displayed frequency. In the −600 mode, the transmitter operates 600 kHz *below* the receiver frequency. In the +600 mode, the transmitter operates 600 kHz *above* the receiver frequency. An AUX (auxiliary) position is provided for an alternate frequency split, should you require one. Do not use this position if you have not installed an auxiliary crystal, because the transmitter will not operate.

Tone Switch. Some repeaters require a subaudible continuous access tone. This switch allows you to select one of three tones (adjustable internally) or a no-tone (off) condition. This switch should normally be OFF when you use simplex operation.

Channel-Selection Switches. Use the lever switches to select the 1 MHz, 100 kHz, and 10 kHz digits of the desired receive frequency. Use the toggle switch to select either 0 kHz or 5 kHz. The left-hand lever switch must be set to 4, 5, 6, or 7 (also 3 or 8 for CAP or MARS operation). The displayed frequency is always the receiver frequency and will be the transmit frequency only when the mode switch is in the SIM (simplex) position.

NOTE: You must add the displayed frequency to 140 MHz to obtain the correct operating frequency, for example:

$$6.940 = 146.940$$

CAUTION: In the +600 and −600 modes the transmitter frequency is 600 kHz higher or 600 kHz lower than the receiver frequency. You must use care to avoid out-of-band transmission in these modes. A smiliar condition exists in the auxiliary mode if it is used.

Power Supply

A DC voltage between 12.6 volts and 16 volts will operate the transceiver. The voltage can be furnished by an AC-operated power supply or a 12-volt system, such as an automobile battery. The supply must have a negative ground and be capable of at least a 2.6-ampere output.

CAUTION: Before you connect this transceiver to a mobile "12-volt" power source, check the voltage at the battery with the engine running above a fast idle. *The voltage must not exceed 16 volts* or the transceiver may be damaged.

POWER AMPLIFIER FOR 2-METERS

The Heath Model HA-202 amplifier (Fig. 8-2) is a compact 2-meter amplifier designed for mobile FM operation in conjunction with a transmitter or transceiver capable of supplying 5 to 15 watts of FM driving power. The output power of the amplifier will be between 20 and 50 watts, depending upon the driving power.

For alignment, a wattmeter (or SWR bridge) is preferred, but you may use a voltmeter. A 50-ohm noninductive load should be available for the output.

Installation

Refer to Fig. 8-2 for the suggested arrangement of components and their interconnections. All installation steps should be accomplished before the 2-meter FM amplifier is aligned, except for installing the amplifier cover and securing the completed amplifier in place. In the absence of excitation, the Heath amplifier draws less than 1 mA of current, and on-off switching is therefore not required.

Although the standard installation instructions suggest connecting the power wire to a fuse near the battery, it is possible that there is an unused circuit available on the accessory fuse block of your vehicle. Such a circuit normally has provision for a fuse, and in this case the red power wire can be connected to this unused terminal. A 1/4-inch push-on connector should be used. The vehicle ignition switch will usually control this circuit in the same manner as the other accessory circuits.

Low-power operation can be secured in two ways. First, you can reduce the excitation below the pull-in point of the amplifier relay (1.5 watts). Second, you can connect a single-pole switch in series with the power wire to prevent the amplifier from turning on. Straight-through operation will result.

Decide where the amplifier will be installed. It should be located as close to the antenna as is convenient. Mark the mounting holes for the amplifier. Use the amplifier assembly as a template. Drill the mounting holes with a #21 or 5/32-inch drill bit. Sheet-metal screws (10-32) will be used to mount the amplifier, later.

Wiring

1. Carefully measure the lengths of transmission line required between the exciter and the amplifier and between the amplifier and the antenna. Cut the RG-58A/U coaxial cable to the measured lengths.
2. Refer to Fig. 8-7 and install a phono plug on one end of each cable. To avoid an impedance mismatch in the transmission line, be sure to install the plugs as shown.
3. Refer to Fig. 8-8 and install the fuse block close to the battery. Use a #6 × 3/8-inch sheet-metal screw in a hole made with a #35 or 7/64-inch drill bit.
4. Cut a length of red stranded wire to reach from the fuse block to the battery positive terminal. Solder one end of this wire to the fuse block. DO NOT connect the free end yet.
5. Install the fuse in the clips on the fuse block.

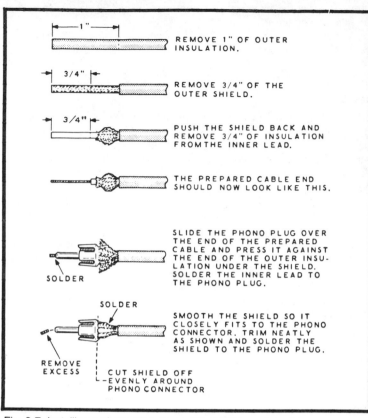

REMOVE 1" OF OUTER INSULATION.

REMOVE 3/4" OF THE OUTER SHIELD.

PUSH THE SHIELD BACK AND REMOVE 3/4" OF INSULATION FROM THE INNER LEAD.

THE PREPARED CABLE END SHOULD NOW LOOK LIKE THIS.

SLIDE THE PHONO PLUG OVER THE END OF THE PREPARED CABLE AND PRESS IT AGAINST THE END OF THE OUTER INSULATION UNDER THE SHIELD. SOLDER THE INNER LEAD TO THE PHONO PLUG.

SOLDER

SMOOTH THE SHIELD SO IT CLOSELY FITS TO THE PHONO CONNECTOR. TRIM NEATLY AS SHOWN AND SOLDER THE SHIELD TO THE PHONO PLUG.

REMOVE EXCESS

CUT SHIELD OFF EVENLY AROUND PHONO CONNECTOR

Fig. 8-7. Installing a phono plug on an RG-58A/U coaxial cable.

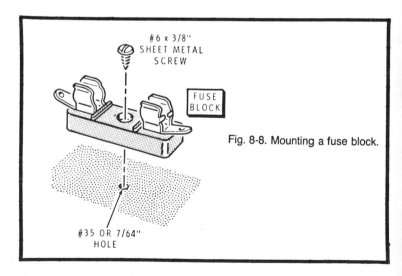

#6 x 3/8" SHEET METAL SCREW

FUSE BLOCK

Fig. 8-8. Mounting a fuse block.

#35 OR 7/64" HOLE

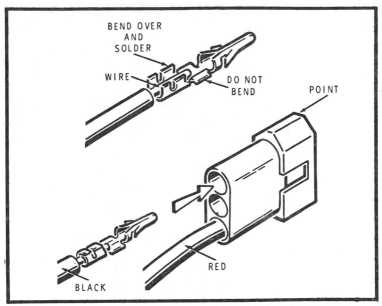

Fig. 8-9. Installing male pin on wire and then into housing.

6. Cut a 12-inch length of black stranded wire and a 12-inch length of red stranded wire. Remove 1/4-inch of insulation from both ends of each wire.
7. Install a spade lug on one end of each wire.
8. Refer to Fig. 8-9 and solder a male pin to the remaining end of each wire.
9. Cut off and discard the two ears from a female-connector housing (Fig. 8-10). Position the female-connector housing with the point

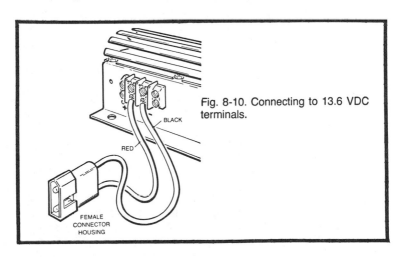

Fig. 8-10. Connecting to 13.6 VDC terminals.

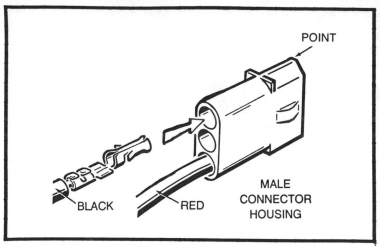

Fig. 8-11. Installing pin in male-connector housing.

up and push the male pin on the black wire into the upper hole, as shown, until the pin locks into place.

10. Similarly, push the pin on the red wire into the lower hole, leaving the center hole open.

11. Refer to Fig. 8-10 and connect the spade lug on the red wire to the plus (+) screw of the 13.6 VDC terminal strip. Connect the spade lug on the black wire to the other (−) screw. Be sure to tighten both screws securely.

12. With the amplifier temporarily in its permanent location, cut the length of red stranded wire required to reach from the female connector housing to the fuse block (or the accessory fuse block, if used).

13. Cut the length of black wire required to reach from the female-connector housing to the ground point selected (negative battery terminal, auto body, etc.).

14. Remove 1/4-inch of insulation from both ends of the red and black wires.

15. In the manner shown in Fig. 8-9, solder a female pin to one end of each wire.

16. Refer to Fig. 8-11 and position the male connector housing with the point up and push the female pin in the black wire into the upper hole, as shown, until the pin locks into place.

17. Similarly, push the pin on the red wire into the lower hole, leaving the center hole open.

18. Route the free end of the red wire toward the battery and solder it to the remaining lug of the fuse block.

19. Make sure the male and female connector housings are not plugged together. Then connect the free end of the red wire coming from the fuse block to the battery.

General Alignment Notes

To avoid overheating and damaging the transistors, do not key the exciter continuously during alignment. A cycle of 5 seconds on, followed by 10 seconds off, is recommended until alignment has been completed.

Although it is unlikely, you could encounter low-frequency oscillation (squegging) under certain conditions of mistuning. When it is properly tuned, the amplifier will not exhibit these oscillations, but low-frequency spurious output can destroy the RF transistors if it is allowed to exist for any length of time. A portable broadcast receiver makes a good indicator when it is tuned to an unused frequency and placed near the amplifier. The existence of squegging will be easily recognized as an unusual noise from the broadcast receiver.

If you use your battery as a power source, check the voltage across its terminals with the engine running and all accessory equipment and lights off. Most amplifiers are designed for 16 volts maximum input, and if the voltage is in excess of this figure, you should have your voltage regulator adjusted or replaced.

It is good practice to start the tuneup procedure at 11–12 volts input. If you are using your battery as a power source, leave the engine off during the initial alignment steps. Then start the engine (in a well-ventilated area) for the final tuneup.

The antenna relay may chatter until the input capacitor is peaked. This is normal and is due to the low input impedance possible when the amplifier is mistuned.

The alignment of a power amplifier requires the following:

- A 2-meter exciter (transmitter) capable of 5–15 watts output.
- A 50-ohm nonreactive load, such as the Heath *Cantenna*, connected to the amplifier's output. An antenna may be used, but its VSWR should be as low as possible and in no event more than 2:1.
- An output indicator. A wattmeter (or SWR bridge) is preferred, but a voltmeter may be used.

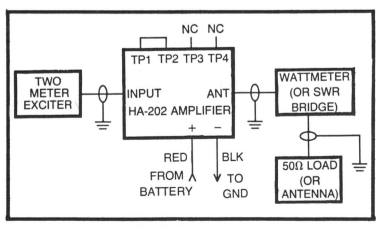

Fig. 8-12. Equipment lineup for alignment.

Before starting alignment, tune your exciter for maximum output in the portion of the 2-meter band in which you expect to operate. If a wattmeter or SWR bridge is used for alignment, it is important that it be capable of accurate measurements at the operating frequency of the amplifier; otherwise there may be a false indication of peak power output, and result in possible misalignment.

1. Interconnect your equipment as shown in Fig. 8-12. Be sure to use RG-58A/U coaxial cable for all leads which carry RF.
2. Plug the power-line connectors together. While keying the exciter 5 seconds on and 10 seconds off, use an alignment tool to adjust the four trimmer capacitors.
3. Repeat the trimmer adjustment at least twice to ensure maximum output.
4. Disconnect the wattmeter, the 50-ohm load, and the power-line connectors. This completes the alignment.

Chapter 9
CB Antennas

There are two types of mobile CB antennas: the full-length whip and the loaded whip. A vertically polarized whip antenna is best suited for mobile service. It is omnidirectional and can be the loaded type or a full quarter-wave (quarter-wave being more desirable).

LOCATIONS

There are many possible antenna locations on a car. Four of the most popular are as follows (see Fig. 9-1):

Roof Mount—In this position the antenna radiates equally in all directions. Since the normal 1/4-wavelength whip antenna is too long (102 in.) for roof mounting on a vehicle, the antenna is shortened and a loading coil is used to provide the proper electrical length.

Front-Cowl Mount—The radiation pattern of an antenna in this position is slightly greater in the direction of the rear fender opposite the side on which the antenna is mounted. However, this position offers a number of advantages. First, the CB antenna can be easily mounted. Second, it can double as both the CB and the standard-radio antenna by employing a 2-way coupler. Radio Shack's Catalog Number 21-930 front-cowl-mount antenna is designed for CB, AM, and FM operation.

Rear-Deck Mount—The radiation pattern at this location is strongest in the direction of the front fender opposite the side on which the antenna is mounted. In this position you can use a full quarter-wave antenna or a shorted, loaded whip. Here you might consider Radio Shack's Catalog Numbers 21-926 or 21-908, or one of the full (102 in.) whips.

Bumper Mount—Here, the antenna radiates in a pattern directly in front of and to the rear of the vehicle, with maximum radiation directly away from the vehicle, in a horizontal plane. Despite its fairly irregular pattern, a bumper-mounted full-length whip antenna will normally give the best results. Also, removing the antenna is simple and will leave no holes in the car.

A few general rules should help you install any mobile antenna properly:

1. Keep it as far as possible from the main bulk of the vehicle.
2. Keep as much of it as possible above the highest point of the vehicle.
3. During operation, keep it vertical. It should be mechanically rigid so it will remain vertical when the vehicle is in motion.
4. Mount it as far as possible from sources of noise (ignition system, gauges, etc.) and keep the transmission line away from these noise sources.

An antenna or transceiver mounted in a boat requires a ground plane. This can be either a metal hull or a ground made of tinfoil or copper sheeting. This ground should cover an area of 12 square feet (approximately 1.5 square meters) or more. Be sure the transceiver and antenna have an adequate ground. However, if you use Radio Shack's 21-912 fiberglass marine antenna, you won't have to worry about a ground—it is designed so no ground is required.

DEFINITIONS

Here are some definitions you'll need to know as you read about antennas and their installation:

beam antenna—an array of elements, approximately one-half wave in length, which concentrate the transmitted and received signal into a narrow arc.

bidirectional—Transmits (or receives) in two directions, usually 180° apart. This is the pattern of the half-wave dipole.

dB gain—The power increase of an antenna compared to that of a standard half-wave dipole (or isotropic radiator). For each 3 dB (decibel) increase,

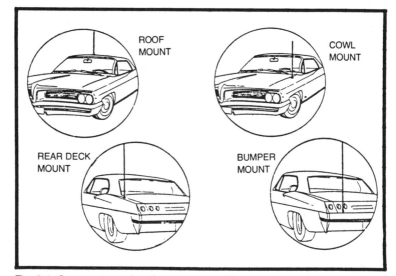

ROOF MOUNT

COWL MOUNT

REAR DECK MOUNT

BUMPER MOUNT

Fig. 9-1. Some antenna locations on a car. (Courtesy Radio Shack)

power is doubled. For example: If a 10-watt signal is increased 3 dB, it becomes 20 watts; for 3 dB more, it becomes 40 watts.

dipole antenna—A basic half-wave antenna (approximately 18 feet long for CB), fed at the center. It forms the driven element of the beam antenna and is the standard against which other antennas are measured.

direct wave—The portion of the radiated signal which travels directly, or via line-of-sight, between transmitter and receiver. This is the principal path taken by CB signals. The *ground wave*, which follows the earth's curve, is extremely limited on CB.

effective radiated power (ERP)—The CB transmitter produces a fixed amount of watts, but this may be varied by antenna gain, height, and other factors. The ERP is the result of these variations. For example: A 3-watt signal applied to a directional antenna with 3 dB gain has an ERP of 6 watts. The gain, however, occurs within a confined pattern.

front-to-back ratio—Applied to directional beams, this rating describes the amount of signal pickup from the front compared to that picked up at the rear. Stated in decibels, the higher the better. High ratios (say, 30 dB instead of 20 dB) mean less signal is lost to the rear during transmission. Less interference is also heard during reception.

gamma match—This is a special rod assembly added to the driven element of a beam antenna for impedance matching. It allows a 52-ohm coaxial cable to be mechanically connected to the driven element at an electrical 52-ohm point for best transfer of energy.

ground plane—A basic antenna type, usually 9 feet in height for CB, with three or four drooping radials to form an electrical ground plane.

impedance—A rating, given in ohms, which describes the amount of opposition to a flow of current. The most common impedance in CB is 52 ohms— the rating for transmitter outputs, receiver inputs, coaxial cables, and antennas. These items may then be interconnected for maximum power transfer since their impedances are the same, or matched.

loading coil—Turns of wire embedded or positioned in an antenna element to electrically create the effect of a physically longer antenna. Although the coil consumes part of the energy, the loss is often outweighed by such physical advantages as a small antenna for rooftop mounting on a car, or compact elements in a beam.

omnidirectional—Transmits (or receives) equally well in all directions. Also known as *nondirectional*.

sky wave—The part of the antenna signal which travels above the horizon and is lost in space, unless reflected back toward earth by the ionosphere. Communication via sky wave, or "skip," is illegal in CB.

splitter—A device which recovers AM and FM broadcast signals from a CB antenna for reception on the car radio. Also prevents CB transmitter from overloading the car radio when antenna is shared.

SWR—Standing-wave ratio, or the amount of forward power compared to reflected power. This figure tells the efficiency of the antenna system; the lower the ratio, the better. High SWR means something's mismatched and the transmission line or antenna is reflecting power back to the transmitter. The result is power loss due to heating in the line or signal cancellation. An

SWR of 1:1 is theoretically perfect; 3:1 means about 25% of the power is being lost. Your system should ideally indicate less than 2:1.

transmission line—A pair of wires designed to transfer radio currents between transmitter and antenna. The most common pair for CB is the coaxial cable, constructed of an outer shield and an inner conductor and rated at 52 ohms (RG-58/U). Because of its electrical shield, the line may run close to other wires, metal, or underground.

wavelength—The distance, usually measured in meters, between corresponding points of radio wave. It is also expressed as the distance traveled during one cycle. The wavelength of CB is 11 meters, or approximately 36 feet. Therefore, the basic half-wave antenna is 18 feet; the quarter-wave is 9 feet.

CABLES AND PLUGS

Antenna cables for CB radio are usually of either the RG-58 or RG-8 type. The RG-58 is smaller (typically 0.195 inch outside diameter) and well suited to mobile-unit applications, where good flexibility is required. The RG-8 is larger (typically 0.405 inch) and capable of handling the higher power requirements of base stations and with lower signal losses.

UHF CB Plugs and Receptacles

Series UHF connectors are rugged, general-purpose RF connectors for small- and medium-size coaxial cables. They are commonly used for all types of communications applications where frequencies usually do not exceed 300 MHz. (Class D CB frequency is 27 MHz.) Top-quality UHF connectors (such as Amphenol's) are machined from brass rod stock.

The standard plug, commonly called PL-259, is used on RG-8 antenna cables, or RG-58 and RG-59 cables when used with the proper reducing adapter. The screw-on coupling connects to the receptacle on your CB set, as well as the base-station antenna.

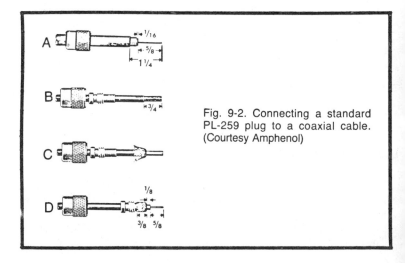

Fig. 9-2. Connecting a standard PL-259 plug to a coaxial cable. (Courtesy Amphenol)

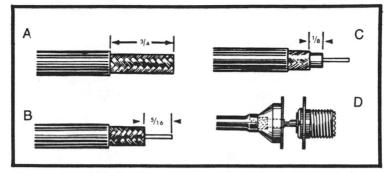

Fig. 9-3. Assembling the SO-239 receptacle. (Courtesy Amphenol)

Assembly Instructions. Cut the end of the cable even and strip jacket, braid, and dielectric to dimensions as shown in Fig. 9-2A. Tin exposed center conductor and braid. Slide coupling ring on cable. Screw the plug sub-assembly on cable. Solder assembly to braid through solder holes, making a good bond between braid and shell. Refer to the solder procedure below. Solder center conductor to contact. For final assembly screw coupling ring on plug subassembly.

Recommended Soldering Procedure for UHF Plug. Use a 50–60-watt soldering iron, Kester solder #44 (60/40, flux #58) or equivalent. Apply heat to rear to be soldered until solder flows. Time required to solder cable braid to body is approximately 15 to 20 seconds. Clean flux from connector after soldering.

Assembling SO-239 Receptacles. These receptacles are commonly used on CB sets and accessory items such as VSWR meters, antenna matchers, power meters, and antenna switches. Assemble as follows: Cut end of cable even. Remove cable jacket to dimension shown in Fig. 9-3A. Tin exposed braid. Remove braid and dielectric to expose center conductor as shown (B). Remove braid to expose dielectric to approximate dimension (C). Tin center conductor. Slide hood (Amphenol 93IH) over braid and force under cable. Place inner conductor in contact sleeve and solder. Push hood flush against receptacle. Tack-solder hood to braid through solder holes. Tape this junction or use vinyl tubing.

See Fig. 9-4 for illustrations of various coax connector adapters and accessories which may be found helpful during antenna installations.

ANTENNA TESTS

Make certain the antenna lead-in shield is grounded at both ends. Insulation should be inspected, and all connections must be clean and tight. Here are three ohmmeter checks you should make on an antenna (see Fig. 9-5):

1. On lowest scale, touch test probes to antenna rod and center contact of plug. Resistance should be a fraction of an ohm.
2. On highest scale, touch test probes to antenna rod and vehicle ground. You should read an open circuit (on most antennas). Some

DOUBLE FEMALE—83-1J

Commonly called PL-258, this double-female adapter is used to connect two plugs together where a cable splice is necessary.

DOUBLE MALE—83-877

The double-male adapter connects two receptacles together. Used when two or more instruments are connected together within the same antenna system.

ANGLE ADAPTER—83-1AP

Commonly called M359, this adapter is used to make connections more convenient where space limitations exist, and to prevent a sharp bend in the antenna cable, which could result in a signal loss.

BULKHEAD ADAPTER—83-1F

Used for permanent installation where female connections are required on each side of a panel. Mounting hole diameter: 41/64 in.

TEE ADAPTER—83-1T

Commonly called M358, this adapter is used where two antenna leads are required to be connected to one instrument.

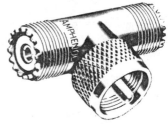

PIN-PLUG ADAPTER—83-10

This adapter is commonly used when a transition is required from the cable plug to a Motorola or RCA type of jack.

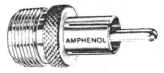

POWER-OUTPUT INDICATOR/ 83-888

Used to check power output of your transmitter. By substituting the power-output indicator for the antenna, unlawful transmissions are prevented while your set is being tested or tuned. Light glows when the microphone is keyed and brightens when someone talks into the microphone.

DUMMY LOAD—83-887

Prevents unlawful transmission when tuning and testing your transmitter (50-ohm nominal load, 5 watts).

LIGHTNING ARRESTOR—83-23

Eliminates static buildup from the antenna. Protects your valuable equipment against lightning damage. Should be properly grounded with 12-gauge, or larger, wire.

ALTERNATOR FILTER—575-654

Reduces or eliminates noise caused by automobile alternator systems.

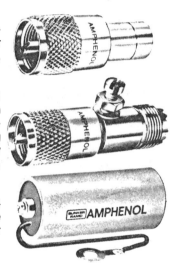

Fig. 9-4. UHF CB adapters and accessories. Adapters are used to link components where coupling would otherwise be impractical. For example, two components having female connectors cannot be mated without the use of a double-male adapter. Amphenol adapters for various types of connections are shown along with Amphenol part numbers.

high-gain antennas with built-in matching transformers will be short-circuited.

3. On lowest scale, touch test probes to outside of antenna plug and vehicle ground. It should measure close to zero resistance.

VHF MONITOR ANTENNAS

Depending on the transmitter power and antenna height, the whip antenna on a VHF scanner receiver should provide a reception range of 15 to 20 miles. The terrain of the surrounding areas can increase or decrease this range, depending on the location of the scanner in relation to the transmit-

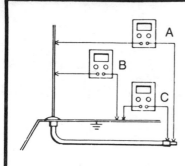

Fig. 9-5. Antenna tests. (Courtesy Pace Two-Way Radio Products)

ter, nearby hills, mountains, flatlands, etc. Adjust the whip antenna so the antenna tip is 18 inches above the top of the cabinet.

To increase the receiving range to 20 to 30 miles, you should use an external (outside) antenna. If you use an outside antenna, use one of the communications-type antennas for the 150 to 160 MHz range. Connect the antenna lead into the HI VHF antenna socket (be sure you completely collapse the built-in whip antenna). A directional-gain antenna is recommended for fringe-area reception.

The antenna mentioned above is available from many electronics distributors. Or, if you prefer, you can make a ground-plane antenna as shown in Fig. 9-6. Cut each of the elements to correspond to receive crystals, locate a frequency that is halfway between your two frequency extremes and cut the antenna radials to that length.

HI BAND VHF
ANTENNA CHART

FREQUENCY (MHz)	1/4 WAVELENGTH (INCHES)	FREQUENCY (MHz)	1/4 WAVELENGTH (INCHES)
146	19	161	17 1/4
147	18 7/8	162	17 1/8
148	18 3/4	163	17
149	18 5/8	164	17
150	18 1/2	165	16 7/8
151	18 3/8	166	16 3/4
152	18 1/4	167	16 5/8
153	18 1/8	168	16 1/2
154	18	169	16 1/2
155	17 7/8	170	16 3/8
156	17 7/8	171	16 1/4
157	17 3/4	172	16 1/8
158	17 5/8	173	16
159	17 1/2	174	16
160	17 3/8		

MAGNETIC-MOUNT (NO-HOLE) ANTENNA

Refer to Fig. 9-7 and route the coax through an open door and down the side of the door post. Pieces of tape placed intermittently will hold the coax in place. After running it to the floor of the car, run it under the front seat and along the center hump.

CAUTION: Do not route the coax through a window. If you were to close the window and open the door, the antenna would be pulled off.

Plug the coax connector into your transceiver and you are ready to operate. To preserve the magnetic strength when the antenna is not mounted, always replace the keeper disk on the magnet.

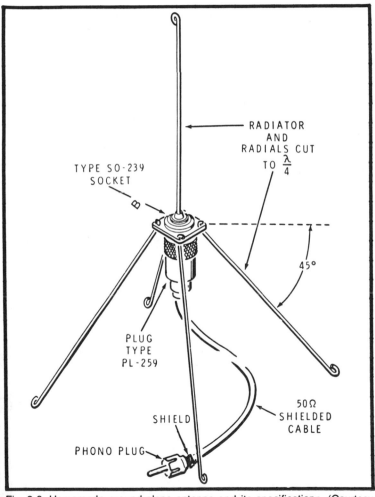

Fig. 9-6. Homemade ground-plane antenna and its specifications. (Courtesy Heath Company)

CAUTION: It is very important to note the following limitations when using a magnetic-mount antenna. The magnet has a holding strength of 25 lb. (usually), and is capable of holding at speeds in excess of 80 mph. It has been carefully designed and tested to offer reliable holding power under normal conditions. However, it cannot be used on vinyl roofs; it must be set upon a perfectly flat metal surface. Variations in paint thicknesses and properties of metal on which it is placed can reduce its effective holding power. The surface must be perfectly clean, oil-free, and dry.

A wall of wind precedes passing vehicles two to four times the speed of the vehicle. The "suction" produced by passing vehicles tends to pull the opposite vehicle toward it. This is especially true of trailers or large trucks. Similar conditions are turbulence caused by overpasses and vehicles meeting under bridges or overpasses, etc. Also, rain forcing its way under the mount can reduce the effective holding power. Therefore, consider these factors when approaching other vehicles or objects since it is possible that the magnetic antenna may be subjected to forces that exceed its ability to hold.

ARCHER CB-AM/FM COWL-MOUNT ANTENNA

This antenna, sold by Radio Shack, is a combination telescoping mobile topper antenna and coupler (see Fig. 9-8). This combination gives a complete antenna system for both CB and AM/FM. The coupler is a unique switching device that allows the antenna to operate both as a CB antenna and an AM/FM antenna for the car radio.

Construction

The telescoping antenna is made of stainless-steel and chrome-plated sections with a chrome body mount. The coupler is extremely small and rugged in construction. It comes complete with all necessary cables for a

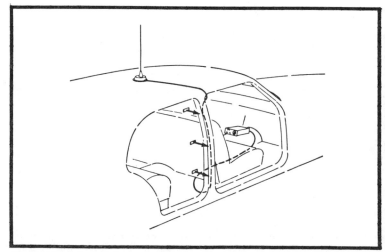

Fig. 9-7. How to install a magnetic-mount antenna.

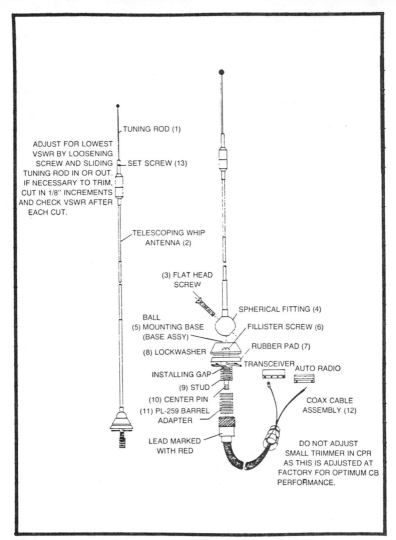

Fig. 9-8. Details of a CB antenna. This is a cowl-mount model that can also be used for AM/FM reception. (Courtesy Radio Shack)

normal front-fender installation. The loading coil is encapsulated in molded polystyrene and is virtually indestructible.

Installation

The installation of an *Archer* 21-930 antenna will illustrate the typical installation of cowl-mount antennas. (Refer to Fig. 9-8).

1. Select the mounting site for the antenna. Normally, the present hole that the existing car radio antenna is mounted in will do.

185

2. Drill or enlarge the present hole to 1-inch diameter on car body. Scrape away paint, burrs, undercoating, etc., on the underside of car body to ensure a good ground.

3. Select the coupler and plug the auto plug into your car radio. Attach the unmarked PL-259 on the coupler to your CB transceiver.

4. Now route the other coupler cable through the car to the hole where the antenna is to be mounted. If the cable is not long enough, you will need to install another length of cable between the coupler and the CB transceiver.
   NOTE: *Do not* lenghten the cables going to the antenna or the car radio.

5. Pull the PL-259 marked with red through the 1-inch hole you made and tighten the connector onto the antenna base. Make sure the center-conductor pin goes into the center pin on the antenna base.

6. Now, unscrew the flathead screw and remove the spherical fitting from the ball-mount base.

7. Loosen the fillister-head screw until it will no longer turn.

8. Place the antenna-base assembly in the hole by positioning the mount with the edge of the hole inserted in the gap of the lockwasher. The stud should be against the edge of the hole.

9. Now, roll the assembly on the edge of the hole *counterclockwise* until the lockwasher is completely beneath the surface of the car body.

10. Center the mount in the hole while securing the assembly by tightening the fillister-head screw.

11. Place the spherical fitting with the whip into the ball-mount base and secure using the flathead screw.

12. Extend telescoping section of whip to maximum height.
    NOTE: To aid in properly adjusting your antenna length, the tuning rod has been premarked.

13. For high-band CB operation (channels 16-23), slide the tuning rod in to the third mark. This shortens the antenna and thereby resonates it at a higher frequency. For midband operation (channels 8–15), slide the tuning rod out to the second mark. For low-band operation (channels 1–7), slide the tuning rod out to the first mark. This gives the antenna maximum length and resonates it at a lower frequency.

14. For a more precise tuning of the antenna, obtain an SWR (standing-wave ratio) bridge and adjust length for the lowest SWR in the manner described below.

15. Insert the SWR bridge between the transmitter and the antenna (as close to the transmitter as possible).

16. Adjust the top portion of the whip for the lowest SWR at the frequency you wish to favor. Do this by loosening the screw located at the top of the loading coil and sliding the tuning rod in or out as necessary. Due to differences in mounting locations, etc., the tuning rod may have to be trimmed to obtain the lowest SWR. To do this, remove the tuning rod, cut off in 1/8-inch increments, and check the SWR after each cut.

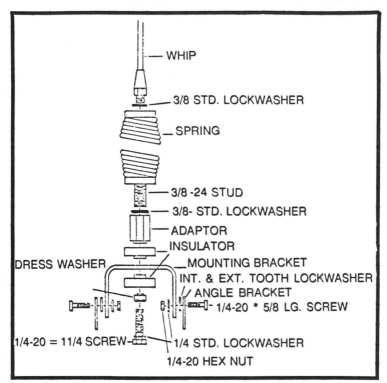

Fig. 9-9. Details of mounting bracket for bumper-mount antenna. (Courtesy Radio Shack)

17. Turn on your car radio and tune to a station around 1000 kHz. Tune the antenna trimmer (refer to your owner's manual for location) for maximum received signal.
18. If antenna trimmer on car radio will not tune for maximum signal, remove top cap (end with no cables) on the coupler and loosen large trimmer capacitor 1/8 turn and tune antenna trimmer for maximum signal. Repeat this process, loosening the large trimmer capacitor 1/8 turn each time until the antenna trimmer on car radio will tune for maximum signal. Replace cap and tuning is complete.

ARCHER 102 INCH FIBERGLASS-WHIP BUMPER-MOUNT ANTENNA

The bumper-mount antenna, as exemplified by the *Archer* 21-927 (available at Radio Shack), is another no-hole antenna. Here is how to install such antennas:

1. Assemble mounting bracket as shown in Fig. 9-9.
2. Mount angle brackets to mounting bracket, leaving 1/4-20 screws and hex nuts loose.
3. Examine bumper to determine whether mounting option No. 1 or No. 2 (shown in Fig. 9-10) adapts to your bumper.

4. Mount bumper-tie assembly to bumper, using mounting option chosen. Either of the mounting chains provided may require shortening (Fig. 9-10).
5. Assemble lower bracket assembly (two required) as shown in Fig. 9-11, leaving 1/4-20 hex nuts on end of eye bolts to allow for secure tightening of bumper mount.
6. After tightening bumper mount assembly securely to bumper, align mounting bracket for vertical mounting of spring and whip assemblies shown in Fig. 9-9.

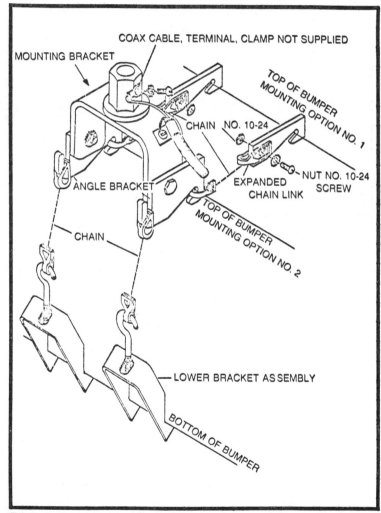

Fig. 9-10. Mounting options for bumper-mount antenna (refer to text). (Courtesy Radio Shack)

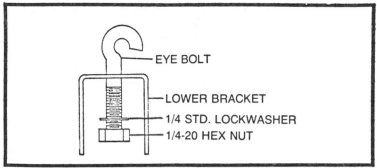

7. After mounting spring and whip assemblies to bumper mount, tighten hardware securely. Route coax cable to mounting bracket and antenna as shown in Fig. 9-10.

MARINE AND FIBERGLASS-CAMPER CB ANTENNA

The *Archer* (Radio Shack) 21-912 1/4-wavelength CB antenna has a snapout feature when mounted on the horizontal plane, and a rotating feature when mounted on the vertical plane, with 17 feet of RG-58 coax and with connector. The antenna is shown in Fig. 9-12. It requires no ground plane and works equally well on fiberglass or wood.

NOTE: Do not cut or coil coax. Coax may have to be repositioned for best SWR reading.

The base mounts on a flat surface with three mounting screws (supplied). A leveling plate is supplied for mounting on a sloping surface. If the plate is not needed, discard it. A rubber grommet is also supplied on the cable to fill a hole for routing the cable.

Mounting instructions:

1. Use base to locate and mark three mounting holes. Drill holes, 9/32-inch diameter.
2. If required, drill a 3/4-inch diameter hole for the coax assembly. Use a rubber grommet (supplied) to plug hole after installing coax, as shown in Fig. 9-12.

MOTORIZED CB ANTENNA

The *Archer* 21-970 CB antenna, sold by Radio Shack, does a disappearing act to help keep your CB radio from disappearing. The telescoping antenna is raised or lowered by an electric motor at the flip of a switch.

Location is an important consideration, as it will affect the antenna pattern. Suggested locations are as follows:

• Rear deck, between trunk and rear window (right is preferred).
• Rear fender, next to trunk (right is preferred).
• Front fender, next to hood (left is preferred).

Do not mount motor where it is directly exposed to tire splash, as salt and water should not enter motor.

Choose a location that does not slope more than 30° from horizontal and which also provides clearance for door, hood, or trunk opening. *Be sure there is enough room beneath location to fit the lower portion of the antenna. Be certain the antenna, even if extended, is not hit by opening trunk or hood.* Antenna should mount as nearly vertical as possible. If installation is on a plastic vehicle body, an artificial antenna ground plane and a return ground path must be provided for the motor power.

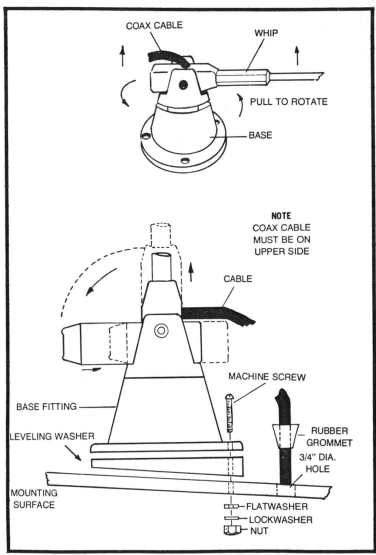

Fig. 9-12. A CB antenna for boats and campers—the Archer Model 21-912. (Courtesy Radio Shack)

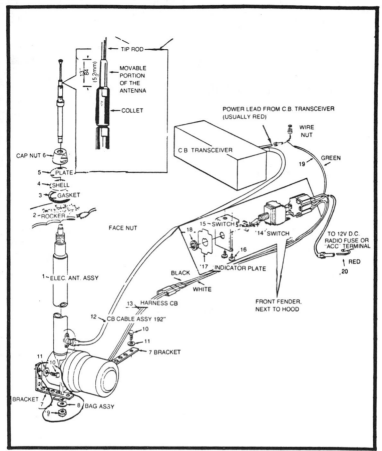

Fig. 9-13. A disappearing CB antenna for CB theft prevention is available at Radio Shack and is installed as shown.

Installation

1. Mark desired location and drill a 7/8-inch (22 mm) hole. A 3/4-inch (19 mm) hole will suffice on a horizontal surface.

2. Position antenna (1, Fig. 9-13) with rocker/lower spacer (2) through hole. A good sealant, such as RTV silicone rubber should be put around top threads and the mounting hole to prevent leakage if the antenna base is in the trunk or other interior area. With antenna in this position, add rubber pad (3), upper spacer (4), and cover plate (5). Lightly tighten upper cap nut (6).

3. Attach brackets (7) to antenna bottom mounting stud and secure with washer (8) and self-locking nut (9). Bend brackets to fit your installation. Brackets should be at nearly 90° angles relative to each other for optimum support. Set antenna so it will be vertical; now mark and drill two 9/64-inch (3.5 mm) holes. Secure the

brackets using #10 × 1/2-inch (#10 × 12.7 mm) screws (10) and washer (11).

4. Position cover plate (5) over opening in upper spacer (4) for proper water sealing, then tighten upper cap nut (6) a little more than hand tight.

5. Route RF coax cable (12) and power harness (13) from dash to antenna. Be sure to place all wires and cables in areas where they will not be pinched, worn, or rubbed. Connect RF cable to connector on antenna support tube. Do not overtighten. Connect power cable to T-connector on lead from antenna motor.

6. Switch Installation—In Dash: The antenna control switch (14) may be mounted on bracket (15) under the dash, or in the dash without the bracket. For in-the-dash switch installation, be sure that the drill does not damage the normal wiring, hoses, etc., behind the dash. Also, be sure there is sufficient room behind the dash for the rear of the switch and the large connector on the power harness. The connector will plug into the switch back. A 1/2-inch (1.27 cm) hole is necessary for in-the-dash mounting. Install the switch with the keyway in the threads *up*.

   Under-the Dash: Mount bracket (15) by drilling two 0.12-inch (3 mm) holes and using #8 × 3/8-inch (#8 × 9.5 mm) self-tapping screws (16). Place switch in position, keyway *up*, and place indicator plate (17) on front of bracket over switch. Adjust hex nut behind bracket so two or three threads show on switch front. Place black knurled circular nut (18) on front of switch and tighten. Be careful to hold switch level near center position when starting black knurled nut so as not to cross threads.

7. Plug large 5-pin female connector from power harness into back of switch (14). This may be easier before final switch tightening in some installations.

8. Connect green lead wire out of connector to CB positive power wire with solderless wire nut. This method of connection is necessary if you want power to the CB set to be automatically switched off when the antenna is fully retracted (this way you won't damage the transmitter circuitry by attempting to operate without a properly tuned antenna).

9. Connect red lead with universal male-female end to radio fuses or other fused area that is switched off by the ignition. Do not connect to a permanently live lead such as the cigarette lighter, brake light, etc.

10. Switch antenna to UP. Radio should be powered (lights come on) and antenna should extend. Do not attempt to transmit unless receiver appears to work properly. After being assured that antenna extends and retracts fully, proceed to tune antenna for lowest SWR. Antenna will clutch (hum after stopping) once or twice up and two or three times down. This is normal. Do not reverse direction until antenna finishes clutching and turns itself off.

Fig. 9-14. Mounting a CB antenna on the mirror mount of a truck. (Courtesy Radio Shack)

11. Using an SWR meter *with antenna fully extended,* check SWR on channels 1, 12, and 23. If the SWR is lowest on channel 1, shorten the antenna. If the reading is lowest on channel 23, lengthen the antenna. Adjust (see next section) until channel 12 is lowest and channels 1 and 23 are nearly equal. Minimal readings under 1.5:1 are considered excellent on channels 10, 11, or 12. SWRs of 2:1 are acceptable.

Tuning Adjustment

For optimum efficiency this antenna must be tuned. If you are not going to tune the antenna, set the movable portion of the antenna to be exactly 13/64 inch (5.2 mm) above the top edge of the collet when fully tightened.

1. Retract the antenna approximately halfway and stop it by turning off ignition.
2. With wrenches, loosen collet above coil. Lengthen or shorten the 0.2-inch (5 mm) diameter section that comes out the top of the collet.

   CAUTION: Adjustment is critical. Move in 1/16- to 1/8-inch (1.5-3 mm) steps and retighten collet.

3. Turn ignition back on. Antenna will continue earlier retraction. Let antenna fully retract and clutch out. Then raise antenna fully and recheck SWR.

4. Repeat 1, 2, and 3 above, until channel 12 is lowest and channels 1 and 23 are nearly equal in SWR. Remember, lengthen (pull up) the small 0.2-inch (5 mm) diameter section that is above collet (the piece the tip rod comes out of) to lengthen antenna. Lower the 0.2-inch (5 mm) section to shorten antenna. When you have obtained the optimum SWR, be sure to tighten the collet securely.

Operating Considerations

CAUTION: Do not operate your transmitter until the antenna is fully extended. You may damage the transmitter circuitry if you try to transmit with a partially extended antenna.

At extremely low temperatures, the antenna may not extend or retract consistently and completely. So, if the outdoor temperature is −10°F (−25°C) or lower, try it a few times till the motor warms up and will extend or retract the antenna fully.

Always retract your antenna fully before you turn the ignition off. Only the fully retracted position will gain maximum security for your CB set (no giveaway antenna to show would-be thieves that you have a CB). Of course, the antenna will not retract when the ignition is off (power has been removed from both the CB set and the antenna).

SINGLE TRUCKER MIRROR-MOUNT ANTENNA

The *Archer* single trucker mirror-mount antenna (21-941), a-vailable at Radio Shack, has been designed for convenient mounting on mirror mounting brackets, for either vertical or horizontal brackets (see Fig. 9-14).

Be sure the mirror mount is well grounded to the body of the vehicle — no rusting between mount and body and no insulators. This is absolutely necessary for proper operation of the antenna system. You can mount this antenna to the luggage rack of a station wagon, or any other convenient location (or other mobile-type installation); just be sure you obtain a good electrical ground connection back to the body of the vehicle and don't allow the door to pinch or cut the coaxial cable.

Assembling the Antenna

Assemble the antenna as illustrated in Fig. 9-15. Be sure all pieces are fastened securely (nuts tight, rods threaded firmly in place, and Allen-head setscrew holding the tip rod securely.

Mounting the Antenna

Determine the best position for the antenna. This establishes if you will have to use the horizontal mount (Fig. 9-16) or the vertical mount (Fig. 9-17).

Remove thumbscrews, if necessary, and reposition the bracket clamp (for horizontal or vertical mounting as required). Mount the bracket-and-

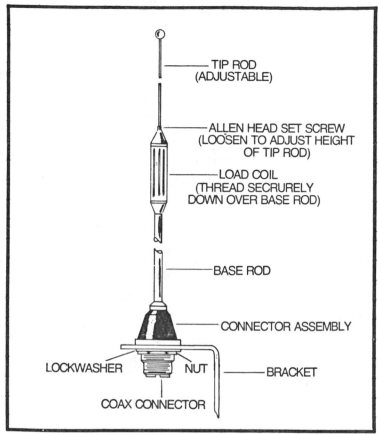

TIP ROD
(ADJUSTABLE)

ALLEN HEAD SET SCREW
(LOOSEN TO ADJUST HEIGHT
OF TIP ROD)

LOAD COIL
(THREAD SECRURELY
DOWN OVER BASE ROD)

BASE ROD

CONNECTOR ASSEMBLY

LOCKWASHER   NUT   BRACKET

COAX CONNECTOR

Fig. 9-15. Details of a mirror-mount antenna. (Courtesy Radio Shack)

clamp assembly as shown in Fig. 9-16 or 9-17. Tighten the Allen setscrew so it bites firmly into the mirror-mount bracket (this ensures a good ground connection for the antenna system, and it's very important that it be firm).

Connecting the Cable

Connect one end of the cable to the back of your transceiver; connect the other end to the base of the antenna. See Fig. 9-18. This completes the assembly and mounting of your antenna system.

You will achieve excellent results with the system just as it is, but if you have an SWR meter available (such as Radio Shack's catalog No. 21-521), you can tune the antenna for optimum results. Connect the SWR meter between the transceiver output and the coaxial cable from the antenna. Measure SWR on channels 1, 12, and 23. (Remember the readings.)

If the reading is lowest on channel 1, shorten the antenna; if the reading is lowest on channel 23, extend the antenna. To change the length of the antenna, loosen the Allen setscrew at the base of the tip rod and raise or

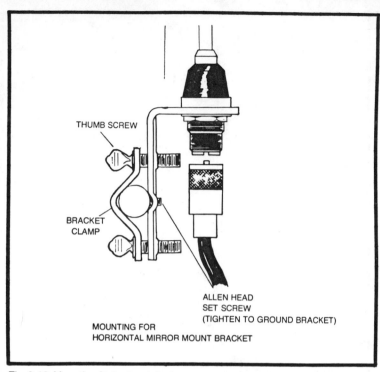

Fig. 9-16. Mounting for horizontal mirror-mount bracket. (Courtesy Radio Shack)

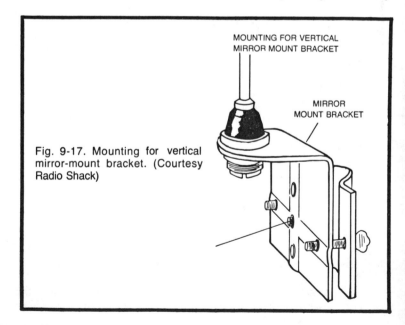

Fig. 9-17. Mounting for vertical mirror-mount bracket. (Courtesy Radio Shack)

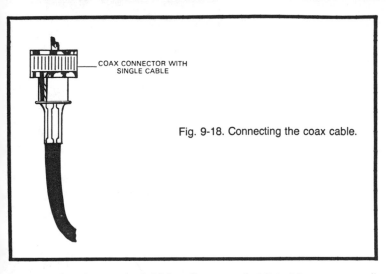

Fig. 9-18. Connecting the coax cable.

lower the tip rod as required. Make adjustments in 1/8-inch increments until you obtain the lowest SWR. Be sure to retighten the setscrew securely.

COPHASE HARNESS FOR CB ANTENNAS

A cophase harness permits you to use two CB antennas at one time, thus effectively increasing your signal coverage. Mount the two CB antennas in appropriate locations. Normally this will be at the two rear corners of the vehicle or boat. (See Fig. 9-19.)

The *Archer* (Radio Shack) catalog No. 21-935 is one such harness. As supplied, the cophase harness is cut for matching Archer full-length 102-inch CB whip antennas. (Proper length of these special cables is 22 ft. 4 in.) If you are using loaded antennas (that is, antennas shorter than the quarter-wave 102-inch whip), the cables will have to be trimmed (to about 19 ft. 4 in.).

The cables come with spade lugs, which provide the most common and simple connection for full-length whips. Each antenna type may require a

Fig. 9-19. Truck and auto installations requiring a cophase harness. (Courtesy Radio Shack)

slightly different form of connection for the cable. Follow the instructions supplied with the antennas and make appropriate connections to the bases of the antennas. When you have made proper and firm connections to the antennas, connect the coaxial fitting to the antenna connector on the rear of your CB transceiver.

If you are going to use the *Archer* cophase harness with *Archer* loaded antennas, you should cut the length of the cables to 19 feet 4 inches. For other brands of loaded antennas, use an SWR bridge (such as Radio Shack's catalog No. 21-576 or 21-575) to achieve a precise matching of the cable to the antennas.

The 19 ft. 4 in. length for loaded antennas is based on a typical installation on full-sized automobiles. Installations on smaller vehicles (or on boats) may result in higher than desired SWR. In such cases, you can follow the trimming instructions that follow.

Cable Trimming

When you cut and trim the cable ends, follow the illustration in Fig. 9-20. Dimensions of inner and outer insulation (and braiding) will depend on your needs.

If you don't have an SWR bridge, cutting to the 19 foot 4 inch length will certainly be adequate, and in most cases may be the best length anyway.

If you are going to use an SWR bridge, trim the cables to about 19 feet 10 inches (this leaves 4−6 inches for experimental trimming to precise length). Set up your equipment as shown in Fig. 9-21 (antennas mounted). Now, turn the transmitter on and check SWR. Turn transmitter off. Cut about 1 inch off the ends of the cable and reconnect the cables to the antennas. Turn transmitter on again and check SWR; it should have gone down. Continue doing this trimming of the cable ends until you achieve an SWR of about 1.5.

NOTE: As you get closer and closer to the approximate ideal length, cut off shorter and shorter pieces. With careful trimming, you may be able to get an SWR of about 1.2 (anything lower than that is not worth the precise effort required).

This is the only method you can use to obtain *optimum* matching for your particular antenna installation. When you have the optimum cable

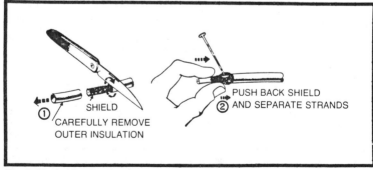

Fig. 9-20. Cable trimming for an antenna installation. (Courtesy Radio Shack)

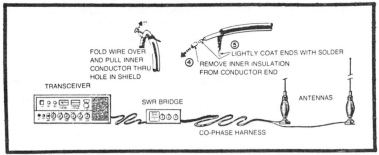

Fig. 9-21. Hookup for SWR check. (Courtesy Radio Shack)

length (lowest SWR), permanently attach the ends of the cable of the antennas. Be sure all connections are firm and secure.

DOUBLE TRUCKER MIRROR-MOUNT ANTENNA

A double trucker mirror-mount antenna provides increased signal-pulling power to make the trucker's signal speak with greater authority on the CB Band. *Archer's* Model 21-942 (Fig. 9-22) is designed for convenient mounting on mirror mounting brackets for either vertical or horizontal mounting brackets.

Be sure your mirror mounts are well grounded to the body of the truck—no rusting between mounts and body and no insulators. This is absolutely necessary for proper operation of the dual-antenna system.

The coaxial cable assembly has been precisely cut to match the antenna provided. Do not cut or trim the coaxial cable. Coil any excess cable inside the cab in a convenient place. Don't allow the doors to pinch or cut the coaxial cable.

Assembling the Antennas

Assemble each antenna as illustrated in Fig. 9-15. Be sure all pieces are fastened securely together (nuts tight, rods threaded firmly in place, and Allen-head setscrew holding the tip rod securely).

Mounting the Antennas

Determine the best position for the antennas. The system should be balanced—each mounting in exactly the same location on each side of the cab. Determine if you will have to use the horizontal mount or the vertical mount (Figs. 9-16 and 9-17).

Remove thumbscrews, if necessary, and reposition the bracket clamp (for horizontal or vertical mounting as required). Mount each bracket-and-clamp assembly as shown. Tighten the Allen setscrew so it bites firmly into the mirror-mount bracket (this ensures a good ground for the antenna, and it's very important that it is firm).

Connecting the Cable

Connect the center connector to the back of your transceiver. Fasten the other coax connectors to the base of the antennas. See Fig. 9-23. This completes the assembly and mounting of your dual-antenna system.

You will achieve excellent results with the system just as it is, but if you have an SWR meter available (such as Radio Shack's catalog No. 21-521), you can tune the antennas for optimum results. Connect the SWR meter between the transceiver output and the coax connector from the antenna system. Measure SWR on channels 1, 12, and 23 (remember the readings).

If the reading is lowest on Channel 1, shorten both antennas; if the reading is lowest on channel 23, extend the antennas. To change the length of the antennas, loosen the Allen setscrew at the base of the tip rod and raise or lower the tip rod as required. Make adjustments in 1/8-inch increments until you obtain the lowest SWR. Be sure to retighten the setscrew securely. Both antennas must be extended to the same length.

ARCHER VHF MONITOR ANTENNA

The *Archer* mobile antenna (No. 20-180) is designed to give you the maximum signal capture of those elusive low-level calls, yet provides a sleek modern 54-inch overall height. It features an extruded PVC coil housing, a stainless steel whip, and a heavy chrome spring. It is supplied with cable and solderless connector.

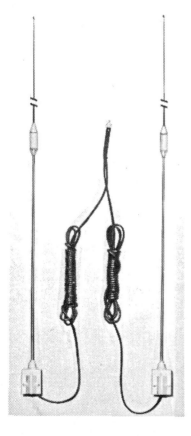

Fig. 9-22. Double trucker antenna for 18-wheelers. (Courtesy Radio Shack)

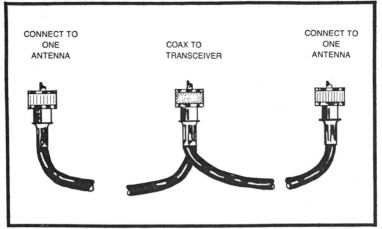

CONNECT TO
ONE
ANTENNA

COAX TO
TRANSCEIVER

CONNECT TO
ONE
ANTENNA

Fig. 9-23. Connecting the coaxial cable. Note: Do not cut or trim the cable assembly.

Assembly and Installation

1. Route coax cable from radio to mounting position, thread through mounting bracket, and attach braid as shown in Fig. 9-24. Antenna may be mounted off center of trunk lid or on the side of trunk lid to avoid antenna striking rear window when opening trunk.
2. Assemble mount to trunk lid as shown in Fig. 9-25. Do not screw on lower load coil at this time.
3. Thread center conductor through threaded adapter as shown in Fig. 9-26).

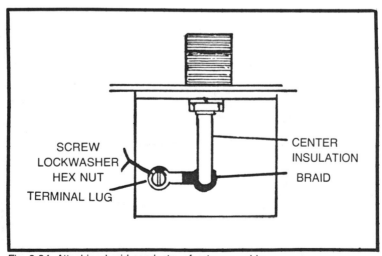

SCREW
LOCKWASHER
HEX NUT
TERMINAL LUG

CENTER
INSULATION
BRAID

Fig. 9-24. Attaching braid conductor of antenna cable.

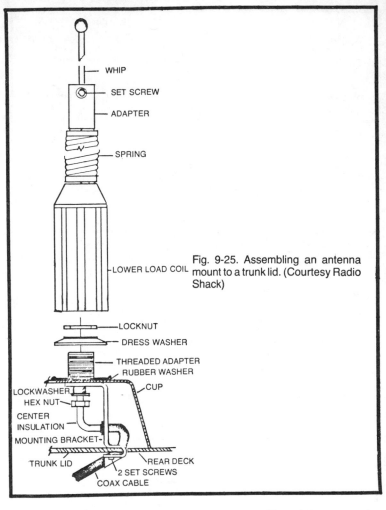

Fig. 9-25. Assembling an antenna mount to a trunk lid. (Courtesy Radio Shack)

4. Thread lower load coil onto thread adapter. Hand tighten securely.
5. Loosen setscrew in adapter, insert whip, and tighten setscrew securely.

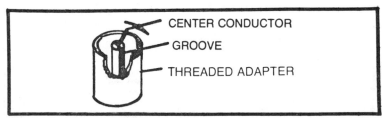

Fig. 9-26. Threaded adapter for antenna.

Chapter 10
Bicycle Radio

No coverage of radio installations for vehicles could be complete without mention of the bicycle radio. At least you should know that they exist. Radio Shack's *Road Patrol* receiver (Fig. 10-1) is more than a frivolous gadget or an ordinary "transistor" receiver that has been especially styled for bicycle use and carefully engineered for outdoor use. (Don't leave it out in the rain or snow, though; it's not completely waterproof.)

BATTERY INSTALLATION

Remove the cover from the battery compartment by gently pushing down and outward. Load four AA penlight batteries into the battery compartment as indicated by the diagram in the compartment. Replace the battery-compartment cover.

INSTALLATION OF RECEIVER

1. Place the bicycle radio on top of the upper mounting bracket; then insert the large plastic screw up through the bottom of the bracket and into the radio and tighten.
2. Place the bracket on the bicycle's handlebar in a convenient place; then attach the two lower brackets around the bottom of the handlebar so they match up with the position of upper bracket. Fasten with four screws provided.

You can quickly and easily remove the radio from its bracket (just loosen the large plastic screw) and then you can take it with you indoors, on a hike, camping, etc.

OPERATION

1. Turn the ON-OFF/VOLUME control knob (small knob on left side) toward you to turn the power on.

Fig. 10-1. Radio Shack's Road Patrol receiver is an AM/FM model that's especially styled and engineered for bicycle use.

2. Slide the FM/AM band selector to the desired band.
3. Use the tuning knob (large knob, right side) to select the desired station.
4. Adjust the volume to the desired level by turning the VOLUME knob.

Chapter 11
Burglar Alarms

One of the most important installations you can make in your car is one that will help keep your other installations intact. The more electronic accessories you install in your car, the more you will need the protection of one of the alarm systems discussed next. Even if you have only one accessory installed, the cost of a burglar alarm is justified. Either of the alarms discussed costs but a fraction as much as a CB radio, and the theft of CB radios is epidemic. In some areas the police report that the average lifespan of a CB radio on the street is only 21 days. Either of the installations discussed next will help keep your CB installed—in your car instead of someone else's.

SIREN ALARM FOR DOORS AND CB SET

Radio Shack's CB-250 is a self-contained alarm system that requires no connection to existing lighting or horn wiring. It includes a siren to frighten off a thief by attracting attention. It also includes switches to mount at the doors, hood, and trunk. Opening any of these accesses causes a switch to operate and the siren to wail. Once the siren is in operation, it can only be shut off by the ignition-type key-lock switch included with the kit. There is even a direct connection to the CB set itself, just in case some agile thief crawls through a window or attempts to remove the set through a window.

Installation

1. Mount the siren under the hood against the fender wall (preferably on the left side), concealed from view as much as possible. Using the siren bracket as a template, drill three 1/8-inch holes and mount the siren with three #8 × 1/2-inch screws.
2. Decide on a location for the key-lock switch on the front-left fender of the vehicle so that the terminal end of the lock will protrude into

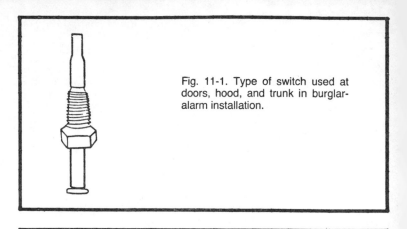

Fig. 11-1. Type of switch used at doors, hood, and trunk in burglar-alarm installation.

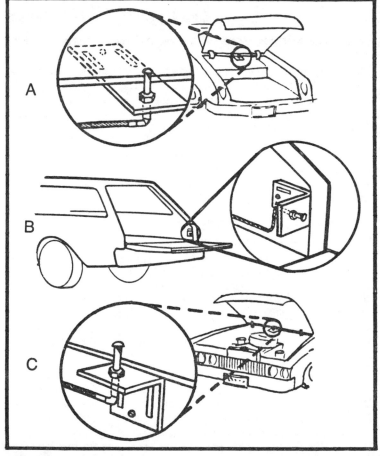

A

B

C

Fig. 11-2. The use of brackets may be required to mount some switches. (Courtesy Radio Shack)

the engine compartment. The size of the lock hole is 3/4 inch. Drill the appropriate hole and install the lock with the washer on the inside. Lock it in position with the nut.

3. Determine location of hood- and trunk-lid switches so that the switches will be depressed when the hood and trunk lid are closed. Drill 1/4-inch mounting holes as appropriate. Use a wrench to mount these switches (Fig. 11-1). Threads are self-tapping and will bite into the metal as you fasten them.

   Brackets may be used when necessary. Three #8 × 1/2 inch screws are used to mount each bracket (Fig. 11-2). Brackets can be made for alarm systems not already so equipped.

4. The switch for each door should be located on the door jamb or hinge side of each door. It should be in such a position that when the door closes, the switch will be hit. The door switches supplied by Radio Shack are self-adjusting and will adjust themselves to the door automatically the first time the door is closed. Drill a 11/32-inch hole for each door switch. Again, use a wrench to thread these switches into their mounting holes. (See Fig. 11-3.)

5. Using a sufficiently long length of insulated wire, begin wiring under the hood of the vehicle. Make sure that throughout the entire wiring no wires are ever pinched so as to cut through the insulation. Start by running a wire from the red wire of the siren unit to one terminal of the key-lock switch. Next, connect a wire from the other terminal of the key-lock switch to the accessory terminal on the fuse block. The remainder of the wiring must be as shown in Fig. 11-4. To make the connection, follow the illustrations in Fig. 11-5.

6. Connect a wire between the white wire of the siren unit and the hood switch. Continuing onward with this same switch wire, drill a hole in the firewall or use an existing hole so as to allow the switch wire to pass into the car.

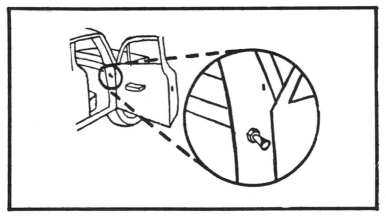

Fig. 11-3. Door-jamb switch to detect the opening of a door. (Courtesy Radio Shack)

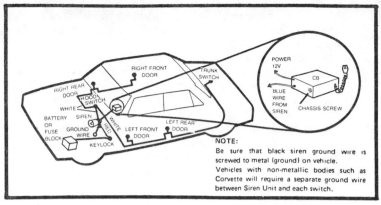

NOTE:
Be sure that black siren ground wire is screwed to metal (ground) on vehicle. Vehicles with non-metallic bodies such as Corvette will require a separate ground wire between Siren Unit and each switch.

Fig. 11-4. A complete burglar-alarm installation. (Courtesy Radio Shack)

7. The front-door-jamb switches can normally be reached by removing the kick pads below the dashboard. After splicing in the front-door switches to the main switch wire, remove the metal threshold strips on the floor near the front-door opening and run the wire under the carpet. (If the vehicle is a four-door, install the rear-door switches in the jambs in the same manner as the front doors and splice the rear-door switches into the main switch wire.)

8. Remove the rear-seat cushion (not the backrest) and pass the switch wire up under the backrest into the trunk compartment. Connect the switch wire to the trunk switch.

9. Continue with the wire around to connect to the remaining door-jamb switches, or use another wire from the white siren wire to the other doors as shown.

10. Connect the hank of blue wire provided to the blue wire from the siren. Run it into the car as in step 6.

11. Connect the blue wire under a convenient screw on the CB or stereo unit so that the wire is grounded through its chassis. In cases where the unit mounts to a plastic dashboard, it may be necessary to run a separate ground wire to the unit. If it should become necessary to remove the unit from the car, ground the blue wire. The CB-250 will then work as a conventional auto alarm. Now, check to be sure all wires are properly and securely connected and will not be pinched by movement of door. Refer to the wiring diagram to be sure everything is in order. You may want to insulate bare wire ends with tape.

Testing and Operating

Close all doors plus hood and trunk. Turn key clockwise in lock (to ON position). If the siren should sound before any door, hood, or trunk lid is opened, check each switch to be sure the plunger is depressed when door is closed. Check also that bue wire is grounded through chassis of CB or stereo unit.

Open one of the doors. The siren will sound. Close the door. The siren will continue to operate until the key is turned to the OFF position. Proceed in same manner to test each protected location. Test CB alarm by turning key on; then, without opening doors, disconnect blue wire from CB or stereo unit momentarily. The siren will operate until the key is turned to the OFF position. Replace all upholstery panels and threshold strips.

LOW-COST HORN SYSTEM

If you have a horn in working condition, you already have half of an effective system installed. For the rest of the system, you'll need the following parts (available at auto-parts stores):

2   Horn relays
1   Keyed switch lock
6   Door-jamb switches (single-terminal, self-tapping, contact made when plunger is out)
6   Connectors for door-jamb switches
2   Switch-mounting plates (for trunk and hook, if desired)
25 Feet of hookup wire

Mounting and Wiring the Relays

Locate both relays as near as possible to the horn relay of your car. Mount both relays with their terminals facing each other as per Fig. 11-6. Use one mounting screw to attach both relay 2 and the short green ground lead. Attach other end of green lead to terminal marked H on relay 2.

Installation of Key-Lock Switch

IMPORTANT: Always install key-lock switch so that terminal end of lock protrudes into either the trunk or engine compartment and is not accessible from outside the car except through the trunk or engine openings. It may be necessary to make an access hole in the inner fender to accomplish this.

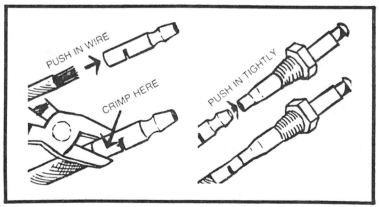

Fig. 11-5. Crimpon pins provide easy connection to door and other switches.

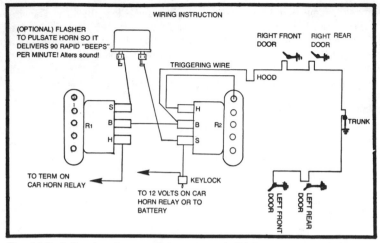

Fig. 11-6. A burglar-alarm system you can build from scratch, using parts commonly available at auto-parts stores.

Cut a 3/4-inch hole at desired location. Attach heavy wire to both terminals of lock, leaving ample length to work with. Wires may be attached to key-lock switch either by soldering or crimping, or using screw terminals provided on some models. Insert lock in hole and mount. Tighten retaining locknut so that switch is off when key is vertical with notches up. OFF is left position.

Simplified Door-Jamb-Switch Hookup

NOTE: Do not connect a jamb switch to emergency brake when using this shortcut method. You can use your existing courtesy-light switching arrangement in place of the door-jamb switches on all doors so equipped. Just follow the wiring diagram, and attach the alarm-triggering wire to the same point as the wire already on the courtesy-light switch. If all doors are equipped with courtesy-light switches, you can save even more time by running a single wire to the ungrounded side of just one switch. (On most switches the ungrounded side is the single wire leading in. The ground side is the body of the switch.) If necessary, add switches as per diagram to unprotected doors. These added switches will then operate the courtesy lights as well as the alarm (when alarm lock is on). This will protect all doors; hood and trunk must be protected by addition of switches as described.

IMPORTANT: This will work only on cars that use *grounding* to activate the courtesy lights.

Regular Installation of Door-Jamb Switches

Locate door-jamb switch on the hinge side of each door opening so that the switch plunger will be depressed when the door is closed. Drill a 1/4-inch hole for self-tapping door-jamb switch. Do not fasten door-jamb switches until wiring is completed.

Installation of Trunk-Lid and Hood Switches

Determine location of hood switch so that switch plunger will be depressed when hood is closed. Proceed in like manner to install trunk switch. Drill a 1/4-inch hole and install self-tapping door-jamb switch. Auxiliary brackets (Fig. 11-2) may be used in installing trunk and hood switches.

The installation procedure for the emergency-brake switch will vary, depending on the make and model of automobile. In general, the switch must be mounted so that the switch plunger is depressed when the brake is on, and released when the brake is released. An auxiliary bracket may be formed from aluminum or steel plate (Fig. 11-2).

The procedure for protecting the rear opening in station wagons will depend on the make and model of automobile. It is usually best to mount a switch on the side of the opening so that switch plunger is depressed when door is closed.

Wiring

In accordance with Fig. 11-6 and using insulated wire, run a wire as indicated to connect all door, hood, and trunk switches in series. Starting at the hole drilled for right-front door-jamb switch, proceed to right-rear door, trunk, left-rear door, and left-front door. Remove threshold strips to pass wire under door openings. Door-post upholstery panels and rear-quarter upholstery panels may be removed to facilitate wiring. A weighted string, fish tape, or stiff wire may be used in threading wire through places where access is difficult.

At each point where a switch is to be installed, the wire should be cut and both ends stripped of insulation, twisted together, and inserted in a plug-type terminal (Fig. 11-5). The terminal should be crimped solidly over these wires with diagonal pliers or a terminal tool, or the wires may be soldered into the terminal. Insert the plug-type terminal in the door-switch terminal receptacle and start the threaded portion of switch in the 1/4-inch hole. Use a wrench to screw switch tight against car body.

If the emergency brake is to be protected, run a wire from the left-front door-jamb-switch terminal to the emergency-brake-switch terminal.

When making connections to your existing horn relay, you will find that many cars have a male and female press-in connector rather than screw terminals. Since there is very little current used in the alarm system, you can just strip the wire from the alarm relays and attach it to the horn-relay connection by pulling the horn-relay connector out, laying the wire over it, and just pressing it back in.

Run short jumper wire between the B-terminals of the two alarm relays. Run another short jumper wire between the S-terminals on the alarm relays.

Run a short jumper wire from the H-terminal on relay 1 to the S-terminal on your existing horn relay. To test and identify the S-terminal (if not properly marked), briefly ground the terminal in question on your horn relay and see if the horn blows. Do this with caution since the B-terminal is connected to the battery and will cause a temporary short if briefly grounded.

IMPORTANT: Do not reverse relays 1 and 2. Take the two long wires coming from your key switch and run one end to the S-terminal of relay 2 and the other end to the B-terminal on your present horn relay (or direct to + terminal of the battery if more convenient).

There is no current flowing in this circuit, except when the alarm is activated. When the alarm is activated, there is a very moderate amount of current flowing in the circuit, which is adequate to trigger the relays. There is no need for heavy wire at any point in this circuit.

Testing and Operating

Close all doors and both hood and trunk lid. (If emergency brake is protected, pull emergency brake on.) Turn key in lock to the right to ON position. If the horn should sound before any door, the hood, or the trunk lid is opened, check each switch to be sure the plunger is depressed when door is closed. Spacing washers may be placed under door-jamb switches, if necessary, to provide more movement of the switch plunger.

Open one of the doors. The horn will sound. Close the door. The horn will continue to operate until the key is turned to the OFF position. Proceed in same manner to test each protected location. Replace all upholstery panels and threshold strips.

Chapter 12
CB Units

The units covered in this chapter include one of the new 40-channel transceivers, a 23-channel set with single sideband, and a listen-only CB converter for an existing car radio.

40-CHANNEL TRANSCEIVER

The *Realistic* TRC-452 is a completely solid-state transceiver, designed for class D 27 MHz citizens band use. It uses a frequency-synthesizing circuit with digital phase-lock-loop techniques to provide crystal-controlled transmit and receive operation on all 40 channels.

Installation

Location of the transceiver is very important. Installations in cars are usually made somewhere under the dash. Things to consider when planning its location are:

1. Will I bump my knees getting in or out of passenger or driver side?
2. Will the microphone be convenient to reach while I am driving?
3. Will the mounting-bracket bolts that go through the dash interfere with any electrical or mechanical operation in the car?
4. Will the transceiver block the air-conditioning or heater venting into the car?

After you have satisfied yourself that you have selected the most desirable location, proceed as follows:

1. Use the mounting bracket (see Fig. 12-2) as a template to mark the position for the mounting holes.

Fig. 12-1. A 40-channel CB unit. (Courtesy Radio Shack).

2. Observe the size of the mounting bolts and choose a drill that will make the bolts fit snugly, holding the mounting bracket tight against the dash.
3. Drill mounting holes, taking great care not to damage wiring, trim, or other accessories.
4. Secure mounting bracket to dash, using mounting bolts.
5. Install transceiver into mounting bracket, using thumbscrews as shown, and mount the microphone bracket in a convenient location. Before proceeding with electrical-power hookup, verify that OFF/VOLUME power switch is rotated to OFF.
6. Determine if the car has a negative or positive ground. This can be done by simply raising the hood and observing whether the positive or negative post on your battery is connected to the engine block or car body. Most late-model cars have negative-ground systems.
7. Using the appropriate figure (A or B, Fig. 12-3) as a guide, complete the electrical hookup to the transceiver.
8. If the antenna has already been installed, attach the PL-259 coax cable plug from the antenna to the ANT connector at the rear of the transceiver.

Operation

NOTE: Do not transmit unless a suitable load or antenna is attached to the transceiver.

The OFF/VOLUME control (Fig. 12-1) is used to apply and remove power from the transceiver and to control the sound level coming from the receiver section.

The SQUELCH control is used to eliminate receiver background noise in the absence of an incoming signal. This control is very effective in accomplishing its task. However, as the control is adjusted clockwise, effective sensitivity is decreased, thereby eliminating weaker signals which you would otherwise receive. To properly adjust the control, proceed as follows: With no incoming signals, turn control fully counterclockwise, then slowly clockwise until the receiver noise abruptly stops. Any signal to be received now must be slightly stronger than average receiver noise. Only very strong signals will be heard when the control is set in its maximum clockwise position.

The RF GAIN control is used to adjust the transceiver's receiver section to the signal strength in your area. Adjust as required to receive the weakest signals in your area.

The channel-selector control is used to select the channel on which the transceiver transmits and receives.

NOTE: Channel 9 has been reserved by the FCC for emergency communications involving the immediate safety of life of individuals or immediate protection of property. Channel 9 may also be used to render assistance to motorists.

The PA-CB switch selects the mode of operation for the transceiver. The PA-CB switch should not be in PA position unless an 8-ohm, 5-watt speaker is attached to PA SPKR jack, located on the rear panel of the transceiver. In the PA position, the transceiver operates as a public-address system. In the CB position, the unit operates as a transceiver (transmitter and receiver).

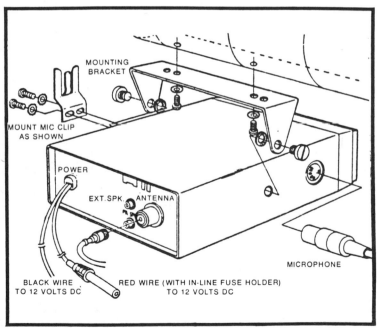

Fig. 12-2. Mounting and connection details for a typical CB transceiver. (Courtesy Radio Shack)

The ANL-OUT switch, when in the ANL position, engages an automatic-noise-limiter circuit, which helps to eliminate low-level impulse-type external noise. When the switch is in the OUT position, the automatic noise-limiter circuit is deactivated.

The RF/S meter measures input signal strength when receiving and RF output power when transmitting.

The modulation lamp (to the right of the meter) flashes as the transceiver transmits. The brightness of the lamp is directly proportional to the percentage of modulation.

NOTE: The modulation-lamp circuitry in the Radio Shack CB incorporates a special feature you should be aware of. If you operate the transmitter with an open transmission line or high SWR, the modulation lamp will come on and stay on (will not flicker with modulation). The TRC-452 will not be damaged under such conditions, but your signal will not be getting out with much "punch." Check your antenna system. Be sure the coax cable is not open. Be sure you are using 52-ohm cable (RG-8 or RG-58) and antenna.

When the press-to-talk switch (on the mike) is pressed, the transmitter is in operation. When released, the receiver is operating.

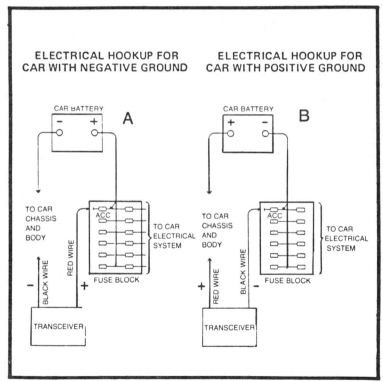

Fig. 12-3. Wiring diagrams for electrical systems with negative ground (A) and positive ground (B). Most cars, including all modern American cars have a negative-ground electrical system.

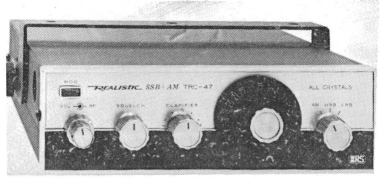

Fig. 12-4. Radio Shack's Realistic TRC-47 CB provides communication through the use of single sideband modulation.

SINGLE SIDEBAND TRANSCEIVER

Radio Shack's *Realistic* TRC-47 (Fig. 12-4) is a completely solid-state AM/SSB transceiver for Class D 27 MHz citizens band use. While you can't buy a new 23 channel unit (FCC Regs of 1/78) millions are still available and are legal to use. They use a frequency-synthesizing circuit to provide crystal-controlled transmit and receive operation on 23 channels. You can use such a set on any one of the 23 channels in the conventional AM mode as well as the same 23 channels in either the upper single-sideband or lower single-sideband mode.

This flexibility doubles the effective number of channels from 23 to 46. The SSB mode also increases the effective range of communication because all the power is concentrated in one sideband. Single-sideband reception also adds advantages in sensitivity and selectivity, plus lower signal-to-noise ratio. This of course also contributes to an increase in operating range.

Ordinarily, an SSB signal will reach farther and be heard more clearly than an equivalent AM signal. Reception of SSB is simple—just adjust the CLARIFIER control to bring in the voice transmissions.

SSB (Single Sideband)...What Is It?

To understand SSB, we first need to know what an AM (amplitude-modulated) signal is.

Amplitude modulation is a form of heterodyning—mixing two signals together electrically. In the process of mixing, three signals result. Example: An RF signal at 27.005 MHz (channel 4) is mixed with (modulated by) a 1000 Hz tone.

The resulting signals are:

27.005 MHz = original or *carrier* signal

27.005 MHz − 1000 Hz (27,005,000 minus 1000) = 27.004 MHz, the lower sideband.

27.005 MHz + 1000 Hz (27,005,000 plus 1000) = 27.006 MHz, the upper sideband.

217

Figure 12-5 shows these signals. Note that the communication or intelligence (the 1000 Hz tone) is contained in each sideband. The carrier contains no intelligence; this fact is vital!

For the sake of communication, all we need to receive is the 1000 Hz tone. The receiver only needs to recover one signal, and yet we are transmitting three signals. Not only are we sending three signals, but also we are wasting most of our power in one of them (the carrier, which actually carries none of the intelligence). The two sideband signals duplicate each other.

Thus, if we can eliminate the carrier (not needed for communication) and send only one of the sidebands (since they duplicate each other's information anyway), we concentrate all of the transmitting power into one sideband. This is exactly what single sideband accomplishes.

Single sideband transmissions incorporate only one of the sidebands — i.e., in the example above, only the upper sideband, at 27.006 MHz, or only the lower sideband, at 27.004 MHz. The second sideband and the carrier are eliminated in the early stages of the transmitter circuitry.

When only one sideband is transmitted, we can concentrate all of the available power in this one sideband, greatly increasing the effective power of an SSB signal as compared to an AM signal (see Fig. 12-6).

Controls and Their Functions

This short description of the function of each control and connector supplies background information for proper operation of a typical SSB transceiver.

RF—Varies the sensitivity of the RF amplifier stages of the receiver circuitry. For normal operation, set RF to maximum and adjust VOL for a suitable listening level. Under high-signal conditions, you may want to turn RF down a little and raise VOL as required.

VOL (with ON/OFF switch)—Turn clockwise to apply power to the unit and then adjust for the desired level of sound from the speaker.

SQUELCH—Sets the level of the internal squelch circuitry to cut out the background noise when no signal is being received. When properly set, it allows signals to come through; but it cuts off the receiver sound when no

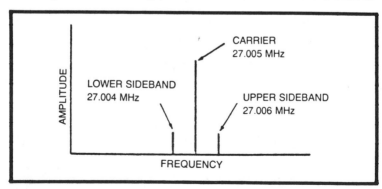

Fig. 12-5. Carrier and sidebands of an ordinary AM signal.

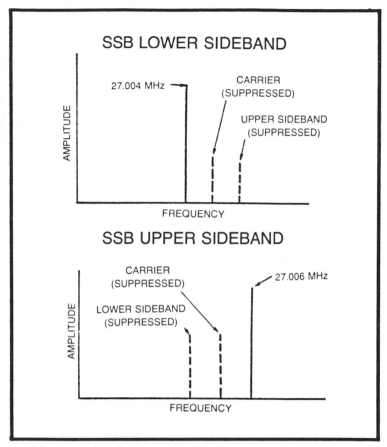

Fig. 12-6. Lower and upper sidebands produced by an SSB transmitter.

signal is being received, thus eliminating annoying background and atmospheric noise during standby and monitoring conditions. If SQUELCH is set too high, you may miss some of the weaker signals. Operating conditions will determine the best setting.

CLARIFIER—Functions as a fine-tuning (or *delta*-tuning) control for reception of single-sideband and AM signals when the mode switch is set to either LSB or USB. It also shifts the transmit frequency by a small amount. This permits you to tune your receiver and transmitter to exactly the same frequency of any other station which you are communicating with.

AM-USB-LSB—Selects the desired mode of operation for both transmit and receive. When in the AM position, both transmitter and receiver sections are operative for AM. When set to the LSB position, the receiver operates to receive only the lower-sideband portion of a signal; the transmitter will transmit only the lower sideband of the modulated waveform. In the USB position, the receiver operates only to receive the upper-sideband portion of a signal; the transmitter will transmit only the upper sideband of the modulated waveform.

Channel Selector—Selects one of the CB channels.

MOD—A modulation lamp which provides a relative output indication for both AM and SSB.

During AM transmissions, the lamp will light up to about one-half normal brightness and will brighten as you talk into the microphone. The first brightness level indicates the strength of the AM carrier. Full brightness will be achieved when you talk at a level causing 100% modulation. (The carrier peak output increases with modulation.)

In the SSB mode, the lamp lights only when you talk since an SSB signal does not transmit an RF carrier. During normal SSB operation, the lamp will blink in time with your voice peaks, thus indicating RF output.

Microphone—The dynamic microphone must be connected to the jack on the side. To transmit, press the button on the mike and talk into the mike. To receive, release the button. When transmitting, hold the microphone at an angle, 2 or 3 inches from your mouth, and speak clearly in a normal voice.

The Rear Panel

ANT—Coax connector for the CB antenna (SO-239 type, accepts PL-259 connectors).

SPKR—External speaker jack. If you want to use an external speaker, plug it into this jack. You should use a standard 8-ohm type. When a standard phone plug is inserted into this jack, the built-in speaker is automatically disconnected.

Power Cable with In-Line Fuse—This cable is to be connected to a source of 12 − 16 volts DC power, negative ground. The red wire with the in-line fuse must be connected to the plus side, and the black wire to the minus side.

Installation

Safety and convenience are the primary considerations in mounting any piece of mobile equipment. All controls must be readily available to the operator without interfering with the movements necessary for safe operation of the vehicle. Be sure all cables are clear of the brake, clutch, and accelerator pedals. Also, thought must be given to the convenience of passengers (will they have adequate leg room?).

Another extremely important requirement is the ease of installation and removal for service and maintenance. Mount the tranceiver so it can be slipped in and out very easily.

The most common mounting position for a transceiver is under the dashboard, directly over the driveshaft hump. Do not mount the transceiver in the path of the heater or air-conditioning air stream. Be sure the chassis of the transceiver is electrically connected to the ground system of the vehicle or boat. Use a separate ground wire to be certain.

Also, before installing the transceiver, be sure the vehicle has the correct ground system. Most vehicles manufactured in the United States

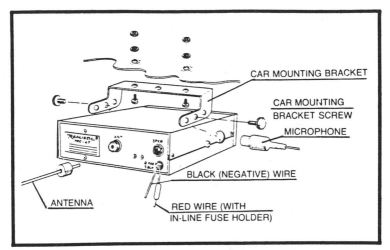

Fig. 12-7. An SSB installation for the citizens band. (Courtesy Radio Shack)

since 1956 have a negative-ground electrical system. Severe damage may result if you attempt to use a transceiver on a positive-ground system.

1. When you have determined the best location for mounting, use the mobile mounting bracket as a template to mark mounting holes. Take care when you drill holes that you do not drill into wiring, trim, or other accessories. Mount in position with bolts, lockwashers and nuts, or self-threading screws. (Refer to Fig. 12-7.)

2. Connect the red (positive) wire (with in-line fuse holder) to the accessory (ACC) terminal on the ignition switch of your vehicle. Make a good mechanical and electrical connection to the frame of the vehicle for the black (negative) wire. You can use an auto-accessory plug (Radio Shack catalog No. 274-331, or equivalent) to connect your transceiver to the vehicle's power source. However, it is better to connect the DC power cord directly to the accessory terminal of the ignition switch. This will prevent unauthorized use of the transceiver and will also prevent you from leaving the transceiver on unintentionally.

CAR RADIO CONVERTER

The *Realistic* 21-500 CB converter is designed to pick up signals in the citizens band and to process them through a standard AM radio in your vehicle. It requires a 12-volt power connection (it will work from either positive- or negative-ground electrical systems) and connection to the antenna-input jack on your car radio and the vehicle's antenna cable.

With the CB converter on you'll be receiving CB channels 1 through 40 on 800 to 1240 kHz on the AM dial. The emergency channel, channel 9, will appear at 900 on the dial. The front of the CB converter has the markings showing the frequencies where you'll pick up the channels. Example: channel 1 will show up at 800, 9 at 900, 23 at 1090, and 40 at 1240.

Installation

Carefully plan the installation. Consider the following:

1. Will the cables reach?
2. Will it be safe and convenient to operate the converter in the chosen location? Can you reach its button?
3. Will you have to drill into trim or existing wiring?

You might want to make electrical connections before mounting the converter (in some cases it's easier that way). Do it as follows:

1. Connect the wire with in-line fuse to an ACC terminal on the fuse block of your vehicle.
2. Disconnect the antenna cable from your AM (or AM/FM) radio.
3. Connect the antenna cable to the ANT jack on the back of the converter.
4. Connect the antenna cable from the converter to the ANT input jack on your AM (or AM/FM) radio.

NOTE: Ground connection is made through the shield wire of the antenna cable.

Mounting

1. Use the converter as a template to mark holes for drilling. Be sure you don't drill into trim or existing wires.

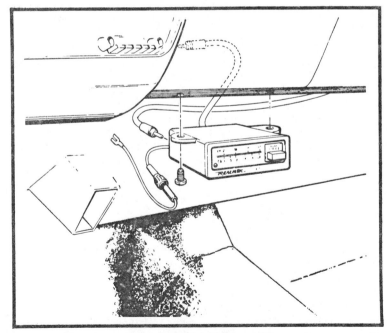

Fig. 12-8. Installing a converter for hearing CB transmissions on your original-equipment AM radio. (Courtesy Radio Shack)

2. Drill 5/32-inch (4 mm) holes.
3. Mount the CB converter with sheet-metal screws (see Fig. 12-8).

Operation

1. Turn ignition switch to ACC or ON. This will make power available to the CB converter, assuming you've made power connection to an accessory terminal on the fuse block. Then, when you turn the ignition switch off, the CB converter's power will go off too.
2. Turn AM radio on.
3. Press in the pushbutton on the front of the CB converter. The CB LED will light up, telling you the unit is functioning.
4. Tune the AM radio from 800 to 1240 and you'll pick up signals from channels 1 through 40.
5. To receive AM (or FM) signals, press the pushbutton on the CB converter and you're back to normal radio operation.

Some automotive radios have special antenna-trimmer adjustments. If your AM radio has one, adjust it for best reception when using the CB converter. Check your owner's manual for location and procedure.

Chapter 13

Depth Sounder/Recorder

Take time to plan the installation of your chart recorder. This could save disappointment and possible installation modifications later.

The main installation considerations are the ease of reading the chart, the physical size of the chart recorder, and the length of the transducer cable.

If you intend to use the chart recorder primarily as a navigational aid, you will want the chart recorder mounting on or near the boat's instrument panel. If you use it mainly to locate fish, expecially on larger boats, you might consider mounting the chart recorder at the rear of the boat where it can be monitored by the fishing party. Do not mount the chart recorder too near the compass or radios, as there could be some interaction between them.

Be sure to allow 2 inches behind the mounted unit for the power and transducer cables. The three most common positions for mounting the gimbal bracket are shown in Fig. 13-1.

POWER CONNECTIONS

The free end of the power cable should be connected to the boat's 12 VDC power with the red wire to the positive (+) connection and the black wire to the negative (−) connection. If these power-cable connections are reversed, the chart recorder will not operate. Normally, wiring the recorder directly to the ignition switch is satisfactory. However, if excessive ignition noise is present, you should connect the power cable directly to the battery, or as close to the battery as possible.

1. Install the gimbal bracket at the selected location in your boat.
2. Install the chart recorder in the gimbal bracket (Fig. 13-2). Secure the unit in the desired position with the thumbknobs.
3. Check to see that the unit is turned off (sensitivity control turned fully counterclockwise, until it clicks).

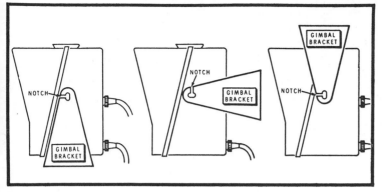

Fig. 13-1. Mounting configurations for the gimbal bracket.

4. Make the necessary power-cable connection to your boat's 12 VDC power source.

This completes the installation of the main unit.

TRANSDUCER INSTALLATION

IMPORTANT: When you choose the mounting location for your transducer, be sure to consider the length of the transducer cable.

Through-Hull Mounting

Choose the location where the transducer is to be mounted. This location should be approximately amidships, but not near any underwater fittings which protrude from the hull, and not so far aft that propeller noise will be picked up. It is important that the transducer be mounted where water flow across the face will be smooth, with no turbulence or air bubbles

Fig. 13-2. The Heath MI-2910 chart recorder is installed with a gimbal bracket and secured with two thumbknobs.

in the stream. Select a location near the keel and as near the point of maximum draft as practicable without actually being on the keel. Running aground may tear the transducer loose and weaken the keel. The mounting place you choose should be as nearly flat as possible, to make fairing out easier.

If the transducer is not mounted on a flat surface, fairing blocks are required to keep the transducer vertical. (Refer to Fig. 13-3.) If the transducer can be mounted on a flat surface, fairing blocks are not required. (Refer to Fig. 13-4.)

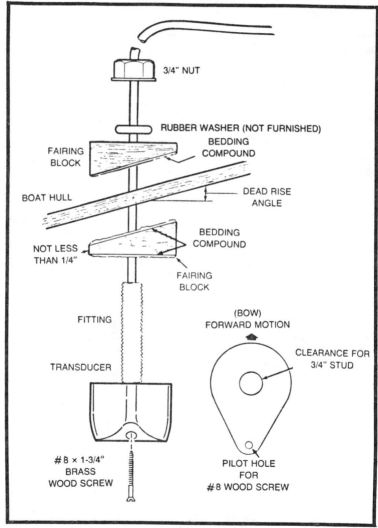

Fig. 13-3. Use of fairing blocks to mount the transducer vertically.

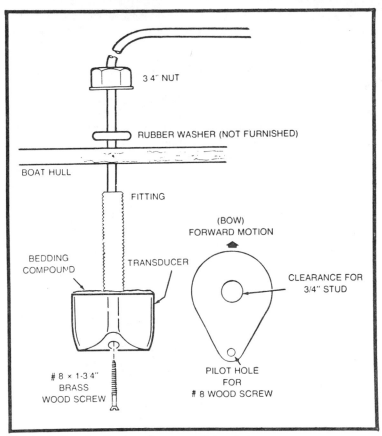

Fig. 13-4. Mounting the transducer on a flat surface.

At the point of mounting, drill a 3/4-inch hole through the hull. Measure the dead-rise angle (angle of the bottom with respect to the horizontal). Transfer this angular measurement to the fairing block and cut the block to the angle. (Refer to Fig. 13-3.) Thoroughly paint both pieces of fairing with a good grade of marine paint and allow it to dry. Coat both flat surfaces of the outside fairing block with bedding compound. If the fairing blocks are not required, coat the mounting surface of the transducer with bedding compound (Fig. 13-4).

Remove the 3/4-inch nut from the fitting on the transducer. Place the transducer and the outside fairing block (if used) together. Then feed the cable and the fitting through the hull as shown. Place the inner fairing block (if used) over the cable and fitting until it butts against the hull. If you feel there is any change of the fairing blocks (if used) or the hull swelling with absorbed water, place a rubber washer on the fitting as shown in Fig. 13-3 and 13-4. Finally, place the 3/4-inch nut on the fitting of the transducer. *Tighten this nut only finger tight* or use only a *small* wrench.

From the outside of the hull, align the transducer so its pointed end is toward the stern. Hold the assembly against the hull and drill a tap hole for the brass wood screw. Start the #8 × 1-3/4 inch brass wood screw through the transducer.

Important: Do not overtighten the 3/4-inch nut. To do so may break the transducer housing.

From the inside of the hull, tighten the 3/4-inch nut on the fitting snugly against the brass washer. Then tighten the #8 × 1-3/4-inch brass wood screw. Position the free end of the tranducer cable as required. Be sure to route this cable away from the boat's ignition system.

Transom Mounting

Locate the position on the transom where the transducer is to be mounted. It is important that the transducer be mounted where water flow across its face will be smooth, with no turbulence of air bubbles in the stream. It's a good idea to observe the boat while it is moving through the water to determine the best mounting location. Also, try to keep the transducer as far away from the motor as possible.

1. Remove the 3/4-inch nut from the fitting on the transducer.
2. Refer to Fig. 13-5 and pass the transducer cable through the slotted hole in the transducer bracket. Replace the 3/4-inch nut over the transducer cable and fitting. Tighten the nut only finger tight at this time.
3. Refer to Fig. 13-6 and mark (with a pencil) the four transducer-bracket mounting holes on the transom of the boat at the selected mounting location. Locate these holes so the face (bottom) of the transducer is *parallel with the surface of the water* and flush with the bottom of the hull. Bend the bottom of the transducer bracket up or down as required (see the inset drawing in Fig. 13-6).
4. Refer to Fig. 13-7 and drill the four required-size mounting holes and mount the transducer bracket to the transom.
5. Check to see that the transducer is still flush with the bottom of the hull as shown in the inset drawing in Fig. 13-6. If it is not, bend the bottom of the transducer bracket as required.
6. Refer to Fig. 13-7 and install the 1/4-20 × 3/8-inch hardware in the two side holes of the transducer bracket. This will keep the face of the transducer flush with the bottom of the hull.
7. Position the transducer so its pointed end is away from the stern. Then tighten the 3/4-inch nut on the transducer fitting so it is snug enough against the flat washer to keep the transducer pointed properly.
   NOTE: When you perform the next step, keep the amount of the transducer cable that is exposed to the water as short as possible to avoid excessive cable movement when the boat is underway. If you notice excessive cable movement, it may be necessary to secure the cable to the transom with one or more cable clamps.
8. Position the free end of the transducer cable as required. Be sure to route this cable away from the boat's ignition system.

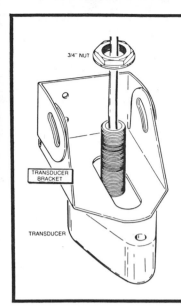

3/4" NUT

TRANSDUCER
BRACKET

TRANSDUCER

Fig. 13-5. Use of transducer bracket to mount transducer on transom.

Inside-Hull Installation

This is a type of installation in which you mount the transducer inside the hull at a location that will allow its face to remain in water at all times. Such a location might be in a bilge that always contains water, or inside some kind of bottomless water-filled container that is sealed to the bottom of the boat.

This type of installation has produced good results on some fiberglass and wooden boats. However, this installation may not work on metal boats, boats that are painted with a metal-impregnated paint, well soaked wooden boats, or in areas of fiberglass boats that have two thicknesses of fiberglass separated by flotation material. Many fiberglass boats of this type of construction, however, have a small section of single-thickness bottom area located near the transom. This area will usually provide enough room to mount the transducer.

An obvious advantage of an inside-the-hull mounting is that it does not require you to drill holes in your boat. Other advantages are: it is not necessary to remove your boat from the water to make the installation; the transducer will not be damaged if your boat should run aground; and the transducer can be easily serviced.

One disadvantage that you should consider is the possible loss of sensitivity in that the overall measurable depth could be reduced. For this reason, you should perform a depth-measurement test to determine if this type of installation is practicable for your purposes. You can perform this test quite easily as follows:

1. Position the boat where the water depth is the maximum in which you expect to navigate.

2. Hang the transducer over the side of your boat and make a test reading. Be sure the transducer is covered with water and that its face is parallel to the water surface. Record the results of this reading.

3. Now make a comparison reading with the transducer inside your boat. If there is no water in your bilge, add sufficient water to cover the face of the transducer. Remember that the transducer must have water between it and the bottom of the boat and that its face must be parallel to the surface of the water. NOTE: It may be necessary to try several locations in the boat to find the one that gives the best results.

If you have decided on an inside-the-hull mounting for your transducer, consider the following points as you select its mounting location.

1. Select a relatively thin area in the hull. Avoid any built-up areas that have been added to strengthen the hull.

2. Mount the transducer below the boat's waterline. Water must be under the transducer outside the boat, as well as inside, for the transducer to operate.

3. Mount the transducer directly above a flat, horizontal surface. The greater the angle of the boat bottom to the face of the transducer, the greater the loss in sensitivity (measurable depth).

4. The face of the transducer must be parallel to the surface of the water outside the boat. The transducer is a highly directive device that will have less sensitivity when tilted to any side.

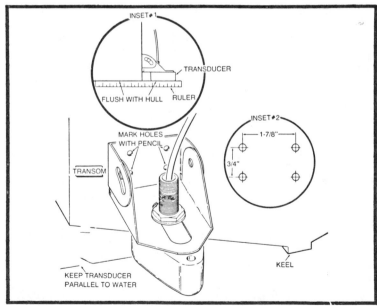

Fig. 13-6. Alignment of transducer. (Courtesy Heath Company)

230

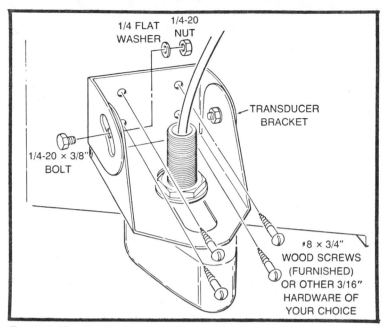

Fig. 13-7. Mounting the bracket to the transom.

If the bilge of your boat does not contain water in which the transducer can be suspended, you must provide some kind of bottomless leakproof container for the transducer mounting. This container can be a wooden box covered with fiberglass, or a copper, brass, or fiberglass tube that is then fiberglassed to the inside bottom of the boat.

The container you provide must be splashproof and yet have some means of adding water when necessary. It must also have a means of supporting the transducer. Figure 13-8 shows only two of the many ways to mount your transducer in this manner.

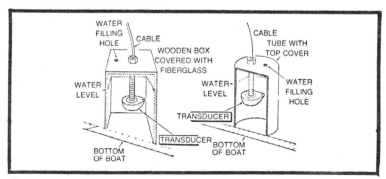

Fig. 13-8. Inside-the-hull mounting of the transducer, eliminating the need for drilling a hole in the boat.

Chapter 14

Digital Clock

▶▶▶▶▶▶▶▶▶▶▶▶▶▶▶

As shown in Fig. 14-1, you can mount the clock on top of or beneath the dash, and with or without the mounting bracket. Most on-top-of-the-dash locations will require that you drill about a 3/16-inch hole in the dash for the cable.

Perform the following steps that pertain to the type of installation you have chosen, either *With Bracket* or *Without Bracket*.

WITH BRACKET

Refer to Fig. 14-2 for the following steps:

1. Loosely mount the mounting bracket to the clock. Slide each bracket slot between the screw head and the large lockwasher on the clock.
2. Set the clock in the position you want it to be mounted. Then, while you hold the mounting bracket firmly in place, lift the clock off the bracket and set the clock aside.
3. Use a pencil to mark the bracket holes.

CAUTION: Drilling through vinyl material can be difficult, as the drill bit will tend to snag and then quickly make a long rip in the vinyl. Therefore, in the next step, *be sure to press the mounting bracket against the dash and then use an ice pick or nail to make the bracket holes.*

4. Use the mounting bracket as a guide and make three 3/32-inch holes. Then mount the bracket with three #6 × 5/8-inch sheet-metal screws.
5. Mount the clock to the bracket. If your location requires a hole in the dash for the cable, temporarily remove the clock, make a 3/16-inch hole, route the cable through the hole, and remount the clock.

232

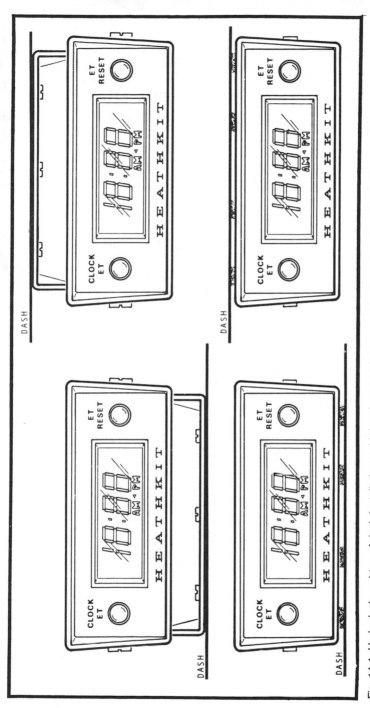

Fig. 14-1. Underdash and top-of-dash installations with brackets and foam mounting tape. (Courtesy Heath Company)

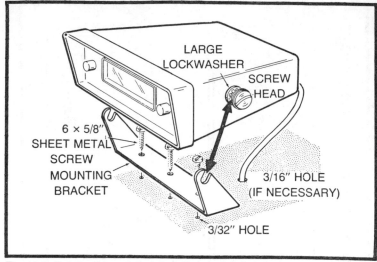

Fig. 14-2. Details of top-of-dash installation of digital clock.

WITHOUT BRACKET

Refer to Fig. 14-3 for the following steps:

1. Set the clock in the position where it is to be mounted. Then make a faint pencil line around the clock. Make sure the line is far enough away from the clock so it can be erased after the clock is mounted.
2. If your mounting location requires a hole in the dash for the cable, carefully drill a 3/16-inch hole at a suitable location, as shown in Fig. 14-3.
3. Remove the protective paper backing from one side of one piece of foam tape and press the tape in place on the clock. Put it on top of the clock for a beneath-the-dash installation and on the bottom of the clock for an on-top-the-dash installation.

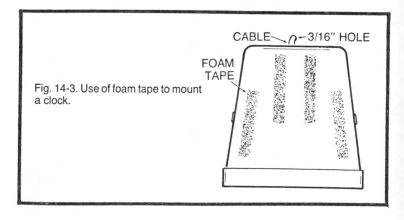

Fig. 14-3. Use of foam tape to mount a clock.

234

4. In a similar manner, install three other pieces of foam tape.
5. Route the cable through the cable hole (if you drilled one), remove the remaining paper backing from the pieces of tape, center the clock over the penciled outline, and carefully press the clock into place.
6. Erase the penciled outline.

WIRING

In the following steps, you will route the cable, cut it to its necessary length, and connect the cable wires at the proper place in the vehicle. Because there can be large differences between vehicles, the following information is general. Therefore, use the information that pertains to your vehicle. Read all the following material before you perform any steps. Connect the cable wires as follows:

- Green wire to a connection that has power applied to it only when the ignition switch is in the ACCESSORY or ON position.
- Red wire to a connection where battery power is always available.
- Black wire to the chassis ground of the vehicle.

If your vehicle has a fuse block:

1. Cut the cable to a length that (when routed as desired) will be long enough to reach and connect to the fuse terminals.
2. Remove the desired amount of outer insulation from the end of the cable.
3. Remove 1/4 inch of insulation from the red and green wires and 3/4 inch of insulation from the black wire.
4. Refer to Fig. 14-4 and connect wire connectors to the green and red cable wires.
5. Push the connector on the green wire onto a fuse block lug marked FUSE ACC, ACC, or RADIO. (See Fig. 14-5.)
6. Push the connector on the red wire onto a lug marked FUSE BATT, BATT, or LIGHTS.
7. Connect the black wire to a screw that is connected to chassis ground. (This is usually the metal part of the dash.)

If your vehicle does not have a fuse block, refer to Fig. 14-6 for the following steps:

1. Cut the cable to the proper length.
2. Connect and solder the green wire to the wire that carries power to the radio or other accessory; then wrap the connection with electrical tape.

Fig. 14-4. Handy terminals supplied by Heath Company for making connections to fuse block of car.

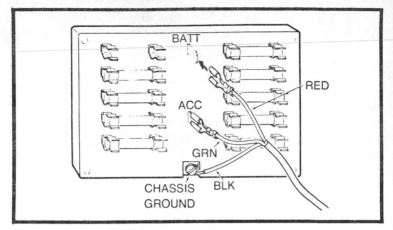

Fig. 14-5. Connecting to the fuse block.

3. Connect and solder the red wire to a wire that carries power to the head lights, horn, etc., then wrap the connection with electrical tape.
4. Connect the black wire to a screw that is connected to chassis ground. (This is usually the metal part of the dash.)

OPERATION

The operation of the Heath Model GC-1093 (Fig. 14-7) is typical of digital clocks.

To set the time:

1. Position the CLOCK ET switch to the "out" position.
2. Push the MIN switch. The minutes of the display will advance 1 minute each second.
3. Push the HR switch. The hours of the display will advance 1 hour each second.

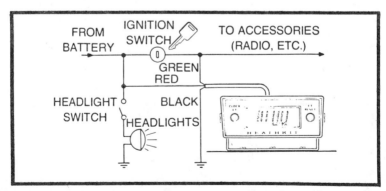

Fig. 14-6. Wiring diagram for a digital clock.

Fig. 14-7. A digital clock offered in kit form by Heath Company, Benton Harbor, Michigan.

To set the elapsed timer:

1. Position the CLOCK ET switch to the "in" position.
2. Push the ET RESET switch. The timer will go to zero and begin timing.

The Heath clock, because it has a normal time mode and an elapsed-time mode, is actually two clocks in one. In the normal clock mode, the ET RESET switch has no effect—except when the ignition is off. Then, when you push this switch, the time is displayed.

When the clock is in the elapsed-time mode, the MIN and HR set switches have no effect.

When the vehicle ignition switch is turned off, the clock and timer both continue to operate, but the digital display is turned off to conserve battery current. To read the display when the ignition is off and the CLOCK ET switch is in the "in" position, you must turn the ignition switch to the ACCESSORY position.

The elapsed-time display shows minutes and seconds up to 19 minutes 59 seconds. Then, hours and minutes are displayed up to 19 hours 59 minutes. The timer than automatically resets to zero and continues to count in hours and minutes.

The display intensity may vary for a few seconds when it is first turned on.

Chapter 15

Direction Finder

The Heath Model MR-1010 radio direction finder (Fig. 15-1) is a sensitive receiver that covers two AM bands: long wave (190 kHz to 10 kHz), and broadcast (535 kHz to 1605 kHz).

This receiver is a rugged unit designed specifically for all types of water craft that travel out of sight of land or travel at night. Stainless-steel hardware is used, as it resists the corrosive effects of salt water.

The null meter and sensitive rotating-rod antenna quickly locate the direction of a station signal. The sense antenna provides further accuracy in determining the direction of a signal. The directional-antenna base is calibrated in 2° increments to provide a compass heading suitable for the most sophisticated navigator.

The receiver is equipped to operate from either a boat battery or its own self-contained battery. The tuned frequency is displayed by a digital readout on the front panel. When the receiver operates from the self-contained battery, the frequency readout remains lit for only 20 seconds to conserve power. The brightness of the readout is automatically controlled by the existing light level.

A switch-controlled front-panel lamp lights up the meter for night use. Also, a sensitivity control allows you to adjust for varying signal strengths to obtain the best direction-finding null.

You may install the radio direction finder at any convenient location in the boat. However, it should be located some distance from the magnetic compass, as the ferrite-rod antenna in the radio direction finder may affect the operation of the compass.

The power cable, which connects to the back of the radio direction finder, must be connected at the other end to the boat battery supply. This can be connected directly to the boat battery or to the switched side of the

Fig. 15-1. A radio direction finder sold in kit form by Heath Company, Benton Harbor, Michigan.

boat ignition switch. Connect the red wire of the power cable to the positive (+) battery supply, and the black wire to the negative (−) battery supply.

The following applies to the Heath direction finder, *but not to all direction finders.*

If you are not sure of the polarity of your boat's electrical system, temporarily connect the radio direction finder to the system and operate the radio direction finder. If it does not operate, temporarily reverse the wiring of the power cable and try it again. Reversing the connections of the power cable will not damage the Heath radio direction finder *but may damage some makes.*

To operate the radio direction finder from your boat's electrical system, the power switch on the back of the chassis must be in the EXTERNAL position. When operating from external power, the frequency display will remain lit any time the receiver is on.

Chapter 16
FM Signal Booster

The *Realistic* FM signal booster (Fig. 16-1) is designed to give increased sensitivity for FM signals in a vehicle or boat. It requires a 12-volt DC power source and will work with either negative or positive electrical ground. This FM booster will give you better FM reception, especially in previously marginal reception areas; this will result in better FM stereo and quieter FM radio signals.

The unit is designed for the standard FM band, 88 to 108 MHz, and will provide more than 6 dB gain (this represents a doubling of signal sensitivity). It can be left on all the time if you wish, as it draws very little current. Since it does not affect standard AM reception, you can use it with an FM-AM radio and will not need to switch it off when listening to AM (no gain is provided for the AM signals).

It's easy to mount and connect—and since it is so compact, you'll probably be able to locate it within easy reach of the driver.

MOUNTING AND CONNECTING

First, select a suitable mounting location. It must be:

- Close enough to the antenna cable and radio so the antenna connections can be made.
- Close enough to a source of 12 volts DC so the power cable will reach.
- Convenient for use (switch on and off if desired).

1. Remove the bracket from the FM booster. Use the bracket as a template to mark mounting holes. Then drill holes for the screw. Take care not to drill into existing wires or trim. Also, don't actually mount the bracket yet!

2. The wire with the in-line fuse holder is the power cable and must be connected to a source of 12 volt DC (this may be either positive or negative ground—there is internal automatic circuitry in the *Realistic* booster which can utilize either polarity of voltage). Typically, the best location to make this connection is at the fuse block in the vehicle. Make connection to the accessory terminal by

Fig. 16-1. The Realistic FM signal booster, sold by Radio Shack, gives improved performance to any existing FM or AM/FM radio.

    loosening the nut, slipping the spade lug under the nut, and then retightening the nut.

3. Disconnect the antenna input cable to the vehicle radio and plug it into the connector at the back of the FM booster.
4. Plug the antenna cable from the FM booster into the antenna connector at the back of the vehicle.
5. Double-check the connection. Refer to Fig. 16-2 to be sure everything is okay.
6. Mount the FM booster onto the bracket and mount the assembly, using the screws provided. Notice that you can place the bracket either under the booster (for underdash mounting) or on top (for mounting on top of the dash).

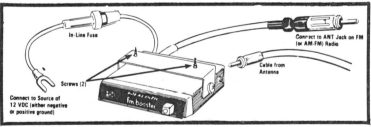

Fig. 16-2. Connections and installation details for an FM signal booster. (Courtesy Radio Shack)

OPERATION

    It's simple to use an FM booster. To obtain extra FM sensitivity, just press the button on the FM booster. This activates the booster and lights up the front. In areas where the FM signals are strong, you may want to turn the booster off—just press again. If you have an AM-FM radio, no need to turn off the booster when listening to AM (the booster does *not* increase the signal strength of AM signals, only FM signals).

    NOTE: If the booster fails to light up when the button is pressed in, the fuse may be blown. Check it. If you make a replacement, use only the same size and type. *Do not use a higher amperage-rating fuse.*

Chapter 17
FM Radio Converter

The *Realistic* FM converter (Fig. 17-1) has been designed for use in an automobile having either a 12-volt negative- or positive-ground electrical system. It utilizes one IC, four transistors, and five diodes in a superheterodyne circuit to function together with an AM radio. An RF amplifier has been incorporated into the converter to provide greater sensitivity in the FM mode of operation.

OPERATION

The FM converter uses your regular radio antenna to receive FM stations. It takes the FM signal received and changes (converts) it into an AM radio signal and then feeds the converted signal into your AM radio. This principle of operation requires that both the AM radio and FM converter be turned on when FM reception is desired. However, to receive the converted FM signal, you must first tune your AM radio to the converted FM signal, which is at 1400 kHz on the AM dial. After tuning the AM radio to 1400 kHz, you may then tune in FM radio stations with the FM converter.

If your AM radio is a pushbutton type, one of the pushbuttons can be set at 1400 kHz. Then, whenever FM reception is desired, you need only press the preset pushbutton, turn the converter on, and tune in FM stations.

ELECTRICAL INSTALLATION

1. Remove antenna lead-in from the antenna receptacle on the AM radio and plug it into the antenna receptacle (ANT IN) on the FM converter (Fig. 17-2).
2. Connect the output cable from the antenna receptacle (TO AM) on the FM converter to the antenna receptacle on the AM radio.

242

Fig. 17-1. The Realistic FM converter, sold by Radio Shack, enables you to hear FM stations as well as AM stations on your car's AM radio.

3. Connect the converter power lead to an accessory terminal on the fuse block or ignition switch, or to any other convenient source of battery power that is turned on and off with the ignition switch.

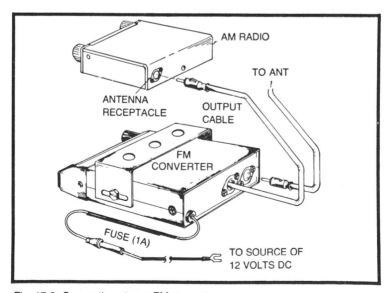

Fig. 17-2. Connections to an FM converter.

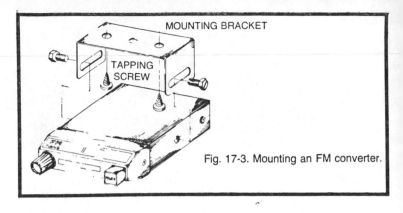

Fig. 17-3. Mounting an FM converter.

ANTENNA

For best FM reception, the car-radio antenna should be extended to 30 inches.

1. Turn the AM radio on and set the AM volume control to near maximum.
2. Turn the AM radio to a weak station around 1400 kHz.
3. Adjust the AM radio-antenna trimmer for maximum volume. The FM converter must be off during this adjustment.

MECHANICAL INSTALLATION

Remove screws from the sides of the FM converter. Using the mounting brackets as a guide, drill two holes (Fig. 17-3). Be careful, when drilling, so as not to damage existing wiring under the dashboard. Mount unit to the dash with two self-tapping screws (see Fig. 17-3).

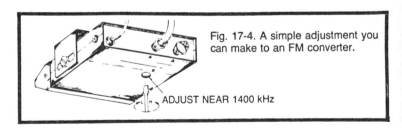

Fig. 17-4. A simple adjustment you can make to an FM converter.

TECHNICAL NOTE

If there is a local AM station on or near 1400 kHz, you can readjust the output frequency of the FM converter as follows:

1. Tune AM radio to 1400 kHz.
2. Tune FM converter to an FM station.
3. Adjust AM radio either slightly above or below 1400 kHz to a blank spot (no station).
4. Use an insulated adjustment tool and slowly rotate the tuning slug through its adjustment hole (see Fig. 17-4).

Chapter 18
Foghorn

The Heath Model MD-19A foghorn-hailer (Fig. 18-1) is a combination foghorn, boat horn, hailer, and listener. When used with accessory speakers, it may also serve as an intercom. A single lever-type switch lets you change quickly from one mode to another.

The foghorn signal can be heard more than a mile away. The duration and rate of the foghorn signal may be adjusted by two rear panel controls to conform with local variations in fog-signal regulations. In the *foghorn* mode the circuits automatically return to the listen mode between foghorn blasts.

The *boat-horn* mode produces a signal higher in pitch than the foghorn signal and may be used for warning other craft or signaling bridges.

In the *hail* mode a microphone push-to-talk switch changes connections from the *listen* circuit to the *call* circuit. The hailer will project your voice up to several hundred yards and is very useful when coming in to dock or when calling to other craft. A CALL VOLUME control lets you adjust the call output to suit conditions. In the *listen* mode the speaker horn acts as a sensitive microphone. A LISTEN VOLUME control lets you adjust the listen sensitivity to a comfortable level.

INSTALLATION

Refer to Fig. 18-2 for the following steps:

1. Mount the gimbal bracket in its permanent position with #6 wood screws. The gimbal bracket may be mounted either underneath or on top of the mounting surface.
2. Install the cabinet in the gimbal bracket and secure it in place with the two 10-32 thumbnuts.
3. Carefully remove the protective backing from the nut inserts; then install one insert in each thumbnut.

Refer to Fig. 18-3 for the following steps:

4. If necessary, loosen the screw at the rear of the horn speaker and turn the horn to meet your installation requirements. Then re-tighten the screw.

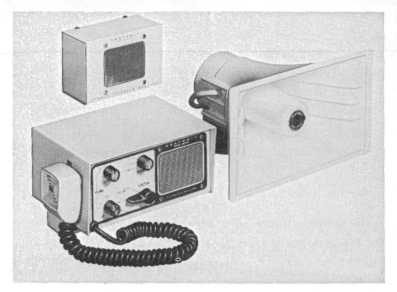

Fig. 18-1. A combination foghorn and hailer, sold by the Heath Company of Benton Harbor, Michigan.

5. Remove the swivel base from the horn speaker by unscrewing the wingnut, as shown in Fig. 18-3.

NOTE: The swivel base may be mounted on either a horizontal or vertical surface, depending on your preference as to function and appearance (see Fig. 18-4). Mount the horn speaker as far away from the microphone as possible and face it away from the microphone to prevent acoustic feedback (a loud squealing noise when the volume control is turned too high). Any structure between the microphone and horn speaker, such as a wind screen or cabin bulkhead, will also help to prevent feedback. Keep the horn back far enough from the bow of the boat to prevent water from being splashed directly into the horn. The horn is protected against normal spray; however, large amounts of water could damage the horn.

6. Mount the swivel base with three brass, stainless steel, nickel-plated, or chrome-plated fasteners. Machine screws, wood screws, or lag bolts may be used, depending on your preference. The horn-speaker cable may either pass through a hole in the mounting surface or be positioned along the top of the mounting surface (see Fig. 18-3).

7. Reassemble the horn speaker to the base. Tighten the thumbnut securely (see Fig. 18-3).

8. Route the horn speaker cable back to the foghorn hailer. Fasten the cable in its permanent position.

9. If necessary, cut the cable a few inches beyond the foghorn hailer so it will not be under tension when it is connected to the terminal strip.

10. If the cable has been shortened, prepare the two leads by removing 1/4 inch of insulation from each lead.
11. Attach a #6 spade lug to each lead.

WARNING: Never connect the horn speaker to another amplifier. Low frequencies will damage the horn speaker.

12. Connect either lead to the HORN terminal and the other lead to the COMMON terminal on the rear of the foghorn hailer.
13. Make certain that the power switch (CALL VOLUME control) is turned off. Plug the power cable into the receptacle in the rear panel of the foghorn hailer. Tighten the retaining nut to hold the plug in place.
14. Route the power cable as directly as possible to the battery or to the master battery switch and fasten it in its permanent location.
15. If necessary, cut the power cable to a convenient length so that it will not be under strain when it is connected.
16. Connect the power cable *directly* to the battery or to the master battery switch to minimize ignition and generator noise. Connect the white wire to the positive (+) terminal, and the black wire to the negative (−) terminal.

A 20-foot length of 16-gauge 2-conductor cable is supplied with the Heath kit. This is more than enough for most installations. For installations that need more than 20 feet of power cable, an extension cable may be used if the wire gauge is large enough (#14 or #12) to avoid causing a voltage drop at the power input of the instrument.

On rare occasions ignition noise (crackling noise from the speaker when the engine is in operation) may be encountered. This can usually be elimi-

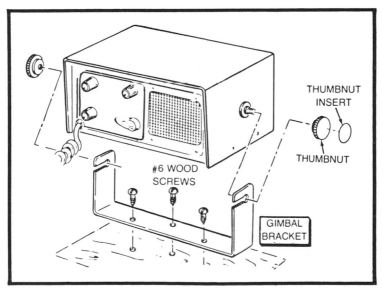

Fig. 18-2. Mounting a gimbal bracket for a foghorn.

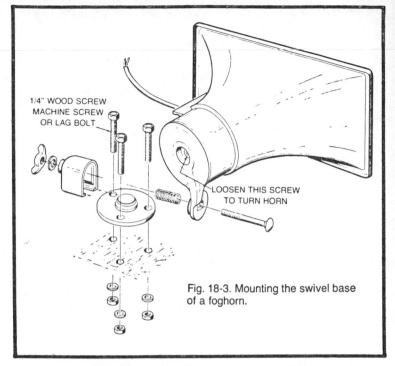

nated by grounding the cabinet of the foghorn hailer. This can be done by connecting one end of the ground wire under one of the screws on the rear of the cabinet. Then, by trial and error, connect the other end of this wire to various metal objects in the boat until the ignition noise is eliminated.

OPERATION AND APPLICATION

The Heath MD-19A foghorn hailer is very simple to operate. Its normal operating condition is the *listen* mode, which permits the pilot to hear signals or warnings that might otherwise be missed in a closed cabin. The LISTEN VOLUME control adjusts the level of the sound coming from the listen speaker.

On small boats it may be necessary to operate the unit with the LISTEN VOLUME control at a position less than full volume to prevent acoustical feedback (a loud squealing noise from the speaker).

To sound a warning or a signal, the operator just has to depress and release the spring-return lever of the FUNCTION switch. This will result in a loud, clear blast from the horn speaker.

In extreme situations, the boat horn may be used for "hound dog" navigation: Sound a blast on the boat horn, and with a stopwatch or a watch with a second hand, time the echo. Divide the time it takes for the echo to return by 2. Then multiply the result by 1100 (the approximate speed of sound in air in feet per second). This will tell you the approximate distance in

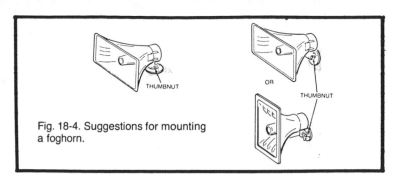

Fig. 18-4. Suggestions for mounting a foghorn.

feet from the object reflecting the echo. An approximate bearing can be made by noting the direction from which the echo came.

To hail other craft or the shore, depress the microphone push-to-talk switch and speak in a normal tone of voice into the microphone. Best performance will result if the microphone is held slightly to the side of the face. The voice level should be kept the same as for normal conversation. The CALL VOLUME control permits adjustment of the voice level coming from the horn speaker.

To sound the foghorn, turn the FUNCTION switch lever to the FOGHORN position. The foghorn will continue to sound at its preset time intervals as long as the switch is in the FOGHORN position. To set the foghorn-repeat rate and duration, adjust the FOGHORN RATE and FOGHORN DURATION controls on the rear panel.

NOTE: For best results, the FOGHORN DURATION control should be set for a relatively short foghorn tone time and the FOGHORN RATE control set for a long listen time. If the foghorn tone time was too long and the listen time too short, it would be almost impossible to hear any other boats in the area. However, you must adhere to the regulations for your area.

For additional convenience the foghorn hailer may be used as an intercom, using auxiliary speakers. These speakers connect to the STATION and COMMON terminals on the rear panel.

Little maintenance is required beyond keeping the unit clean and dry. Although the horn speaker is weatherproof, it is not submersible. When running in heavy seas or when hosing down, it is advisable to position the horn speaker so that is does not ship large amounts of spray or water.

U.S. COAST GUARD RULES FOR FOGHORNS

Rules for the proper use of foghorns and other sound signals are given in the following U.S. Coast Guard publications. These pamphlets may be obtained on request from the Coast Guard Marine Inspection Officers, or from the Commandant (CHS), United States Coast Guard Headquarters, Washington, DC 20226.

CG-169,   *Rules Of The Road*, for use on the high seas, in coastal
            waters, and on certain inland waters.
CG-172,   *Rules Of The Road*, Great Lakes.
CG-184,   *Rules Of The Road*, western rivers.

Chapter 19
Ignitions

A capacitive-discharge ignition (CDI) system is an electronic installation that will improve the performance of any car or other engine that presently has a conventional battery-distributor-coil ignition system. The one covered here—the Heath Model CP-1060 (Fig. 19-1)—is a very popular model that is similar to models sold by Radio Shack under the *Archerkit* label and by Delta Products under the *Mark Ten* label.

A further improvement in performance is offered by Heath's CP-2052 breakerless-ignition adapter (Fig. 19-2), which eliminates the troublesome ignition points. The adapter, which must be used with a CD ignition, uses the magnetic-pickup principle employed in the latest car models.

CAPACITIVE-DISCHARGE IGNITION

The Model CP-1060 capacitive-discharge ignition is a reliable ignition system that outperforms conventional systems. It supplies more energy to the spark plugs and greatly reduces the problems and wear associated with the ignition points. The carefully engineered circuits are backed up with high-quality components to provide many years of high performance and troublefree operation.

The solid-state circuits are designed to deliver increased energy (higher voltage) through the coil to the spark plugs. The increased energy more completely burns the fuel-air mixture. This results in increased engine performance. In addition, there is an increase in the firing duration of each spark plug when it is needed—during starts, low temperatures, and when the battery voltage is low. This firing duration decreases as the engine reaches a higher rpm and is not needed, yet the increased energy continues to the plugs.

Ignition points tend to bounce at high rpm and can sometimes cause false triggering of an ignition system. However, the circuitry of the capacitive-

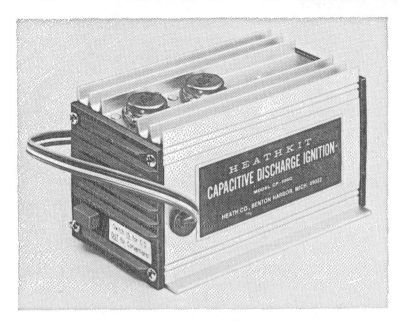

Fig. 19-1. A kit-type capacitive-discharge ignition system.

discharge ignition does not respond to these false trigger pulses. Also, in conventional systems heavy currents flow through the points and cause them to pit, burn, and wear out. The CD ignition system, however, produces a remarkably long point life, as it allows only small currents to flow through the points so that nearly all the wear is associated with the rubbing block as it rides the cam.

Preinstallation Check

The capacitive-discharge ignition is designed to provide optimum performance with standard (original equipment) coils. The use of special coils, such as transistor or high-ratio types, is not desirable and will substantially detract from the performance of the system.

Because of the high output energy of a capacitive-discharge ignition, it is very important that the high-tension system of your engine be in good condition. Defective or cracked distributor caps or rotors, which may cause an occasional misfire on a conventional ignition system, will usually cause extreme engine roughness in the CD (capacitive discharge) mode. High-resistance spark-plug wires, in particular, must be in good condition to prevent hard starting and poor performance. The resistance of these wires must be 30,000 ohms or less, as checked with an ohmmeter, to be considered in good condition. If there is any question as to the condition of your high-tension leads, replace all the high-tension leads, including the lead between the coil and distributor. New leads are available at most stores that carry automotive supplies.

If you find it necessary to reduce radio noise, an inductive high-tension wire may be used. This type wire is available from Triple-A Speciality Co., 5730 W. 51st St., Chicago, IL 60638.

Spark Plugs

To ensure optimum performance, use standard-heat-range plugs that have been gapped at 0.040 inch. Surface-gap plugs are not recommended. Cold-range plugs should be used for racing or extremely high-speed operation. If you install your capacitive-discharge ignition during the winter months in extremely cold climates, gap the spark plugs to 0.045 inch.

Ballast Resistor

The ballast resistor or resistance wire is a part of the electrical system of most automobiles and is normally mounted on the firewall. This resistor (or resistance wire) should be retained if the automobile is to be used for normal street and highway speeds. However, if the automobile is to be used

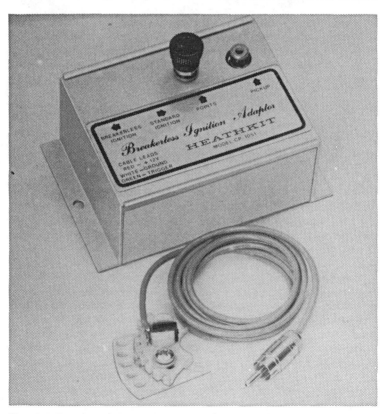

Fig. 19-2. The breakerless-ignition adapter goes a step beyond the CD ignition, completely eliminating the breaker points. This unit is from the Heath Company of Benton Harbor, Michigan.

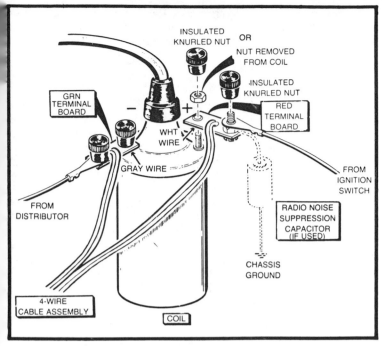

Fig. 19-3. Connections from CD ignition to existing coil.

for racing or operation over 5000 rpm, the resistor should be bypassed for optimum performance. If you elect to bypass the resistor, do not operate your capacitive-discharge ignition in the "switch out" (conventional) mode for prolonged periods of time. To do so may cause burning of the points.

Condenser

The distributor-point condenser should be retained in your system.

Radio-Noise-Suppression Capacitors

These capacitors may be used with your CD ignition system, but they must not be connected to the coil terminals.

Defective Coil

If your ignition coil has shorted turns or primary-to-secondary shorts, it will cause a rapid failure of the SCR in the CD ignition. If you have any doubt as to the condition of your engine coil, check it with a good coil tester or replace it.

CD IGNITION INSTALLATION

To install your capacitive-discharge ignition in a typical vehicle, perform the following steps. To install your ignition system for marine or special-

engine use, first read the paragraph, *Marine or Special-Engine Applica.*
Then perform the steps under *Typical Vehicle Installation* and modif
steps as necessary to fit your application.

Typical Vehicle Installation

Refer to Fig. 19-3 as you perform the following steps:

1. Check to be sure that the vehicle ignition switch is turned
2. Select a mounting location for your unit. Be sure to conside
   length of the 4-wire cable that must extend from the unit t
   ignition coil. Also, the 4-wire cable may require support at o
   more points along its route and must be kept away from all
   tension leads and the exhaust manifolds. Be sure that the
   case of the unit is well grounded to the frame of the vehicle. Us
   a location on the firewall of a fender well provides a satisfa
   mounting location. However, if you have any doubt as to the
   being well grounded, connect the ground wire provided with
   kit.
3. Make a template such as is shown in Fig. 19-4. Use the templa
   mark the location for drilling the mounting holes.
4. Drill a pilot hole (1/8 in. or as appropriate) at each of the
   marked locations.
5. Mount the unit with three #8 × 3/8 in. sheet-metal screw
   three #8 lockwashers.
6. Route the cable assembly, supporting it where necessary,
   the unit to the ignition coil.

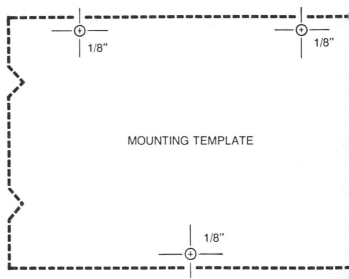

MOUNTING TEMPLATE

1/8"   1/8"   1/8"

Fig. 19-4. A template such as this simplifies the drilling of holes for mount
CD unit. Your template, of course, should be the actual size and shape of
CD unit.

254

7. Disconnect and remove all the leads from the positive (+) coil stud where your ignition-switch lead is connected. Remove any clips, stampings, or washers that may be on this stud.

NOTE: Four insulated knurled nuts are supplied with the Heath kit. Use two of these knurled nuts to connect the leads coming from the distributor and ignition switch. Use the two remaining knurled nuts or the nuts removed from your coil to connect the terminal boards to the ignition coil studs.

8. Install the *red* terminal board with its white wire side attached to the positive (+) coil stud. Then replace *only* the hardware previously removed from this stud or use an insulated knurled nut. Tighten this connection.

NOTE: If your ignition coil has pushon connectors (such as those used on Ford products), be careful not to bend the metal contact strips that are located inside the insulation as you connect the leads to the terminal boards.

9. Connect the leads that you removed from the positive (+) coil stud in step 7 to the red wire (outside) terminal on the red terminal board. Tighten this connection.

10. Disconnect and remove all the leads from the negative (−) coil stud where your distributor lead is connected. Remove any clips, stampings, or washers that may be on this stud.

11. Install the *green* terminal board with its gray wire side attached to the negative (−) coil stud. Then replace *only* the hardware previously removed from this stud or use an insulated knurled nut. Tighten this connection.

12. Connect the leads that you removed from the negative (−) coil stud in step 10 to the green-wire (outside) terminal on the green terminal board. Tighten this connection.

13. Push the button switch on your unit to the "in" position for capacitive-discharge operation.

14. Check all the wiring and connections made during the above steps. Be sure that each connection is tight, and that all wires are routed away from the manifold and supported as necessary. If the cable assembly is too long to be easily accommodated, the excess length may be folded together and secured with tape.

CAUTION: Never short-circuit the connections on the red or green terminal board to each other or to ground (any metal part of the vehicle) when the ignition switch is turned on. To do so may cause permanent damage to the unit.

15. Turn the ignition switch on, but do not start the engine. Then listen for a high-pitched whine coming from the unit. (This sound indicates that the converter is operating.) If no sound can be heard, check again to be sure that the button switch on the unit is in the "in" position.

16. Start your engine and check the unit for proper operation.

Some vehicles that have a generator or alternator warning light may exhibit a tendency to continue running with the ignition turned off. If this problem occurs, it may be solved in either of the following ways:

1. Change the generator or alternator warning-light bulb to one that requires less power for operation, such as a type 1892 or type 53 (available at most radio-supply houses).
2. Install a 100-volt, 1-ampere diode in series with the generator or alternator warning-light wiring. If this method is used, the diode must be installed in the right direction. Temporarily install the diode in one direction; then check to see if the warning light will turn on. If the warning light does not turn on, remove the diode and install it in the opposite direction.

Proper analysis of this system requires the use of a laboratory oscilloscope. Major tune-ups should be performed with the button switch on the unit in the "out" position for conventional operation. This enables the use of standard automotive instruments to perform the tune-up and (with the exception of plug gaps) the use of the manufacturer's tune-up procedures and specifications.

This completes the installation of your unit.

MARINE OR SPECIAL-ENGINE APPLICATIONS

The capacitive-discharge ignition is ideal for use on a marine engine and does not require any modifications to the system. However, the engine must have a standard automotive-type battery-distributor-coil ignition system. *It cannot be used with magnetos*. In addition, engines having a dual ignition (two or more coils) must use a capacitive-discharge-ignition unit for each coil used in the system.

When you install the unit on a marine system, locate the unit in as dry a location as possible. Also, mount the unit on a metal sheet, such as a 0.040-inch aluminum sheet that is about 1 foot square, to help dissipate the heat generated within the unit when running at high speed. If your unit is to be installed inside an engine compartment, mount this metal sheet vertically with 1/4- or 1/2-inch standoffs to ensure adequate air circulation.

Remember that the unit must have a good ground connection to operate properly. You can provide this ground by attaching an 18-gauge or larger grounding wire between the metal case of the unit and the ground terminal of the battery. The use of a standard coil is required in all applications. Standard plugs should be gapped at 0.040 inch for optimum performance.

The CD ignition can also be used on propane, butane, and natural gas fueled engines without modifications. For these engines, be sure to follow the manufacturer's specifications for tune-up procedures in all regards— including standard spark-plug gapping. If, however, the engine is a conversion (gasoline to butane, etc.) type, the plugs should be regapped to 0.040 inch for optimum performance.

BREAKERLESS-IGNITION ADAPTER

The Heath Model CP-1051 breakerless-ignition adapter, which must be used with a capacitive-discharge system, functionally takes the place of the breaker points in the typical (1957 and newer) General Motors V-8

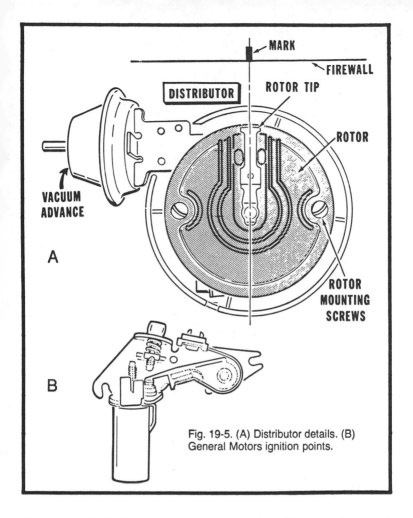

MARK
FIREWALL
DISTRIBUTOR
ROTOR TIP
ROTOR
VACUUM ADVANCE
A
ROTOR MOUNTING SCREWS
B

Fig. 19-5. (A) Distributor details. (B) General Motors ignition points.

distributor. This ignition system generates and conditions a timing signal that is not subject to the mechanical problems associated with breaker points. The adapter eliminates the normal degradation of timing due to wear, and it eliminates high-speed point bounce.

If necessary, the adapter may be easily switched out of the system, and the points will be used as a backup system in their normal manner.

The adapter consists of an easy-to-build unit, which you mount in the engine compartment, and a sensor (or transducer) that is installed inside the distributor in a manner similar to replacing breaker points.

Installation

Read through the following instructions before you perform the actual steps. You will remove and reinstall the distributor. The engine performance will depend on the timing accuracy after the installation. Obtain timing procedure and specifications for your engine before you start. It may be helpful to refer to technical publications, books, and magazines for timing information and techniques. Also keep in mind that you will need a suitable mounting place for the adapter and that the capacitive-discharge system must be installed and working.

Refer to Fig. 19-5 for the following steps:

1. Release the locking clamps on the distributor cap and remove the cap. If it is necessary to remove any spark-plug wires, be sure you identify them and replace them as they were.

2. Carefully examine the points assembly. If the points and condenser are in one unit, as shown in Fig. 19-5B, you must obtain an adapter kit from General Motors to convert your distributor to separate points and condenser. This requires GM kit No. 1876065, which can be obtained from any GM dealer for a nominal cost. If you cannot install this adapter kit, have a mechanic install it for you.

3. Disconnect the vacuum hose from the vacuum advance on the distributor.

4. Locate the points wire coming from the distributor and disconnect this wire from the coil or capacitive-discharge system. The green lead from the adapter will later be connected to this point.

   CAUTION: Mark, or note the position of the rotor and the distributor before you remove the distributor so you can reinstall the parts in the same position. You can extend a centerline through these units to a fixed reference point or mark. Do not turn the engine while the distributor is removed. Remove the ignition key and set the parking brake, or even disconnect the battery cable.

5. Use the ignition switch (or remote starter switch) and turn the engine over until the distributor rotor points backwards. Note the exact position of the rotor tip, and mark this position on the firewall.

6. Also note or mark the exact position of the vacuum-advance mechanism with respect to the engine. It must be in this position when you reinstall the unit.

7. Remove the clamping yoke on the engine block where the distributor enters the engine. Slowly pull the distributor straight up. The distributor may bind or stick, and the rotor will turn slightly. Note (or mark) the position of the rotor as you remove the unit. This will be the starting position to use when you reassemble the unit. If there is a washer or seal on the shaft housing, be careful not to damage or lose it.

8. Remove the rotor.

9. Disconnect the two leads on the breaker-point connection.

10. Remove and save the condenser and the screw. The transducer will be mounted at this position, and the condenser will be mounted elswhere.

Refer to Fig. 19-6 for the following steps:

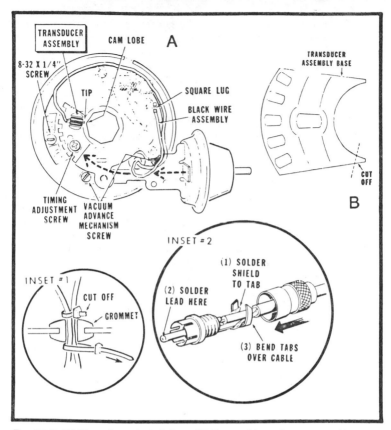

Fig. 19-6. (A) Transducer installation. (B) Base of transducer assembly.

NOTE: There are two critical adjustments to be made as you install the transducer The adjustments provide the following:

- At the instant the points open, the distributor lobe must be at its nearest position to the transducer tip.
- This distance must be 0.005-inch. When the boss on the transducer assembly is positioned against the cam lobe, the gap is correct. Be sure the transducer assembly mounts flat against the breaker plate.

1. Move the transducer to center the timing-adjustment screw in its slot and leave the screw just loose enough so you can move the transducer.
2. Note the direction the rotor normally turns. An arrow through the vacuum advance into the distributor points the direction of rotation.
3. Turn the distributor shaft (in the normal direction) until the points just open.

NOTE: If your distributor has an RF shield that interferes, remove the shield and save it. It is not needed with the breaker-less system.

259

4. Align the transducer tip to the nearest lobe clockwise from the condenser mounting hole in the breaker plate as shown. Move the assembly just enough to use the nearest mounting slot and temporarily mount the assembly with an 8-32 × 1/4-inch screw in the condenser mounting hole. If an oiler interferes, it may be necessary to cut off the corner of the transducer-assembly base (see Fig. 19-6B).

5. Turn the distributor shaft until a lobe is nearest the transducer tip.

6. Position the assembly so the boss contacts the lobe. Tighten the mounting screw.

7. Turn the distributor shaft in the normal direction until the points just open and center the transducer tip on the lobe. Tighten the timing-adjustment screw. Do not overtighten this screw.

8. Remove the points wire and the grommet in the hole in the bottom of the distributor. This may require you to remove the vacuum-advance-mechanism screws and take out the vacuum advance. In this case, be sure and reinstall the vacuum advance.

9. Connect the square lug of the black-wire assembly (supplied with this kit) to the point connection in the distributor, where you removed the points wire and condenser wire.

10. Pass the free end of the shielded cable coming from the transducer and the round lug of the black-wire assembly through the hole in the bottom of the distributor (see inset drawing).

11. Position the wires close to the breaker plate and away from the cam, rotor, and advance mechanism. Then measure the distance to the hole in the distributor. At this point, install a cable tie on the two wires. Bend the tie with the rough side in.

12. Pass the wires through the hole and through the new grommet; then install the grommet.

13. Install a cable tie on the wires next to the grommet, outside of the distributor, as shown in the inset drawing.

14. Check the leads and be sure they are close to the breaker plate and clear of the cam or rotor. Manually move the breaker plate through the vacuum-advance range. Be sure the leads do not touch moving parts and that there is enough slack for free movement.

15. Install the rotor. Look for any orientation guides and be sure this is correctly installed.

16. Prepare the end of the shielded cable and install a phono plug on it, as shown in the inset drawing.

17. Reinstall the distributor in the engine. The rotor must be in the same position you noted earlier. The vacuum-advance mechanism must be in the same position relative to the engine that you noticed before you removed the unit. Tighten the clamping yoke screw so the distributor can be turned by hand but will not move by itself.

18. Use the extra cable tie, if necessary, to position the wires. Do not use tape.

Refer to Fig. 19-7 for the following steps:

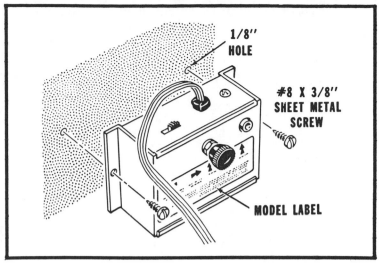

1/8''
HOLE

#8 X 3/8''
SHEET METAL
SCREW

MODEL LABEL

Fig. 19-7. Mounting a breakerless-ignition adapter. (Courtesy Heath Company)

1. Mount the condenser you removed from the distributor on the coil clamp (or a good ground directly on the engine block) and connect the lead to the outside lug on the green terminal board at the coil.
2. Decide where you want to mount the adapter. Use the adapter as a template and mark the two mounting holes. Be sure the wires will all reach the connections.
3. Drill 1/8-inch holes in the position indicated and mount the unit with #8 × 3/8-inch sheet-metal scews.

   NOTE: If you have a Heath CP-1050, Delta Mark 10B, or similar C D system installed on your car, refer to Fig. 19-8 for the following steps. If you have some other system, refer to Fig. 19-9.

4. Connect the 3-wire cable in the following manner:

   • Red wire to the outside terminal of the red terminal board on the coil (connection A in Fig. 19-9).
   • Green wire to the outside terminal of the green terminal board on the coil (connection B in Fig. 19-9).
   • White wire to the engine block or the coil clamp (ground).

5. Install the distributor cap.
6. Place the adapter's BREAKERLESS-STANDARD switch in the STANDARD position.
7. Connect the black-wire assembly (points) coming from the distributor to the points screw on the adapter (thumbnut).
8. Insert the plug on the shielded cable into the socket on the adapter.
9. Start the engine.
10. Make sure the points' dwell is properly set.
11. Time the engine.

12. Switch the adapter to the BREAKERLESS position and note any shift in timing. Turn off the engine.

NOTE: To advance timing, move the transducer in the direction opposite to the normal rotor direction. One tooth is approximately 10°. If necessary, remove the transducer assembly and use the next mounting hole.

13. Remove the distributor cap, loosen the timing-adjustment screw, and position the transducer to correct the difference (within 2°) between the standard and the breakerless ignition systems. Tighten the timing-adjustment screw.

14. Replace the distributor cap and secure it with the clamps.

15. Check the timing and repeat the adjustments if necessary.

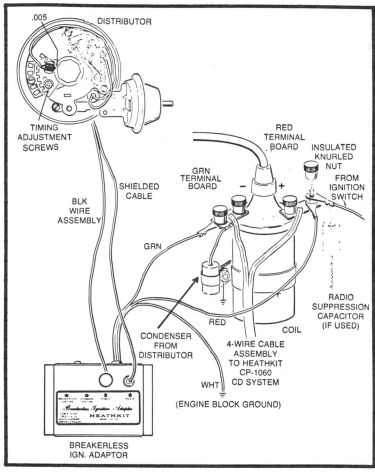

Fig. 19-8. Wiring diagram for use of ignition adapter with Heath CP-1050, or Delta Mark 10B ignition.

262

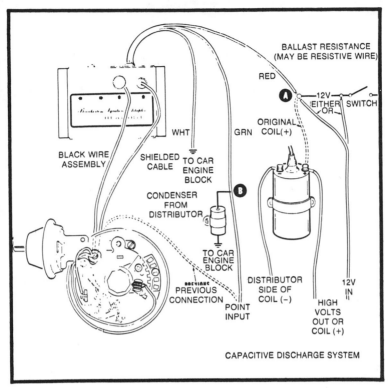

Fig. 19-9. Wiring diagram for systems other than those like the one in Fig. 19-8.

The switches on the adpater and on the capacitive-discharge unit can be used in three of the following combinations. Do not use the adapter in the BREAKERLESS position with the capacitive-discharge systems set in the STANDARD position. Also, keep in mind that the dwell adjustment must be periodically checked in the usual manner to maintain a dependable backup system. The dwell measurement in the breakerless mode is irrelevant.

CD Switch Position	Adapter Switch	Results
Standard	Standard	Operates as standard-ignition system.
Standard	Breakerless	System will not operate.
CD	Standard	CD ignition from points.
CD	Breakerless	CD ignition from adapter.

263

Chapter 20

Intercom for Recreational Vehicles

A mobile intercom is used primarily to communicate between the cab and camper of a mobile camper unit. It may also be used in any vehicle (camper, travel trailer, boat, etc.) where communication between two remote locations is desired. The intercom is an ideal baby sitter. It will continuoutly monitor all activities taking place in the camper while traveling down the highway. Also, music and news from the vehicle's radio can be switched to the camper and provide entertainment to anyone riding in the camper.

One such intercom is Heath's GD-160 *Mobilink*, shown in Fig. 20-1. When the master-unit switch is in the STD BY (stand by) position and the remote unit switch is in the RADIO or STD BY positions, no battery power is applied to the intercom. The all-solid-state amplifier circuit provides instant operation when the master-unit switch is in the MONITOR or TALK position, or when the remote-unit switch is in the TALK position.

Both units are ruggedly built to withstand the vibration and adverse conditions normally encountered in over-the-road vehicles. The electronic circuits are in the master unit. They operate from the vehicle battery and, therefore, need no auxiliary power supply. A 15-foot 5-conductor cable is furnished for connecting the master unit in the cab to the remote unit in the camper.

MOUNTING CONSIDERATIONS

The master unit may be mounted in any location in the truck cab that will allow the wires to be connected to the proper points, as shown in Fig. 20-2. The remote unit can be mounted in any convenient location in the camper.

Figure 20-3 shows the different ways the units can be installed. Refer also to Fig. 20-4 and note that a slightly larger amount of space is needed when you use the gimbal brackets.

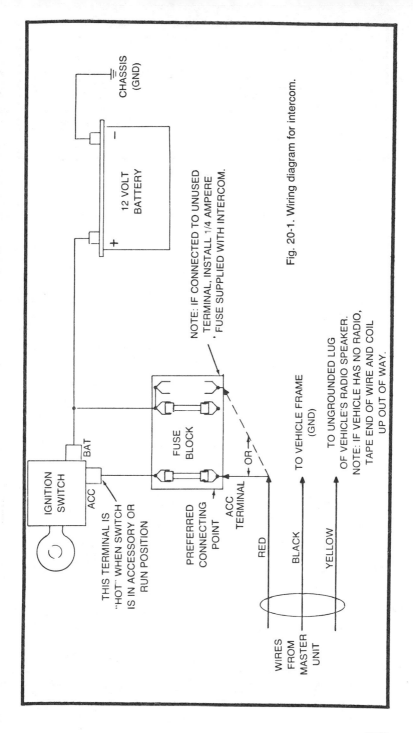

CHASSIS (GND)

12 VOLT BATTERY

NOTE: IF CONNECTED TO UNUSED TERMINAL, INSTALL 1/4 AMPERE FUSE SUPPLIED WITH INTERCOM.

IGNITION SWITCH

BAT

ACC

THIS TERMINAL IS "HOT" WHEN SWITCH IS IN ACCESSORY OR RUN POSITION

FUSE BLOCK

PREFERRED CONNECTING POINT

ACC TERMINAL

— OR —

RED

BLACK

YELLOW

TO VEHICLE FRAME (GND)

TO UNGROUNDED LUG OF VEHICLE'S RADIO SPEAKER. NOTE: IF VEHICLE HAS NO RADIO, TAPE END OF WIRE AND COIL UP OUT OF WAY.

WIRES FROM MASTER UNIT

Fig. 20-1. Wiring diagram for intercom.

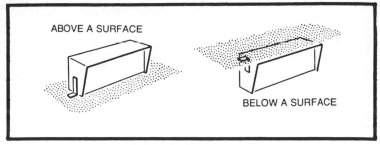

ABOVE A SURFACE

BELOW A SURFACE

Fig. 20-2. Installation possibilities for intercom.

Also consider:

- *Accessibility.* Each unit should be mounted in a handy location that will be easy to reach.
- *Available Space.* Be sure the proper amount of space is available at the locations you select.
- *Cable Routing.* Plan how you will route the cable between the master and remote units, including the locations of the holes where the cable will pass through the walls of the cab and camper.

CABLE INSTALLATION

1. Place one end of the 5-conductor cable in the cab of your vehicle in a location from which the wires can be connected to the master unit when it is installed.
2. Route the 5-conductor cable to the point at which you intend to have it exit from the cab. Place the cable out of sight behind the panels or under the floor mat and door thresholds.
3. Drill a 3/8-inch hole through the cab at the exit location. Remove any sharp burred edge from the hole.
4. Insert a rubber grommet into the hole. This will prevent the cable from becoming frayed where it passes through the hole.
5. Insert the end of the 5-conductor cable through the hole in the grommet. Then pull the cable out through the grommet. Be careful you do not pull the grommet out of the cab body.
6. Seal the exit hole with caulking compound.
7. Determine the location where you intend the cable to enter your camper. If no access panel is provided, carefully drill a 3/8-inch hole through the wall of the camper at the proper location.
8. Remove any sharp burred edge from the hole. Then insert a rubber grommet in the hole.
9. Insert the free end of the cable through the hole in the camper. Then seal the entrance hole with caulking compound. Leave enough slack in the cable between the cab and the camper to produce a "drip loop." This will prevent water from following the cable into the cab or the camper.
10. Inside the camper, route the 5-conductor cable to the planned location of the remote intercom.

INTERCOM INSTALLATION

In the following steps, two holes will be drilled where the units are to be installed. The size and location of the holes depend on whether the units are to be mounted by gimbal brackets or the precut slots.

Installation with Gimbal Brackets

NOTE: If both units use the same mounting method, perform the following steps twice.

1. Drill a hole, using an 11/64-inch drill bit, at each of the two places you marked earlier at the mounting location. Remove the burr if necessary.

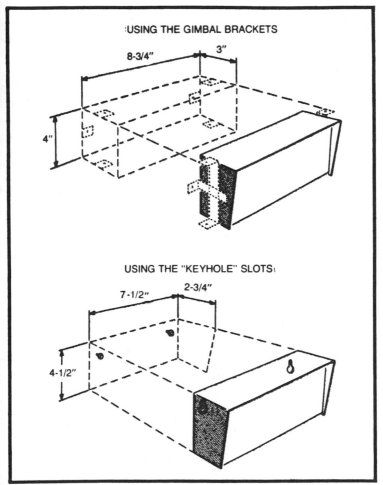

Fig. 20-3. Space requirements for a typical intercom. (Courtesy Heath Company)

2. Position the unit in front of the prepared location to be sure the 5-conductor cable reaches it properly. Then connect the wires of the cable to the terminal strip. Wrap each wire around its terminal and make sure no wire touches an adjacent terminal.

3. If this unit is the master intercom, route the power (black, red, and yellow) wires toward the fuse block of the truck. The electrical connections will be made later.

4. Secure the unit to the prepared location with 8-32 hardware.

Installation Using Keyhole Slots

NOTE: If both units use the same mounting method, perform the following steps twice. The diameter of the pilot holes that you drill in the next step will depend on the size of the screws you use to hold the unit in position. The pilot hole should not be larger than the diameter of the screw shank (screw body without the thread spiral).

1. Drill a pilot hole in each of the two locations you marked earlier at the mounting location.

2. Turn a screw into each pilot hole until there is a 1/8-inch gap between the mounting surface and the underside of the screw head.

3. Position the unit in front of the prepared location to be sure the 5-conductor cable reaches it properly. Then connect the wires of the cable to the terminal strip. As before, wrap each wire around the terminal. Make sure no wire touches an adjacent terminal.

4. If this unit is the master intercom, route the power (black, red, and yellow) wires from the back of the unit toward the fuse block of the truck. The electrical connections will be made later.

5. Mount the unit on the two screws and pull it downward about 3/8 inch into the secured position.

NOTE: If the unit rattles when the vehicle is in motion, remove the unit and turn the screws to reduce the size of the gap between the mounting surface and screw heads.

ELECTRICAL CONNECTIONS

Refer to Fig. 20-2 and connect the black, red, and yellow wires from the master unit to the points indicated in the figure and as described in the following steps:

1. Connect the black wire to any good ground on the instrument panel or dash. This can be under any screw or bolt through the instrument panel.

2. Connect the yellow wire to the *ungrounded* lug on the speaker of the vehicle's radio. If there is no radio in the vehicle, tape the end of the wire, then coil it up out of the way.

3. Connect the red wire to one of the three following locations:

   • To an unused terminal on the vehicle's fuse block. Then place the 1/4-ampere fuse supplied with the intercom in the appropriate empty fuse clip.

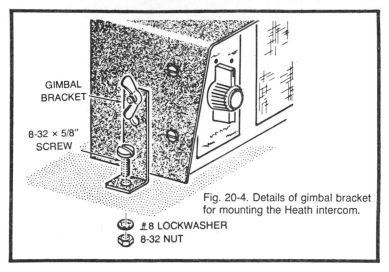

GIMBAL BRACKET

8-32 × 5/8″ SCREW

Fig. 20-4. Details of gimbal bracket for mounting the Heath intercom.

⊕ #8 LOCKWASHER
⊕ 8-32 NUT

NOTE: The 1/4-ampere fuse will not be used if the red wire is connected as follows:

- To the already used ACC (accessory) terminal on the fuse block.
- To the ACC (accessory) terminal on the ignition switch. This completes the installation of a typical intercom.

OPERATION

The following procedures are used to operate a typical RV intercom.

1. Turn the ignition switch to the ACC (accessory) position.
2. Turn the master unit FUNCTION switch to the MONITOR position. Have someone enter the camper and speak in a normal tone of voice. You should hear the person speaking and any other sounds that occur within the pickup range of the remote unit. Adjust the GAIN (volume) control to the desired level.
3. Turn the master unit FUNCTION switch to the TALK position. Speaking in a normal manner, your voice should be heard anywhere in the camper.
4. Turn the master unit FUNCTION switch to the STD BY position. Have the person in the camper turn the remote unit FUNCTION switch to the TALK position and at the same time speak in a normal manner. His voice should be heard in the cab. This is a call-origination feature from the remote to the master unit.
5. Turn the remote-unit FUNCTION switch to the RADIO position and the master-unit FUNCTION switch to the STD BY position.
6. Turn on the radio in the cab. This program material should now come from the speaker in the remote unit as well as the regular radio speaker in the cab. The radio's volume control will determine the volume of the program material.

Chapter 21
Inverters

Inverters are used to supplement the battery as a source of power in cars and other conveyances. A *power* inverter, such as the Heath Model MP-10, converts the 6- or 12-volt direct current of an automobile battery to the 120-volt 60-hertz alternating current required by most electrical devices used in the home. It makes it possible to use your AC-powered phonograph in your camper, or to use your electric razor in your car, for example.

A *voltage* inverter, as exemplified by the *Archer* Model 22-129, is a DC-to-DC converter. It makes it possible to operate standard automobile accessories, which are designed for the 12-volt negative-ground electrical system of modern cars, from the positive-ground and 6-volt electrical systems found in some foreign cars and in old American cars.

HEATH POWER INVERTER

The inverter should be installed in a location providing a free flow of air and protected from water spray. Remember that the case, or housing, is ventilated to help cool the transformer. Because of this, protect the inverter from the elements as much as possible. Do not mount it in a dead air space, as the air temperature may become excessively high.

Figure 21-1 shows two mounting positions for the MP-10. A third position might be an upside-down mounting, such as on the ceiling; in this event the cooling fins should be oriented as for mounting on a horizontal surface.

For connecting the inverter to the battery, use #10, solid-conductor copper wire. Preferably, this should be 2-conductor, plastic-covered wire such as that used for home electrical wiring. The wire length between the battery and the inverter should not be more than 10 ft. Longer battery wires or wire smaller than #10 would cause an appreciable power loss, lowering performance of the inverter.

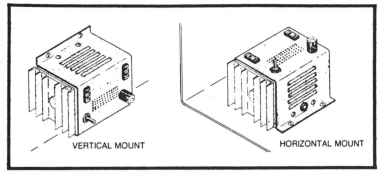

Fig. 21-1. Mounting arrangements for a power inverter. (Courtesy Heath Company)

In installations where the inverter will be frequently disconnected from the battery, the method of making battery connections shown in Fig. 21-2 will be satisfactory. For this purpose, drill holes in the center of each battery terminal. Then mount battery studs in each terminal as shown. Terminal lugs should be attached to the battery wires as shown in Fig. 21-3.

For permanent installations, do not use the battery studs and terminal lugs. Instead, form small hooks at the ends of the battery wires. At the battery, the wires should be connected under the bolt or nut that secures the regular cable clamp. The other end of the battery wires should be connected to the input terminals of the inverter.

Because the battery wires to the inverter should not be longer than 10 ft., it may be desirable to turn the unit on and off remotely. The inverter and the necessary relay can then be mounted close to the battery. Remote switching can be accomplished using the relay circuit shown in Fig. 21-4. A suitable relay can be obtained from an auto-supply store.

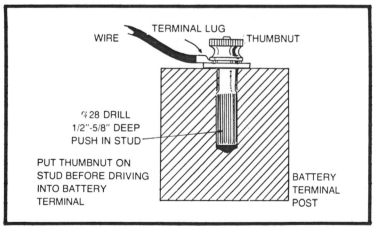

Fig. 21-2. How to make a power connection directly to a battery post.

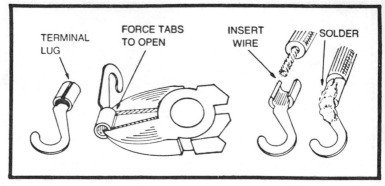

Fig. 21-3. Use of terminal lugs. (Courtesy Heath Company)

ARCHER VOLTAGE INVERTER

The *Archer* voltage inverter is designed to provide 12-volt DC negative-ground power from a 12-volt DC positive-ground or 6-volt DC negative-ground electrical system. You can use it to power any auto radio or other vehicle electrical accessory which requires a source of 12-volts DC, negative ground, and no more than 3-amperes of current.

CAUTION: Before mounting or making any connections, set the switch on the side of the voltage inverter to the appropriate position. Set to 12V POS GND. for use with 12-volt positive-ground electrical systems. Set to 6V NEG GND. for use with 6-volt negative-ground electrical systems. Failure to set the switch to the proper position may cause permanent damage to your radio or other accessory.

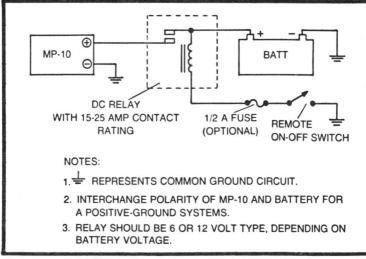

Fig. 21-4. Use of a relay to permit shorter power leads to an accessory. (Courtesy Heath Company)

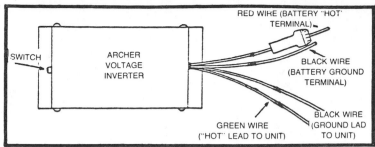

Fig. 21-5. Connections of DC-to-DC voltage inverter. (Courtesy Radio Shack)

Mounting

1. Locate a convenient position for mounting. Do not mount in the engine compartment (heat and grease will degrade its performance). Do not mount where metal parts will touch the transistor cases on the bottom of the voltage inverter.
2. Drill mounting holes (1/8-inch holes for #8 screws) where appropriate. Take care that you do not drill into other wires. Mount with screws and lockwashers.

Electrical Connections

Refer to Fig. 21-5 for the steps that follow:

1. The black and red wires are for the battery connections. Connect the black wire to the battery ground terminal. Connect the red wire (with in-line fuse holder) to the "hot" terminal of the battery or to the accessory terminal on the ignition switch. If you connect the red wire to the accessory terminal on the ignition siwtch, the ignition switch can be used to turn the unit on and off.
2. Connect the green wire to the power-input terminal on your car radio (or other accessory). The power-input terminal may be a wire lead or other form of connection (see notes). In any case, the green wire is the "hot" power lead for your accessory.
3. Connect the remaining black wire to the chassis ground-connection point of your radio or accessory. This may be a wire (see notes).

NOTES: If your car radio (or other accessory) has power-connection leads coming from it, connect them as follows:

- Connect the red lead from the radio to the green wire from the voltage inverter.
- Connect the black lead from the radio to the remaining black wire from the voltage inverter.

Operation

When properly connected, the voltage inverter needs no attention. Operate your radio or accessory as you normally would. If you do not obtain power, check the fuse; always replace with only the original type and rating.

Chapter 22

Marine Scanner

A great safety and entertainment boon for boaters, the marine scanner lets you automatically monitor several frequencies on the 156-163 MHz VHF marine band without twisting knobs or touching any controls. You can listen to weather frequencies, marine emergency channels, harbor instructions, fishing reports, ship-to-shore and ship-to-ship communications, and more.

One such receiver is the Heath RM-1134, shown in Fig. 22-1. The Heath scanner includes channel lockout, priority scanning, and manual as well as automatic scanning.

OBTAINING CRYSTALS

If you wish to obtain receiving channel crystals from some source besides the radio manufacturer, you will have to provide the following information:

Holder
Frequency tolerance
Type
Service resistance
Drive level
Load capacitance
Crystal frequency

PROGRAMMING THE SCANNER

The following steps show how to install crystals in a typical scanner, the Heath Model MR-1134:
Refer to Fig. 22-2 as you perform the following steps:

1. Disconnect the power cable from the scanner.
2. Unscrew the whip antenna and set it aside.
3. Remove the screws from the cabinet shell; then remove the cabinet shell and set it aside.

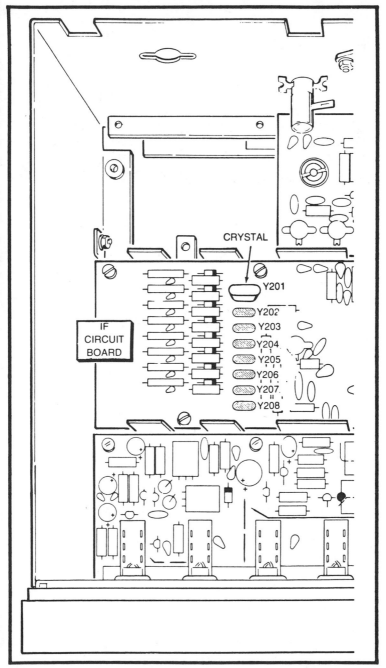

Fig. 22-1. A scanning receiver that automatically tunes you in to all the action on the marine band.

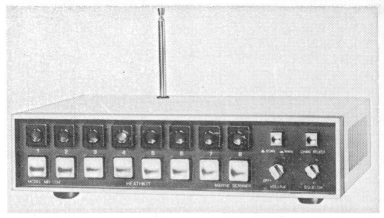

Fig. 22-2. The crystals in a marine scanner.

The scanner circuits momentarily monitor channel 1 every 3 – 5 seconds. If a signal is present on channel 1, the scanner immediately switches to channel 1. This occurs even though another channel is being received. This means that channel 1 is given priority over all other channels. Crystals for fire frequencies are a good choice for channel 1 (priority), especially for volunteer firemen. However, you can install any crystal you choose in channel 1.

NOTE: When you perform the following steps, you should first install a crystal in the priority position (channel 1); then install your other crystals in the other positions in order of descending priority. However, the crystals do not *have* to be in any specific order.

1. Plug the crystal that corresponds to the frequency you wish to use as a priority channel into the crystal-socket (Y201).
2. Write the operation frequency of the crystal and the name of the service on this frequency in the channel 1 blanks on the label on the cover.
3. Plug a crystal into the next crystal-socket (Y202).
4. Write the operating frequency of this crystal and the name of the service on this frequency in the channel 2 blanks on the label on the cover.
5. Continue in this manner until you have all of your crystals installed (Y202 through Y208).
6. Reinstall the cabinet shell on the scanner.
7. Reinstall the antenna.
8. Connect the power cable to the corresponding socket on the rear panel.

FM BROADCAST INTERFERENCE

If you notice interference from a nearby FM broadcast station, adjust the slug in the FM trap of the scanner to null out the interference. (This is on the rear panel of the Heath scanner.)

276

If strong nearby signals cause adjacent-channel interference, purchase and install the appropriate crystal filter.

INSTALLATION

Home installation:

1. Plug the line cord into the mating socket on the rear panel of the scanner.
2. If you have an external antenna, connect it to the HI VHF socket on the rear panel. If you do not have an external antenna, adjust the whip antenna on the top of the scanner.

Mobile Installation:

1. Connect the red lead of the DC cable to the 13.8-volt negative-ground source.
2. Connect the ground (black) lead of the DC cable to a suitable ground location on the chassis of the vehicle.
3. Plug the DC cable into the mating socket on the rear panel of the scanner.
4. If you have an external antenna, connect it to the proper socket. If you do not have an external antenna, adjust the whip antenna on the top of the scanner.

A gimbal bracket should be used if you wish to mount the scanner in your vehicle. If you mount the scanner in a boat, make sure you select a mounting location that will protect the scanner from water spray.

Before you install a scanner in your vehicle, check your state and local regulations concerning the use of a scanner to listen to official frequencies.

Chapter 23
Microphone
with Built-In Amplifier

One of the most popular and least expensive ways of enhancing the communicating ability of your CB is to add a power mike, such as Radio Shack's Model 21-1171. This microphone incorporates a built-in preamplifier to assure high modulation levels. It utilizes a 2-stage transistorized amplifier specifically designed to provide communications-type frequency response. It comes complete with a 5-pin DIN plug on the end of a coiled cord. The clip hanger can be mounted in any convenient location with the screws provided.

The microphone is designed for use with CB transceivers (and other equipment) where the additional gain provided by the preamplifier may be helpful in maintaining maximum modulation level and thus maximum talk power and signal "punch." It can be used as a direct replacement in the following *Realistic* CB transceivers: 21-126/128/136/139/144/146/149. With 21-124, the DIN plug must be rewired as follows:

1. Move wire from pin 1 to pin 2.
2. Move wire from pin 4 to pin 1.
3. Move wire from pin 2 to pin 4.

With some other units on the market it may be necessary to rewire the DIN plug, or the microphone jack on the transceiver. Use the information provided below to aid you in making the proper connections:

Function/Operation of Microphone Connector Pins

Pin Number	Button Out (Receive)	Button In (Transmit)
1	Shield/ground for audio	Shield/ground for audio
2	Connected to + bus of preamplifier	Floating free
3	Floating free	Grounded (to pin 1)
4	Audio "hot"	Audio "hot"
5	Grounded	Floating free

Chapter 24
Mobile Radio

For those who qualify under the FCC Rules, the professional-type communications gear used by police and fire departments offers many advantages over a CB installation. This gear, which is considered to be in the land-mobile (or just *mobile*) radio category, uses FM and relatively high power (compared to CB) to obtain greater range, better reliability of communications, and less interference from electrical apparatus and other stations. Those licensed in the land-mobile service are assigned their own frequencies to operate on, much as a broadcaster is assigned a place on the radio dial. This makes for more privacy as well as less interference among stations. Businesses and professionals of every description are elegible for mobile-radio station licenses—taxi operators, tow-truck operators, clergymen, doctors, loggers, motion-picture producers, newspaper publishers, truckers, and many others. If you need radio communications in your business and you've found the world's biggest party line (CB) inadequate for your purposes, check with your local distributor of FM two-way radios (under "Radio Communication Equipment" in the telephone Yellow Pages). You will find the equipment more expensive and more complicated to install than a CB set, but you can save by installing it yourself according to the following guidelines. Some of the suggestions given here will also help you to make a professional-type installation of CB or other gear in your car.

RECOMMENDED TOOLS

The hand tools and drills listed delow will be helpful in installing the mobile station:

Screwdrivers: #1 Phillips, #2 Phillips, standard 1/4 in. blade.
Open-end wrenches: 1/2 in., 9/16 in.
Nut drivers (spin wrench): 1/4 in., 5/16 in., 3/8 in.

Hammer: 8 oz.

Centerpunch

Twist drills: 3/8 in., 9/16 in., #17 (.173 dia.), #26 (.147 dia.), #31 (.120 dia.), #36 (.106 dia.)

Circle saw or punch: 1 in. dia.

DASH-MOUNT TRANSCEIVER INSTALLATION

As shown in Fig. 24-1, this type of installation is possible in a van or camper as well as a car. Attach the four brackets to the transceiver unit mounting base as shown in Fig. 24-2, then use them as a drilling template for the four mounting holes. Allow sufficient clearance at the rear of the unit for insertion and removal of the power and antenna jacks. The power-cable wiring is detailed in the power cable wiring section.

TRUNK-MOUNT TRANSCEIVER INSTALLATION

Select a location in the vehicle where the transceiver will be protected from mechanical damage and the possibility of water getting into the case. Allow clearance for access to the top of the unit for servicing. Sufficient room should be provided for insertion and removal of the antenna and system cables on the front of the unit.

Generally, the transceiver is mounted in the vehicle trunk, but any available space, such as a shelf or upright panel behind the front or rear seat, may be employed.

CAUTION: If the transceiver is to be used in a vehicle subject to high vibrations—such as an earth mover, concrete mixer, etc.—mount the transceiver to something solid and rigid, such as the frame of the vehicle. Avoid mounting to thin parts of the cab that will vibrate at high amplitude. Thin body parts can be stiffened with heavy plywood or metal plate if no better alternative is available.

Mounting

The transceiver usually locks to a base plate in the trunk. This plate is secured to the vehicle with self-tapping screws. When the location has been

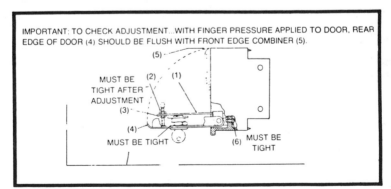

Fig. 24-1. Latch adjustment.

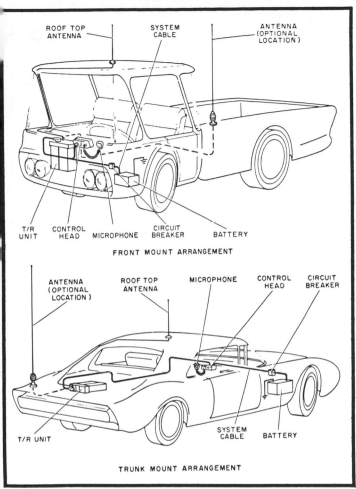

Fig. 24-2. Mobile-station equipment: trunk- and front-mount stations. (Courtesy RCA Corporation)

established, drill or punch appropriate holes, using the base plate as a template, and fasten the plate in place with hex-head screws. Punched holes with extruded sides improve the installation of self-tapping screws, but care must be taken not to exceed the specified hole size.

CAUTION: Be careful not to drill or punch into the gasoline tank. Some units, such as RCA's *Super-Carfone 500* and *Super-Fleetfone 500* transceiver units have latch adjustment. Swing the door on the combiner unit downward and place the T-R unit on the mounting (See Fig. 24-3.) Push the unit to the rear so that the bolt heads at the rear of the transceiver engage in the slots on the base plate. Close and lock the door. This action engages the two dog latches to the base plate and secures the transceiver. Approximately 50

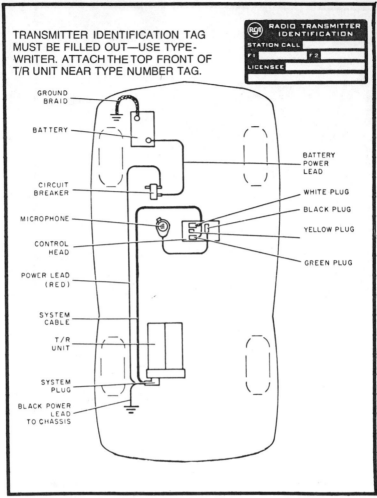

TRANSMITTER IDENTIFICATION TAG
MUST BE FILLED OUT—USE TYPE-
WRITER. ATTACH THE TOP FRONT OF
T/R UNIT NEAR TYPE NUMBER TAG.

RADIO TRANSMITTER
IDENTIFICATION
STATION CALL
F1   F2
LICENSEE

GROUND BRAID
BATTERY
CIRCUIT BREAKER
MICROPHONE
CONTROL HEAD
POWER LEAD (RED)
SYSTEM CABLE
T/R UNIT
SYSTEM PLUG
BLACK POWER LEAD TO CHASSIS

BATTERY POWER LEAD
WHITE PLUG
BLACK PLUG
YELLOW PLUG
GREEN PLUG

Fig. 24-3. Typical cable routing for trunk-mount stations. (Courtesy RCA Corporation)

pounds of pressure should be required to close and lock the door and prevent vibration.

Latch tension may be adjusted as follow: With the transceiver placed on the base plate, swing the door up until resistance is felt. The curved top edge of the door should be even with the front edge of the combiner unit. Open the door and adjust both top adjustments nuts, which hold the tension springs, until the edges meet when the door is closed to the spring resistance. Securely tighten the two locknuts under the tension springs. If latch tension is properly adjusted, both hands will be required to close and lock the door.

CONTROL UNIT INSTALLATION

A separate control unit (head) is mounted on the dash when the transceiver itself is mounted elsewhere (Fig. 24-4). The control unit is designed to be mounted under or on top of the vehicle instrument panel. A location under the panel edge is preferable, as it permits cables to be dressed out of the way, under the dash. Consider also the location of the microphone hangup and choose a location that will be convenient for the operator. Install the control unit as follows:

1. Disassemble the mounting bracket.
2. Using the bracket as a template, locate and drill mounting holes in the instrument panel. For metal panels or locations with no access to the other side, drill 3/16-inch holes and use 1/4-inch self-tapping screws with flatwashers. For molded-plastic panels or where nuts and washers can be installed, drill 9/32-inch holes and use two 1/4-inch bolts with flatwashers and nuts.

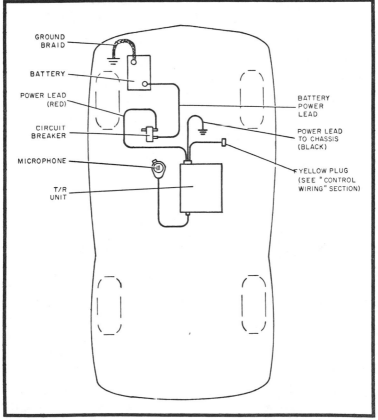

Fig. 24-4. Typical cable routing for dash-mount stations. (Courtesy RCA Corporation)

3. Temporarily reassemble the control unit in the mounting bracket. Wiring connections are made in the *System Cable Installation* section.

MICROPHONE HANGUP INSTALLATION

The microphone hangup should be mounted on the face of the instrument panel. Choose a location that provides for easy removal and replacement of the microphone by the operator. Install the hangup as follows:

1. Using the hangup as a template, drill three holes. For metal instrument panels or locations with no access to the far side, drill 0.106-inch (#36 drill) holes and use #6 self-tapping screws. For molded-plastic panels or where nuts and washers can be installed, drill 0.173-inch (#17 drill) holes and mount the hangup with #6 machine screws, flatwashers, and nuts.

2. Place the microphone in the hangup. Remove the control unit from the mounting bracket, and attach the strain-relief clip to the raised loop directly under the microphone jack on the back on the control unit. Connect the microphone plug to the jack and temporarily reassemble the control unit.

HANDSET AND HANDSET-HOLDER INSTALLATION

For systems which include an optional handset instead of the standard microphone, use the following installation procedure. The handset holder should be mounted on a vertical surface of the instrument panel in a location that provides for easy removal and replacement by the operator.

1. Mount the handset holder on a vertical surface of the instrument panel, using the instructions outlined in step 1 of *Microphone Hangup Installation.*

2. Remove the control unit from the mounting bracket. Attach the strain-relief clamp on the handset cable to the raised loop directly under the microphone jack on the rear of the control unit, then connect the handset plug to the microphone jack. Attach the strain-relief clip on the handset-holder cable to the raised loop directly under the red receptacle, then connect the red handset-holder plug to the red receptacle on the rear of the control unit. Temporarily reassemble the control unit.

SYSTEM CABLE INSTALLATION

The system cable consists of a molded, multi-pin system plug, which typically connects to the front of the transceiver, a multi-conductor control cable from the molded system plug to the control unit, and two power leads (red and black) from the system plug to the vehicle electrical system (see Figs. 24-5 and 24-6).

Select a route through the vehicle, from the transceiver to the control unit, which affords adequate mechanical protection. In trunk-mount installations, run the cable beneath the vehicle's carpets or floor mats. Avoid running the cable beneath the floor of the vehicle unless mechanical and

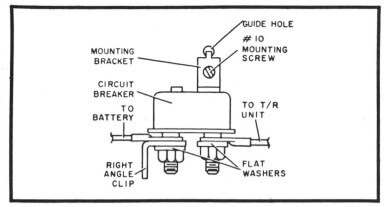

Fig. 24-5. Circuit-breaker wiring.

weather protection, such as flexible conduit, is provided. Install the system cable as follows:

1. Route the system cable and the red power lead loosely in position from the transceiver to the control unit. It may be necessary to cut a 1-inch hole in the rear-seat panel for access between the trunk and the vehicle interior. A rubber grommet is provided to insert in this hole. To pass the cable through this grommet, it is necessary to cut the grommet, fit it around the cable, and then tape the cut.

2. Connect the molded system plug to the transceiver. This plug is keyed so that the cable is directed to the left. Secure the knurled ring by hand. *Do not tighten with pliers or wrench.*

NOTE: For vehicles with a positive-ground electrical system, it will only be necessary to mount a positive-ground converter near the transceiver, connect the system plug to the converter jack, and connect the converter plug to the transceiver. No wiring changes are required.

3. Allowing ample length at the transceiver and control unit for servicing, coil the excess cable at a convenient location under the dash or in back of the seat. Secure the cable at several points along its run with the cable clamps and #8 self-tapping screws (#31 drill). If drilling holes is prohibited, plastic tie straps may be used to fasten the cable to existing wiring or structural members of the vehicle.

4. Remove the control unit from its bracket. Attach the strain-relief clip on the system cable to the raised loop to the right of the white receptacle on the control unit, and if a multi-frequency station, do the same with the green plug and receptacle.

POWER LEAD AND CIRCUIT-BREAKER INSTALLATION

Route the black power lead to a convenient ground point on the vehicle frame. Secure the wire lug to the frame with a #10 self-tapping screw (#26 drill). *Be careful not to drill into the gasoline tank.*

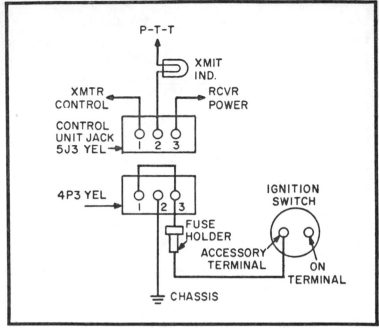

Fig. 24-6. Ignition-switch control for a trunk-mount station. (Courtesy RCA Corporation)

Route the red power lead through an opening in the firewall to the engine compartment. If no convenient hole is available, cut a 2-inch hole and install a rubber grommet. These radios often use a circuit breaker in the power circuit (Fig. 24-7).

The circuit breaker must be mounted within 3 feet (preferably less) of the vehicle's battery. Vehicles which are equipped to minimize air pollution tend to have high ambient temperatures in the engine compartment. The circuit breaker, which may be affected by this high temperature, should be mounted on a metal surface (such as the fender well) which has one side exposed to an outside flow of air. Install the circuit breaker and red power lead as follows:

1. Drill a guide hole (#26 drill) at the circuit-breaker mounting location. Insert the tap of the mounting bracket into the hole. Position so that the red button faces up, and drill a second hole (#26 drill), using the bracket as a template. Secure the bracket with #10 self-tapping screws.

2. Connect the red power lead from the transceiver to the circuit-breaker terminal directly under the mounting bracket. Use a #10 flatwasher between the nut and the wire lug.

3. Connect the smaller wire lug on the red battery power cable to the circuit-breaker BAT terminal below the reset button. Place the right-angle clip, the flatwasher, and nut on top of this lug and securely tighten.

IMPORTANT: Check the position of the control unit OFF/ON switch. Keep the switch in the OFF position while performing the remainder of the installation.

4. Connect the free end of the power cable to the "high" side ("hot" lead) of the battery or, preferably, to the starter solenoid. The solenoid connection avoids the battery-terminal corrosion.

VEHICLE GROUND

The power return for the transceiver is carried through the vehicle chassis. To ensure adequate current capacity between the "low" side of the battery and the chassis, install a braided cable between the grounded battery terminal and the vehicle frame. Secure the braided cable to the frame by drilling a 3/8-inch hole and installing a 5/16-inch bolt, flatwasher, and nut.

In installations where it is necessary to run the transceiver unit's power ground directly to the grounded battery cable, the ground wire extension is connected between the wire lug on the black power lead and the battery's ground terminal.

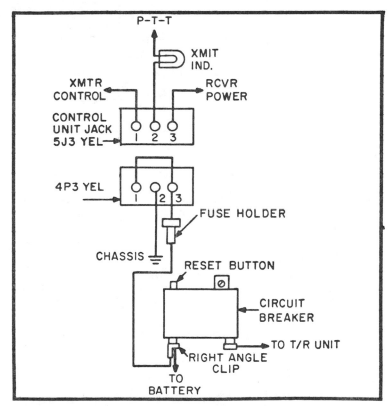

Fig. 24-7. Control-unit ON-OFF switch control for trunk-mount station. (Courtesy RCA Corporation)

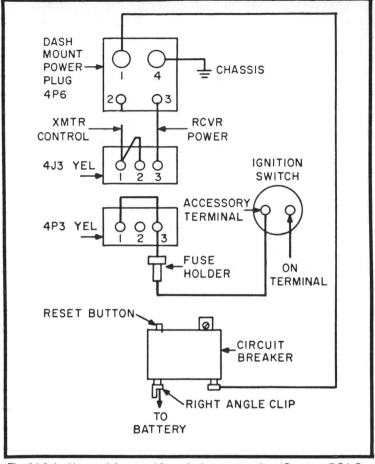

Fig. 24-8. Ignition-swtich control for a dash-mount station. (Courtesy RCA Corporation)

CONTROL WIRING

The installation procedure for the control wiring is determined by the desired ignition-switch interlocking as well as the particular model being installed.

Four versions of control wiring as recommended by RCA follow. All of the versions listed below allow the use of the radio OFF/ON switch to turn the unit off, even though the vehicle ignition switch is in the ON or ACCESSORY position.

Version 1: Trunk-Mount Stations—Ignition Switch Control

1. Plug the yellow connector into the yellow receptable on the rear of the control unit. (Refer to Fig. 24-8.)

2. Connect the brown wire, which includes the in-line fuse, to the accessory terminal of the ignition swtich. If the switch has no accessory position, connect this lead to the ON terminal.
3. Coil and tape the excess wire to a convenient wire harness or structural member, allowing slack to permit servicing.
4. The black wire connects to chassis ground. Use a #10 self-tapping screw.

Version 2: Trunk-Mount Stations—
Control-Unit OFF/ON-Switch Control

1. Plug the yellow connector into the yellow receptacle on the rear of the control unit. (Refer to Fig. 24-9.)

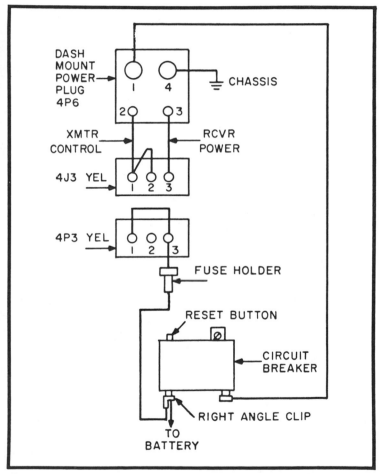

Fig. 24-9. Control-unit ON-OFF switch control for a dash-mount station. (Courtesy RCA Corporation)

2. Route the brown wire, which includes the in-line fuse, through the firewall, and to the circuit breaker. Connect the pushon connector to the right-angle clip on the battery terminal of the circuit breaker.
3. Using cable clamps and #8 self-tapping screws, secure the lead through the engine compartment. Keep all power leads dressed away from the high-voltage ignition leads to avoid ignition interference. Do not coil excess cable in the engine compartment.
4. The black wire connects to chassis ground. Use a #10 self-tapping screw.

Version 3: Dash-Mount Stations—Ignition-Switch Control

1. Insert the yellow plug into the yellow receptacle in the power cable.
2. Connect the brown wire, which includes the in-line fuse, to the accessory terminal of the ignition switch. If the switch has no accessory position, connect this lead to the ON terminal.
3. Coil and tape the excess wire to a convenient wire harness or structural member, allowing slack for servicing.

Version 4: Dash-Mount Stations— Control-Unit OFF/ON-Switch Control

1. Plug the yellow connector into the yellow receptacle in the power cable.
2. Route the brown wire, which includes the in-line fuse, through the firewall to the circuit breaker. Connect the pushon connector to the right-angle clip on the battery terminal of the circuit breaker.
3. Using cable clamps and #8 self-tapping screws, secure the lead through the engine compartment. Keep all power leads dressed away from the high-voltage ignition leads to avoid ignition interference. Do not coil excess cable in the engine compartment.

ANTENNA INSTALLATION

The preferred location of the antenna is in the center of the vehicle roof. Because of its length, a quarter-wave 50 MHz antenna is usually mounted on a rear fender or trunk deck. Usually, the closer the antenna is mounted to the geometric center of the vehicle, the more uniformly circular the radiation pattern will be. Follow the recommendations furnished with the antenna.

Install the antenna according to the instructions furnished with the antenna. Proper shield connections are vital to efficient operation. Care should be taken when preparing the coaxial cable connections. The antenna feed line connects to the coax jack (type SO-239) on the transceiver.

Chapter 25
MPG/MPH Meter

The Heath Model CI-1078 MPG (miles-per-gallon) meter (Fig. 25-1) is an automotive instrument designed to display miles per hour or miles per gallon in a digital format. The meter consists of three main units: a speed transducer to measure forward speed, a flow transducer to measure fuel flow, and a display unit that electronically processes the information from the transducers and displays it on a bright 3-digit display. If you like, you can blank out the third digit (tenths) in the MPH (speedometer) mode. This avoids some excessive display activity that you may consider to be distracting. Other features include:

- A dimming control that adjusts display brightness according to the ambient light level.
- A calibration procedure that compensates for the variables of your particular vehicle.
- An adjustable update control that adjusts the update interval (how often the unit reports on changing conditions) from 1/2 second to approximately 2 seconds.

The miles-per-gallon meter sets the pace in this era of automotive electronics. You will be surprised with the actual miles-per-gallon variations. The meter provides an effective guide for greater fuel economy and is an accessory you may well want to add to your car. The following paragraphs, which show just what is involved in installing and using an MPG/MPH meter, will help you decide.

INSTALLATION

Figure 25-2 is a wiring diagram of the digital speedometer and MPG meter. The speed transducer is basically a miniature generator. The speed transducer is installed in line with the speedometer cable already in the car.

As the cable turns, the transducer generates a voltage that is the analog of the car's speed. Fittings on the transducer allow it to be mounted between the car's speedometer cable and existing automotive hardware. A car's speedometer cable runs from the speedometer head (or meter) in the dash to the speedometer gear on the transmission. Normally the cable connects at the rear of the transmission. The exact nature of the connection varies from manufacturer to manufacturer.

Speed Transducer

The 2-wire cable of the speed transducer is routed next. Cut it to length if necessary. If the transducer is mounted on the transmission or cruise control, the cable must pass through the firewall to get to the location of the plug on the display's relatively short cable. Passage through the firewall can usually be accomplished in one of the following ways:

1. Through the same grommet the speedometer cable passes through.
2. Through a grommet with other wires on the vehicle.
3. Through plastic retainers that hold the insulation to the inside (under the dash) of the firewall. The end of these retainers can be cut off from the engine side of the firewall so that you can pass the cable through (see Fig. 25-3).
4. Through a 3/8-inch hole, which you can drill yourself.

Flow Transducer

The flow transducer is mechanically connected in the fuel line of the vehicle. Its cable is routed through the firewall and under the dash to the vicinity of the display. It will be connected later to the cable coming from the display.

NOTE: A small tube-cutting tool is necessary if you have to cut a metal fuel line. A metal saw is not recommended, as saw fillings can get into the gas

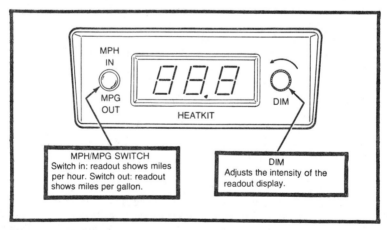

Fig. 25-1. The MPH-MPG unit discussed in the text.

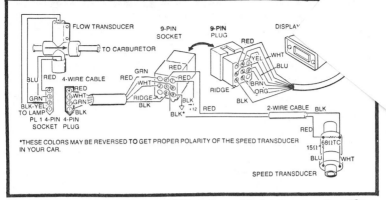

Fig. 25-2. The components of an MPG meter and their interconnection. (Courtesy Heath Company)

line and damage the flow transducer. Use a small container to catch the gasoline that may run out of the line.

Refer to Fig. 25-4 for the following steps. When you install the flow transducer in the following steps, position it so the arrow is in a vertical direction if possible. Decide where you will mount the transducer. If you must reposition the fuel line, be careful not to kink the line when you bend it.

CAUTION: Take great care for personal safety at all times. In the following steps you will open the fuel line to install the flow transducer. Gasoline and its fumes are extremely flammable. Be sure there are no open flames or anyone smoking near the vehicle. Work only on a *cold* engine. If you do not have proper tools and experience, have a qualified mechanic install the flow transducer.

1. Cut out a 5-inch section of the fuel line. If there is a flexible hose connecting a metal fuel line to the filter or carburetor, you may be able to disconnect the hose and bend the fuel line enough to insert the transducer.
2. Align the flow transducer with the openings in the fuel line. If the unit can be centered in the fuel-line gap, cut the gas line tubing

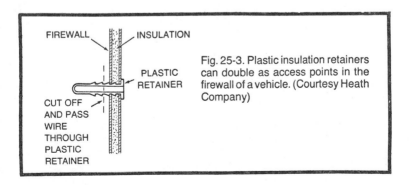

Fig. 25-3. Plastic insulation retainers can double as access points in the firewall of a vehicle. (Courtesy Heath Company)

furnished with the kit into two 2-1/2 inch lengths. If the unit cannot be centered, cut the tubing accordingly, but do not cut a length shorter than 1-1/2-inch.

NOTE: Be careful not to overtighten the clamps in the following steps, as the lines can be damaged. They will be checked for leaks later.

3. Install the gas line tubing on each end of the transducer. Position two clamps over the gas line tubing. Position each clamp *at least* 1/8-inch from the end of the gas line tubing (nearest the transducer) and tighten the clamps.

    NOTE: The 5/16-inch gas line tubing will easily slide on a 5/16-inch fuel line. If you have a 3/8-inch fuel line, it will be a tight fit and you may need to lubricate the *fuel line* (use silicone grease) to reduce friction. *Do not place the lubricant inside the gas line tubing*, as this could damage the transducer.

4. Place one more clamp on each end of the gas-line tubing. Then align the transducer with the fuel line (make sure the arrow points in the direction of the fuel flow) and press the tubing at least 1 inch onto the fuel line.

5. Position the clamps so they are at least 1/8 inch from each end of the tubing. Tighten the hose clamps. Do not overtighten them.

6. Check for a tight fit, then start the engine and let it idle for a minute or so. The engine should run normally and there must not be any leaks. If there is a leak, turn the engine off and tighten the clamps. Then run the engine and check again for leaks. Repeat until no leaks appear.

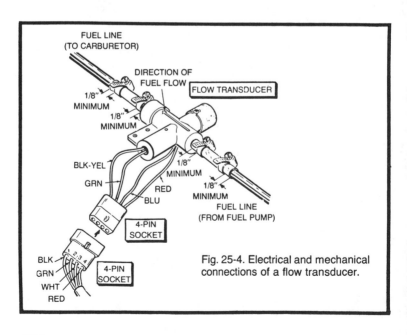

Fig. 25-4. Electrical and mechanical connections of a flow transducer.

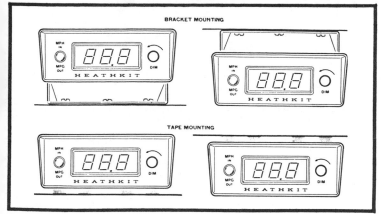

Fig. 25-5. Bracket and tape mounting of MPG display.

All that is left to do is to connect the cables from the transducers to the display unit. In Heath's system, the transducer cables connect to a 9-pin socket, which then connects with the 9-pin plug on the display's cable. Usually it is possible to route the two transducer cables together much of the way. Be sure to secure them to existing wires with cable ties, or by some other reliable method.

Display Mounting

Since the temperature on the top of a dashboard of a vehicle can reach 235°F (112°C) with the sun shining in the windows, it is not a good idea to mount the MPG display unit on top of the dash. If the temperature of the display gets too high, it may stop working until its temperature is lowered, or it may be damaged.

As shown in Fig. 25-5, you can mount the unit on top of, or beneath a suitable mounting surface, with or without the mounting bracket. You can also use double-sided adhesive tape to mount the unit since it is light in weight.

CALIBRATION

Because of variations in transducers, mounting positions, engine-compartment temperatures, fuel-pump and carburetor characteristics, you will need to determine your MPG at a constant speed in order to calibrate this unit. You can obtain this information by keeping track of the fuel you use on a trip involving all expressway driving, where a constant speed (use the vehicle speedometer) is maintained 95 percent of the time. Make sure that the vehicle is level when you fill the gas tank at the beginning and the end of the trip and that the tank gets completely filled each time so you can accurately determine the gallons used. If you divide the number of miles traveled by the number of gallons used, the answer will be equal to the MPG at the constant speed traveled.

However, if you do not know the MPG, you can set the display unit to an estimated value until you have an opportunity to determine the MPG

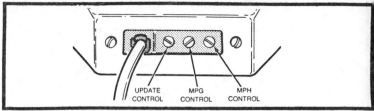

Fig. 25-6. The MPG and MPH adjustments.

figure more accurately. The unit can still be used to indicate the most economical driving habits, even though the indication is not actual MPG.

Before you can adjust the display unit, you must be sure the display numbers change when the vehicle is driven in the forward direction. When the vehicle is driven in reverse or is at rest (with the engine running), the display should indicate 00.0 (for MPG) or 00 (for MPH).

MPG Adjustment

You will need someone to help with the actual adjustments, because it is necessary to drive the vehicle at a uniform speed as the adjustments are made. It is dangerous for one person to both drive and adjust this unit. Also, as you drive, notice if the speedometer needle wavers (more than usual) or is erratic. If this happens, stop and reposition the speedometer cable to smooth out any sharp curves before you proceed with the steps.

NOTE: The MPG adjustment affects the MPH display and must be done first. The MPH adjustment will not affect the MPG display. Refer to Fig. 25-6 for the following steps:

1. Place the MPH/MPG switch to MPG mode (out).
2. Determine the actual MPG for a given set of conditions.

    NOTE: As you drive the vehicle to perform the next step, you will see that the instantaneous MPG indication changes considerably even though the vehicle seems to be traveling at a constant speed. These rapid and wide variations are normal because gas does not enter the carburetor at an even rate. This is due to fuel pump and carburetor characteristics as well as vapor in the fuel line.

3. Repeat the test drive under the same conditions and, as you drive, have a helper adjust the MPG control to indicate the same value you had determined.
4. Press the MPH/MPG switch in for the MPH mode.
5. Drive the vehicle at a steady 50 miles per hour.
6. Have a helper adjust the MPH control until the display indicates 50.
7. Press a piece of tape over the MPH and MPG controls on the rear of the display unit so you do not accidentally change their settings.
8. Adjust the UPDATE control to your preference. This control varies the frequency that the display will update (indicate changes) from every half second to 2 seconds.

    This completes the calibration procedure.

Chapter 26
PA Amplifier

The *Realistic* MPA-10 (sold by Radio Shack) is a 10-watt public-address amplifier. It's designed primarily for use in mobile applications. You can use it in your camper, on picnics, for outdoor events, on buses or trucks, on your boat, at parades—anywhere you'd have a difficult time obtaining 120-volt AC power, but can use a 12-volt battery. The connection of a mobile PA is quick and simple, as these instructions for the *Realistic* MPA-10 show.

INSTALLATION

You can install the PA in almost any location, it takes little room—in or under a dashboard, in a glove compartment, under a seat, against the roof, or in any convenient place.

Before drilling holes, determine the most convenient location. Consider the following:

1. Will other wires be in the way? (Don't drill into them.)
2. Can you route power and speaker wiring easily?
3. How about convenience of use?

If universal mounting brackets (as in Fig. 26-1) are provided with the PA, use them to mount the amplifier either below or above a mounting surface. Drill holes as appropriate (take care not to drill into existing wires or trim) and fasten with hardware as shown.

You can mount the microphone clip to either side of the PA, depending on what is most convenient. Secure with hardware as shown.

WIRING

There are four wires coming from the connector on the rear of the typical PA. The 2-conductor cable is for the speakers. The black and red wires are for power.

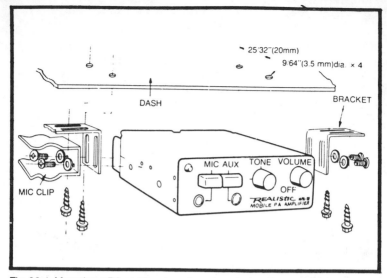

Fig. 26-1. Mounting a PA and its microphone to a dash. (Courtesy Radio Shack)

Connecting Power

The red wire (with in-line fuse holder) goes to the positive (+) side of a source of 12 volts DC. The black wire goes to the negative (−) side of the 12-volt DC source. You can make connection either directly to battery terminals or through a separate power switch (for example, the ignition switch on your vehicle or boat). Determine the best method of connection. Normally, the best way is to make connections at the fuse block. Some models, such as the MPA-10, operate with positive as well as negative grounds. If you've gotten the wire polarity backwards, the pilot lamp will not light up (there won't be any internal damage, because of built-in polarity protection). If your PA is for negative ground only, make sure you get the polarity right.

Connecting Speakers

For maximum efficiency and power, it is necessary that the *impedance* (load that the speakers present to the PA) of the speakers match the output of the amplifier.

For a single speaker:

Connect the 2-conductor cable to the speaker terminals. Then, set the SPEAKER switch on the rear of the PA to the appropriate position—4 or 8 ohms, depending on the speaker used.

For two speakers:

1. If you use two 4-ohm speakers, use the wiring diagram shown in Fig. 26-2. Set rear-panel switch to *8-ohm* position.
2. If you use two 8-ohm speakers, use wiring diagram as shown in Fig. 26-3. Set rear-panel switch to *4-ohm* position.

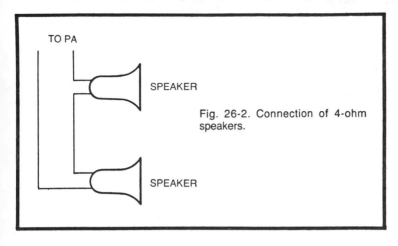

Fig. 26-2. Connection of 4-ohm speakers.

3. If you use two 16-ohm speakers, use wiring diagram as shown in Fig. 26-3. Set rear-panel switch to *8-ohm* position.

OPERATION

OFF/VOLUME control: Use for applying power to the MPA-10 and for adjusting the output level. Rotate maximum counterclockwise to turn power off.

TONE control: Use to decrease the high-frequency or treble response of the amplifier. This control is particularly useful for reducing feedback problems (squeal and other oscillation sounds). To avoid feedback, keep your microphone away from the speakers; don't let speaker sound radiate toward or into the microphone. Set TONE for the best tonal quality of sound and for minimum feedback.

MIC jack and pushbutton: Press in MIC button to activate the MIC jack. Press again to disconnect the microphone function.

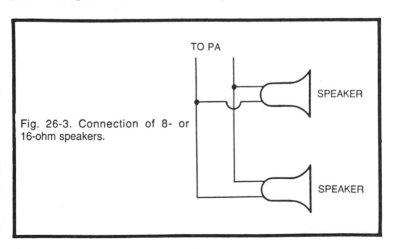

Fig. 26-3. Connection of 8- or 16-ohm speakers.

AUX jack and pushbutton: Press in AUX button to activate the AUX jack. Press again to disconnect the auxiliary-input function.

The microphone supplied with the PA is specifically designed for the rugged usage mobile operation normally demands. However, if you want to use another microphone, the MIC input is designed for other high-quality microphones, such as Radio Shack's *electret* condenser microphone. You might want to take a look at a tie-clip microphone—the ideal for many of those outdoor applications, for a dynamic-type microphone with a cardioid pickup pattern.

You can connect a tuner or a tape-recorder output to the AUX jack. Or, if you have a record changer with a *ceramic* or *crystal* cartridge, you can connect it to the AUX jack and thus play records through the PA system.

If you press both MIC and AUX buttons on the MPA-10, both jacks will be active—thus, you could be playing music and yet make announcements via a microphone.

Chapter 27
Police and Fire Scanner

Radio Shack's *Patrolman* PRO-40 (Fig. 27-1) is an excellent scanner that serves well to illustrate scanner installations. The scanning receiver is a completely transistorized VHF/UHF superheterodyne receiver using dual conversion. It is capable of automatically scanning eight crystal-controlled channels.

It is designed for use in the narrowband FM channels of communications—VHF and UHF police, fire, civil defense, telephone, forestry, and weather service, plus many other industrial radio services and the 2-meter ham band (upper end). These and many other services share the bands of frequencies from 30 to 50 MHz, 148 to 174 MHz, and 450 to 512 MHz.

The PRO-40 features both high sensitivity and selectivity and a sophisticated circuit which includes 10.7 MHz and 455 kHz ceramic IF filters to reduce or eliminate adjacent-channel or strong-signal interference. Such interference is often experienced when operating in urban and metropolitan areas, or where very strong and closely placed signals are present, and good selectivity is something to consider when you are buying a scanner.

This particular monitor receiver is designed to operate from a 12-volt DC negative-ground electrical system. Before you attempt to install such a scanner in a vehicle, check to make sure the vehicle's electrical system utilizes 12 volts and that it is negative ground. If not, check your radio-supply store for a suitable power inverter.

PREPARING A SCANNER FOR USE

To use your scanner, you must do three things:

1. Connect power.
2. Install crystals.
3. Connect an antenna.

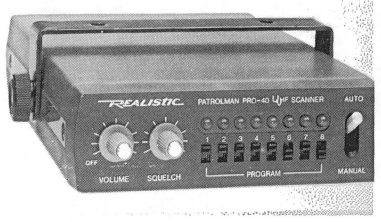

Fig. 27-1. A police and fire scanner from Radio Shack.

To make a quick check, you must connect the 12-volt DC power wires as noted later on under *Mobile Installation*. With an antenna connected and a crystal installed, turn the receiver on by rotating VOLUME clockwise. Rotate SQUELCH maximum counterclockwise. You should hear a "rushing" sound in the speaker.

Crystals are not included with the scanner, because the frequencies are so numerous. The frequencies used in your part of the country will be different from those used in other areas. Order the crystals you want from your radio supplier—specify the model number of the unit and the frequency you want to receive.

Remove the crystal-compartment cover to expose the crystal sockets and program switches. Provision is made in the PRO-40 to install eight crystals; a program switch can be used to obtain either VHF low, VHF high, or UHF reception.

For UHF crystals, position the program switch to U or UHF. For VHF high, set the program switch to H. For VHF low, set the program switch to L. In the example shown in Fig. 27-2, channel 1 will have a VHF high crystal and channel 6 will have a UHF crystal.

INSTALLATION

A good installtion will make the most of the scanner's capabilities. Don't lose any of the weaker signals by using an inadequate antenna or poor-quality lead-in. Use an antenna of proper design and a good-quality foam coaxial cable. The antennas that you choose, and how you install them, will have a great effect on how well your receiver will work.

Mobile Installation

Safety and operating convenience are the primary factors to consider when you install any equipment in a vehicle. Be sure you can easily reach the

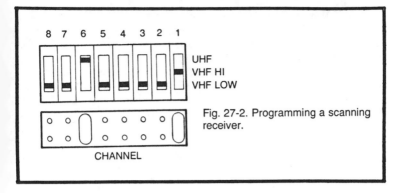

8 7 6 5 4 3 2 1

UHF
VHF HI
VHF LOW

CHANNEL

Fig. 27-2. Programming a scanning receiver.

receiver's controls. Also be sure the connecting cables do not interfere with the operation of the vehicle (brake, accelerator, etc.).

You can mount the receiver to the underside of the dash or instrument panel in the vehicle or boat. Use a universal mounting bracket, such as that in Fig. 27-3. Take care when drilling holes that you do not drill into existing wires or trim.

Be sure you connect power leads with the correct polarity. Use the DC power cable provided. The other end of the wires can be connected to cigarette-lighter plug (Radio Shack catalog No. 274-331), or you can make the connections directly to the fuse block of the vehicle or boat. Be sure to observe correct voltage polarity: red to +, black to −.

IMPORTANT: If your car has been turning out headlamps and other bulbs at a rapid rate, have the voltage regulator checked for proper output. Excessive voltage (more than 16 volts) can cause serious damage to your receiver.

Mobile Antennas

There are many possible antenna mounting locations on a car. Three of the most popular locations for monitor antennas are shown in Fig. 27-4.

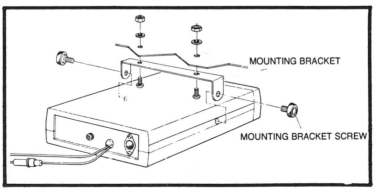

MOUNTING BRACKET

MOUNTING BRACKET SCREW

Fig. 27-3. Mounting a scanning receiver.

Roof Mount. The antenna is mounted in the center of the roof. This position is considered the best by many because it generally results in better reception than the other locations. Radio Shack's high-VHF/UHF mobile mount (No. 20-177) comes complete with low-loss coax cable.

Cowl Mount. If you would rather not cut a hole in the center of your vehicle's roof, you may prefer this location. Radio Shack has a cowl-mount antenna (No. 20-016) which is especially designed for high-low VHF monitoring. For UHF, use their No. 20-183.

Rear Deck. Installation in this location may result in less ignition noise, because it is farther from the engine.

Keep the following points in mind when installing your mobile antenna:

- Mount the antenna as high as possible.
- Mount it rigidly so it will remain vertical while in motion.
- Mount as far as possible from the engine compartment.

SCANNER NOISE SUPPRESSION

A scanner receiver is very sensitive and will pick up signals that are extremely weak. With this extreme sensitivity, you will find that the receiver will amplify any noise that may be present with weak signals.

When operating a receiver in a vehicle, you will find that the vehicle generates electrical noise, and this noise can become very objectionable. Mobile operation will never be as quiet as base operation, but steps can be taken that will greatly improve the noise situation.

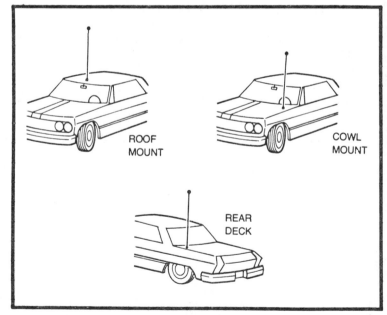

ROOF MOUNT

COWL MOUNT

REAR DECK

Fig. 27-4. Some possible answers to "Where should I put the antenna?" (Courtesy Radio Shack)

Generally speaking, noise can be generated by any device or connection that carries electrical current. Any device that generates a spark should also be suspected. Bypass any suspected wire to ground with a high-quality 1 μF coaxial capacitor.

A very common source of noise is the generator or alternator. This type of noise will sound like a musical whine and will also vary with speed of the engine. Generator and alternator noise can usually be reduced by connecting a coaxial-type capacitor from the armature terminal to the metal case.

The ignition system is the most common source of noise. This noise can be identified by the fact that its speed varies with the engine speed. Ignition noise will sound like a series of popping sounds, while the engine is idling, and will speed up to a buzzing sound as engine speed is increased.

There are a number of things that can be done for this type of noise:

- Use radio-suppression-type ignition wire and resistor spark plugs.
- Check high-voltage wiring for leakage, cracks, etc. Replace any old wiring.
- In extreme cases, obtain an ignition-noise suppression kit—it should shield all ignition wiring. This will provide maximum noise suppression.

SCANNER OPERATION

After power and antennas are connected and crystals have been installed, your scanner is ready to use.

Turn VOLUME on by rotating to the right. Rotate SQUELCH fully counterclockwise. Set all the channel lockout buttons on (button next to LED). You should hear a rushing sound from the speaker. Now, adjust SQUELCH clockwise until you no longer hear the rushing background noise.

If you want to continuously scan the channels for which you have crystals installed, you must adjust SQUELCH as previously instructed, then set the selector switch to the AUTO position. The receiver will constantly scan each channel in sequence; when a signal appears on one of the channels the receiver will lock onto that channel and you will hear the signal.

If you do not want automatic scanning on certain channels, switch their channel lockout switches to the off position (down or away from the LED indicator).

If you want to stay tuned to one channel only, set the selector switch to the center position (stop scanning) and then press to the MANUAL position to advance to the channel you want to listen to (as indicated by the LED above the channel switch). For manual scanning, the receiver can be either squelched (adjusted as previously indicated) or unsquelched (SQUELCH control set to extreme left). For automatic scanning, SQUELCH must be set to eliminate the background noise.

To eliminate the annoying background noise, rotate SQUELCH clockwise until the background noise just stops. You can't adjust SQUELCH properly while listening to a station, so wait until signals cease. If you set SQUELCH as noted above, the scanner will appear dead until a signal comes in. When a signal comes in, the squelch circuit "opens up" and you hear the signal. When the signal ceases, the squelch circuit "closes" and cuts out all sound until the next signal comes in.

Scan Delay

The PRO-40 has a built-in 2-second delay which virtually eliminates missed replies. This circuit holds the receiver on the channel you are monitoring for a period of 2 seconds after the carrier has gone off the air, before the scanner resumes normal scanning.

Skipper Circuit

The PRO-40 scanner has a built-in skipper circuit which is fully automatic and cannot be disabled. It works in both the automatic and manual modes of operation. This feature causes the unit to skip over a locked-out channel so that there is no possibility of the receiver stopping on a locked-out channel.

Accessories

If you want to listen to the receiver from a remote position or just want to use an external speaker, connect it to the EXT SPKR jack. Radio Shack's 40-1244 is a rugged, weatherized 4-inch (10 cm) speaker that is uniquely suited for this type of application.

A pair of headphones can be a very useful accessory. In areas where a high noise level is present (in a factory, at the scene of a fire or accident, etc.), or when you want to listen privately, use headphones. Just plug them into the external-speaker jack.

FREQUENCY COVERAGE

For maximum sensitivity, the channel frequencies you choose should be within certain limits. For the Radio Shack model, you should stay within 3 MHz of 40 MHz on the VHF band (that is, in the spread of 37 to 43 MHz), 4 MHz of 153 MHz on the VHF band (from 149 to 157 MHz). For the UHF band, stay within 15 MHz of 480 MHz (from 465 to 495 MHz). The PRO-40 will function very adequately from 30 to 50 MHz, from 148 to 174 MHz, and from 450 to 512 MHz. The reception spread of 6, 8, or 30 MHz can be moved up or down in this band of frequencies by special realignment of the front-end circuitry by a qualified service techician.

TYPES OF SIGNALS YOU'LL BE ABLE TO MONITOR

Your community is alive with action—action which is constantly being reported on the airwaves. And your scanner will automatically scan the airwaves to bring you that action—your police force at work, a fire truck on a mission, the sheriff's department, the state police, the National Weather Service, ham radio operators, highway and other emergency-type services, some industrial services, some transportation services (taxis, trucks, railroads), plus some government services. Lots of things are going on that most of us just are never aware of. But with the proper frequency crystal in your scanner, you can monitor such exciting signals. You'll have to do a little investigating in your community to find out what services are active and on what frequencies.

What to listen for and where? That is a little difficult for a specific answer. Each area of the country can and will use different channels. All we can do is give you some general pointers and then let you take it from there. Find out if there is a local club which monitors these frequencies. Often a local electronics-repair shop that does work on the equipment can give you the channel frequencies used by local radio services. A volunteer policeman or fireman can also be a good source of this information.

An interesting service is the mobile telephone. The FCC has assigned this service channels in the range of 152.51 to 152.81 MHz at every 0.030 MHz (channels are 30 kHz apart); also 454.375 to 454.95 MHz, with channels 25 kHz apart from 454.375 to 454.625 and then every 50 kHz up to 454.95 MHz.

As a general rule, on VHF most activity will be concentrated between 153.785 and 155.98 and then again from 158.73 to 159.46 MHz. Here you'll find local government, police, fire, and most such emergency services. If you are near a railroad yard or major railroad line look around 160.0 to 161.9 MHz.

In some of the larger cities, there has been a move to the UHF bands for the emergency services. Here, most of the activity is in a spread of 453.05—453.95 and again at 456.025—459.95 MHz.

In the UHF band, the overall spread of 456.025—459.95 and again at 465.025—469.975 MHz is used by mobile units and control stations associated with base and repeater units which operate 5 MHz lower (that is, 451.025—454.95 and 460.025—464.975 MHz). This means that if you find an active channel inside one of these spreads, you can look 5 MHz lower (or higher as the case may be) to find the major base station/repeater for that radio service.

Continuous weather broadcasts are transmitted 24 hours a day in many parts of the country. If you are using a crystal set to one of the two channels assigned (162.55 or 162.40 MHz), your scanner will automatically lock in on that channel since the broadcasts are continuous. To prevent automatic locking, set the channel-lockout button for that channel to the "off" position (button out). When you want a weather report, set the lockout button to the "on" position (press in) for that channel. In areas where two stations are close to each other, one will use 162.55 and the other will use 162.40 MHz. Check with your local FCC office or the National Weather Service for the frequency used in your area.

Chapter 28

High Voltage
Power Supply

The Heath Model HP-13B transistorized DC power supply (Fig. 28-1) was designed to furnish all necessary operating power for Heath mobile amateur transmitters, transceivers, and receivers, as well as for other brands of mobile equipment.

This power supply is actually three DC power sources in one unit. It provides high voltage (750 volts), low voltage (300 or 250 volts), and bias voltage (-130 volts). It also switches DC filament voltage for the equipment with which it is used.

Circuit features include relay control of all primary power, plus individual circuit-breaker protection of the DC input to the power supply and of the DC filament-voltage line to the equipment used with the power supply. The circuit brakers are the automatic-reset, load-delay type. They ensure positive protection for all equipment involved in case of an overload or accidental short circuit.

Because the complete power supply is physically small, it requires a minimum of mounting space.

MOUNTING CONSIDERATIONS

It is recommended that you mount the power supply under the hood. Figure 28-2 shows several possible under-the-hood mounting locations. Choose the location that is best for your particular installation and allows adequate ventilation and protection from water spray.

WARNING: Before you install the power supply in a vehicle, measure the generator or alternator output voltage. The voltage output of the charging system *must not exceed 16 volts*.

Mount the power supply as near to the vehicle battery or starter solenoid as practicable. This will allow the 2-wire battery cable to be connected to either of these two points by the shortest route possible.

Fig. 28-1. A power supply for converting the 12 volts of a battery to the much higher voltages needed by amateur-radio transmitters and receivers. (Courtesy Heath Company)

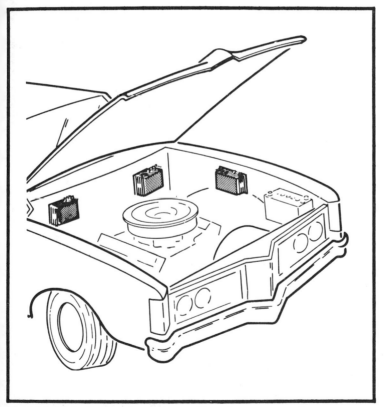

Fig. 28-2. Under-the-hood mounting positions for power supply.

It is preferable that you mount the power supply with the heat-sink fins vertical to provide maximum cooling of the transistor. However, this is not mandatory.

1. When you have decided upon the mounting position, use the power supply as a template and mark the mounting-hole locations on the chassis. (See Fig. 28-3.) Drill a 9/64-inch hole at each of these four points.

2. Refer to Fig. 28-3 and mount the power supply at the prepared location. Start four #10 × 1/2-inch sheet-metal screws into the mounting surface, then tighten them securely.

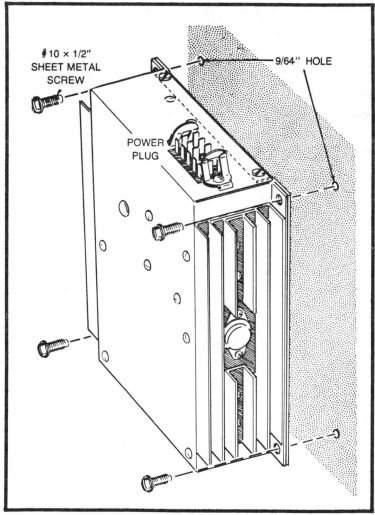

Fig. 28-3. Using the unit as a template for marking holes.

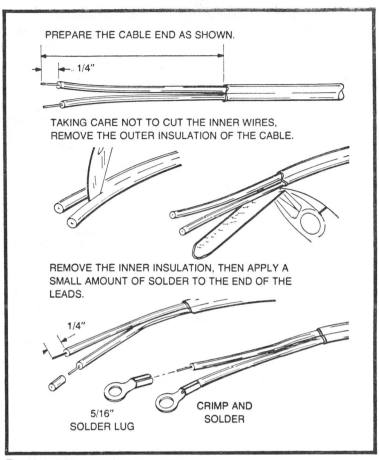

PREPARE THE CABLE END AS SHOWN.

1/4"

TAKING CARE NOT TO CUT THE INNER WIRES,
REMOVE THE OUTER INSULATION OF THE CABLE.

REMOVE THE INNER INSULATION, THEN APPLY A
SMALL AMOUNT OF SOLDER TO THE END OF THE
LEADS.

1/4"

5/16"
SOLDER LUG

CRIMP AND
SOLDER

Fig. 28-4. Adding terminals to a cable.

3. Attach the power-cable connector to the connector on the chassis. Be sure the connectors are coupled firmly together.

BATTERY CONNECTIONS

If the vehicle's battery cables terminate in spring connectors, connect the 2-wire cable to the starter solenoid instead of the battery. Follow the directions for the specific conditions you encounter.

Connecting to Battery

1. Route the 2-wire cable to the battery. Make sure the cable clears all moving parts and is not near the exhaust manifold. Allow sufficient cable length so the wires can be connected to the battery terminals. Then cut off the excess cable.
2. Refer to Fig. 28-4 and prepare the end of the 2-wire cable.

3. Remove the nut from the negative (−) battery cable clamp. Slip the terminal of the brown wire over the bolt. Then replace and tighten the nut securely.

4. In a similar manner, connect the red wire to the positive (+) battery terminal. Tighten the nut securely.

Connecting to Starter Solenoid

1. Route the 2-wire cable to the starter solenoid. Make sure the cable clears all moving parts and is not near the exhaust manifold. Allow sufficient cable length so the brown wire will reach a good ground on the engine and the red wire will reach the starter-solenoid terminals. Then cut off the excess cable.

2. Refer to Fig. 28-4 and prepare the end of the 2-wire cable.

3. Connect the brown wire to a good ground (engine block or starter mounting bolts).

4. Connect the red wire to the battery terminal of the starter solenoid. This is the terminal to which the positive (+) battery cable is connected.

SWITCHING

The relay in the power supply is energized by applying 12 volts DC to the relay coil from an external source. All power to the equipment with

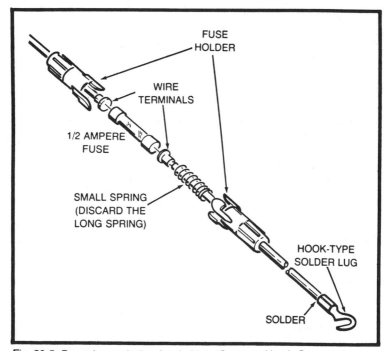

Fig. 28-5. Preparing an in-line fuseholder. (Courtesy Heath Company)

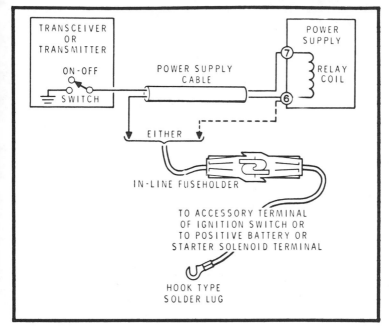

Fig. 28-6. Switching circuit for power supply. (Courtesy Heath Company)

which the power supply is used, as well as the power to the power supply, is controlled by the relay. In effect, the relay is an on-off switch for the entire system.

There are basically two ways to obtain 12 volts DC to control the relay. The first, and preferable way, is from the ignition switch. The second way is directly from the battery. Either source may be used. An in-line fuseholder, a 1/2-ampere fuse, and a hook-type solder lug are used for this purpose. Prepare the fuseholder as shown in Fig. 28-5.

The switching hookup is shown in Fig. 28-6. Connect one lead of the fuseholder to the 12-volt DC source; the other lead should be connected to either pin 6 of the 8-wire cable connector or to the blue wire at the free end of the 8-wire cable.

The relay can be energized by grounding the other side of the relay coil. This is usually accomplished by a simple single-pole, single-throw (SPST) switch in the transceiver or transmitter with which the power supply is used. The brown wire at the free end of the 8-wire cable should be connected to one terminal of the switch. The other switch terminal should be connected to ground. When the switch is closed, it completes the 12-volt DC circuit for the relay coil and energizes the relay. The relay then turns on the complete system.

Chapter 29
Radar Detector

The radar detector is a transistorized *microwave* detector. It is completely self-contained, having a special built-in antenna and battery power supply. When the radar detector intercepts a radar beam, it produces an audible warning that alerts you to check immediately on your speed.

The detector will also react to airport radar and military installations of radar. The "zip-zip" noise heard when near an airport or an airplane with radar tells how frequently the antenna is rotating. It is also possible to use the detector to detect microwave emissions from other locations.

It is a handy device to use for checking leakage from the plumbing associated with microwave installations. Other uses include the detection of transmitted signals from microwave installations and the checking of the alignment of the receiving antenna with the transmitting antenna. Proper alignment of the transmitter antenna with the receiving antenna can reduce the required amounts of radiated RF energy from a microwave transmitter. The louder the sound from the speaker, the stronger the signal being received. A relative indication of just how much leakage is taking place can be found by listening closely to various levels of output. This type of device has been used by telephone maintenance crews for microwave installations, and for all types of microwave applications in military installations.

TESTING FOR PROPER OPERATION

The best test is in the area of a radar speed meter. However, you can often pick up a signal in the vicinity of an airport or military installation. Aeronautical radars search with rotating antennas and produce short, intermittent sounds on the detector. They are easily distinguished from the clean, clearcut tone produced by the speed meter.

Some cities have radar-controlled traffic lights. The radar unit operates in the microwave "S-band" at 2.455 GHz. If you drive under one of these units (a large white pan-like object jutting over the traffic lane), a very loud noise will be emitted from the detector, and you will know that the S-band part of the unit is working. The antenna for the S-band is the slot in the back of the receiver with two radar diodes mounted across it.

INSTALLATION AND OPERATION

Mounting is on the underside of one of the automobile's sunvisors. This ensures maximum range and sensitivity. A clip for mounting the detector in this manner is usually furnished. If necessary, adjust the clip for a horizontal position of the unit.

The unit should be mounted behind the windshield in a location which provides an unobstructed "view" for the antenna (which may be the back plate of the case). Make sure the windshield-wiper arms and blades do not rest in front of the antenna. At microwave frequencies metal can act as a reflector and scatter the waves, thereby reducing the sensitivity of the unit.

Antenna Assembly

Sometimes a special radar antenna is provided with the detector (Fig. 29-1). To assemble, insert the large end of the antenna in the opening in the back of the unit so it fits squarely and is tight. If the antenna becomes loose through taking in and out, put a little glue on the end that fits in the rectangular opening. Be sure the unit is as level as possible when clipped on the sun visor, with the antenna having a clear view of the road.

Operation

Some information about police radar is given in Fig. 29-2.

Advance the OFF-ON-VOLUME control knob until you can hear a slight background noise. This will sound somewhat like radio static. Do not turn it up louder than necessary to hear. The volume control affects only the loudness of the signal produced and does not change the range (sensitivity) of the unit. Increasing the volume also increases the battery drain and shortens the battery life, just as it does in a transistor radio.

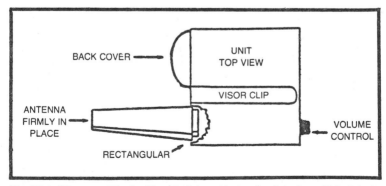

Fig. 29-1. Diagram of Radio Shack's Driver Alert radar detector, which detects police radar on the S and X bands. This device helps maintain driver alertness and is an important aid to safe driving.

```
X-BAND (10,525 MHz)

UNIT ON SIDE WINDOW OR INSIDE CAR.

POWER OUTPUT APPROXIMATELY 100 mW

DISTANCE SPEEDMETER CAN CLOCK:

        SHORT RANGE:    150 FT.
        MEDIUM RANGE:   300 FT.
        LONG RANGE:     500-600 FT.


THE DETECTOR PICKS UP DOUBLE THE ABOVE
DISTANCE.   (IF POLICE ARE OUT 300 FT.,   YOU
WILL PICK THEM UP AT 600 FT. OR MORE.)
```

Fig. 29-2. Some important information about police radar.

When the detector intercepts a radar beam, it will automatically produce a warning sound similar to that which accompanies a TV test pattern. This gets loud very rapidly as you approach the source of the radar beam. It will stop as you pass out of the range of the transmitter.

Traffic conditions, terrain, and the method in which the radar speed meter is pointed determine the range of the detector. Normally, it will give advance warning of radar speed-controlled zones. The detector does not interfere with car-radio reception or with the radar speed meter since it is nothing more than a receiver.

Once the signal is received at 10.525 GHz, it is fed to the radar diode for the X-band and causes instantaneous forward conduction of the diode. This means the resonant conditions of the tuned cavity are shorted by the diode and the cavity ceases to function. Therefore, the diode has no signal to conduct and returns to a nonconduction state. As this happens the resonant conditions of the tuned cavity return; and if a signal is present, the diode conducts once again, shorting the resonant cavity, repeating the previous operation. By conducting and not conducting, the diode causes short bursts to be fed to the flip-flop oscillator causing it to oscillate at about 700 Hz or in the audio range. This is amplified by the audio-amplifier transistor to drive a speaker.

Chapter 30
Radios

The car radio was the first electronic unit to be installed in cars. Today, very few people would consider buying a new car without a factory-installed radio. But, radios offered by after-market suppliers are still very popular accessories. Often they offer special features, and usually they offer a decided price advantage. And, of course, if you install a radio yourself, you can put it where it is most convenient for you.

FM STEREO RADIO

The *Realistic* FM stereo car radio (Fig. 30-1) is designed to meet the needs of value-conscious music lovers.

Installation

Pick an attractive underdash position, taking special care that it is convenient to the driver's seat. Avoid areas with wiring or other mounting obstacles.

1. Remove the two sides screws on unit (Fig. 30-2).
2. Using mounting brackets as a guide, drill two 5/32-inch holes. Be careful, when drilling, not to damage existing wiring under dashboard.
3. Mount unit to dash with two 3/16-inch self-tapping screws.
4. Mount radio to bracket, using hardware previously removed.

Installation Hints

- Use with 12-volt negative- or positive-ground electrical systems, as required.
- Use only original-size fuse in the fuse holder.

Fig. 30-1. A modern high-performance FM stereo radio from Radio Shack (Model 12-1368).

- Do not turn set on until antenna and speaker wires are attached. If radio does not operate, check to see if ground and "hot" power leads are firmly connected. Check fuse and replace if necessary.
- Consider making all wiring connections before installing the unit on the bracket.
- Refer repairs to qualified service personnel.

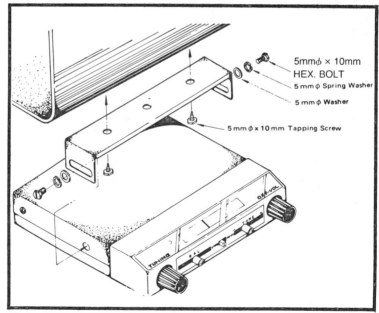

Fig. 30-2. Mounting a car radio under the dash (see details in text).

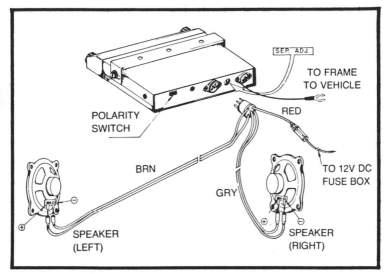

Fig. 30-3. Connecting the speaker wires to an FM stereo radio. (Courtesy Radio Shack)

Connections

Connect the speaker wires as shown in Fig. 30-3. For best sound, observe proper phasing (+ and − connections).

NOTE: For best reception, use a special FM stereo car antenna or the regular telescoping antenna adjusted to about 30 inches.

Determine the polarity of the electrical system of the vehicle or boat. Most domestic vehicles use a negative-ground electrical system. Set the polarity switch to the appropriate position: − for negative-ground systems and + for positive-ground systems.

Connect the end of the power cable (with in-line fuse) to the "hot" terminal of the battery or to a convenient accessory terminal on the fuse block. Connect the separate ground wire (black) to a convenient connection point on the metal frame of the car.

Make antenna connections as shown in Fig. 30-4. If you use only an FM radio, make connection directly between the antenna and the ANT jack. You can connect an AM radio to the same antenna by using a Y-adapter cable as illustrated.

Using the FM Radio

To operate the radio, rotate VOL clockwise to turn power on.

Adjust TUNING for the desired station. If the station is broadcasting in stereo, the STEREO light will come on. To listen to stereo sound, set the STEREO/MONO switch to the STEREO position.

If stereo sound is weak, noisy, or fluttery, use the MONO position of the switch. You are too far away to obtain good stereo signals and thus you are not getting suitable stereo separation and sound.

Adjust VOL, TONE, and BAL for the most suitable sound level, tone, and stereo balance.

If you have an AM radio installed in your vehicle or boat, to listen to it just turn off the FM stereo radio. While both radios can be operated at the same time (both connected to the same antenna), the sound obviously will be distracting if you have both on at the same time.

Maintenance

If the fuse blows after you have made connections, try another one. Use only the same type, size, and rating. If the second fuse also blows, check your wiring with care.

Be sure all wire connections are firm and solid.

If stereo sound is noisy or fluttery, you will have to use the MONO position of the slide switch. A stereo signal must be stronger than a mono signal to obtain stereo sound. Thus, while you'll lose the stereo separation, the sound should no longer be noisy and fluttery (unless you are just too far from the station for good FM reception).

If stereo separation is very poor and you know you have a good, strong signal, you can make a slight adjustment of the SEP ADJ control at the back of the radio. Set this control for the best separation between channels.

AM RADIO

Radio Shack's *Realistic* AM car radio (Fig. 30-5) is a compactly designed radio for installation in or under dash. You get some extra features at a price below that of a factory-installed radio:

- Compact signal unit
- 2-position TONE switch

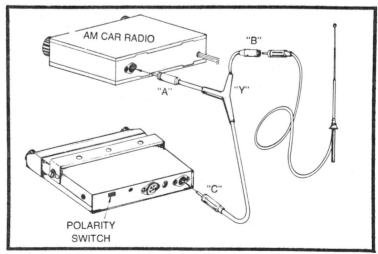

Fig. 30-4. Connecting an FM radio to an existing AM antenna. (Courtesy Radio Shack)

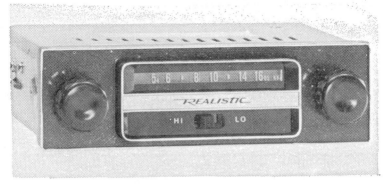

Fig. 30-5. Realistic Model 12-1344 AM car radio from Radio Shack.

- Built-in dynamic-type 4-inch speaker
- Transformerless audio output for superior sound quality
- 12-volt negative or positive ground
- Noise suppressors included

Mounting the AM Radio

You can install your radio either under the dash or in the dash.

Underdash Mounting

Pick an attractive underdash position, taking special care that it is convenient to the driver's seat. Avoid areas with wiring or other mounting obstacles.

Using the L-brackets as a guide (Fig. 30-6), drill a hole on one side of the desired location. Mount the unit to the L-brackets. Drill the second mounting hole. Straighten the unit before tightening the screws.

Use the mounting strap and hardware to attach the radio to the firewall.

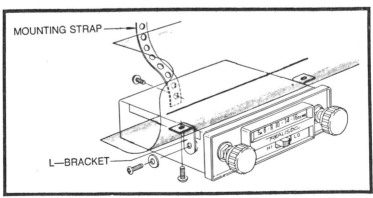

Fig. 30-6. Use of L-brackets and rear mounting strap in car-radio installation. (Courtesy Radio Shack)

321

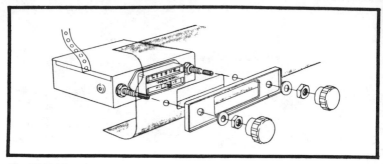

Fig. 30-7. Mounting a radio in the dash. (Courtesy Radio Shack)

In-Dash Mounting

If there is sufficient space provided in the dash cutout, your radio can be mounted right into the dash (see Fig. 30-7).

Carefully pull the knobs off and remove the nuts holding the front panel. Mount the radio from inside the dashboard. Place the front panel over the control shafts and fasten in place with the nuts previously removed. Press the knobs back on.

For additional strength, use the mounting strap and hardware to attach the radio to the firewall.

Electrical Connections

1. Connect the antenna cable to the antenna jack on the radio (Fig. 30-8).

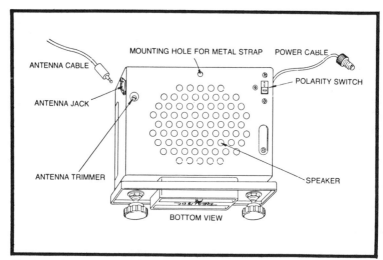

Fig. 30-8. Connections and adjustments for a typical car radio. (Courtesy Radio Shack)

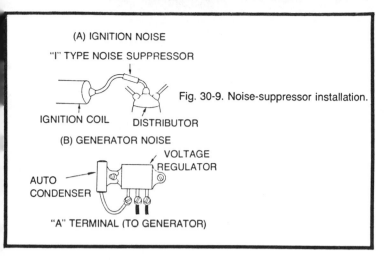

(A) IGNITION NOISE

"I" TYPE NOISE SUPPRESSOR

IGNITION COIL   DISTRIBUTOR

Fig. 30-9. Noise-suppressor installation.

(B) GENERATOR NOISE

VOLTAGE REGULATOR

AUTO CONDENSER

"A" TERMINAL (TO GENERATOR)

2. Determine the polarity of the electrical system. If your car battery is negative ground, set the POLARITY switch so the − mark is showing. If it is positive ground, set the POLARITY switch so that the + mark is showing.
   CAUTION: If the switch is set incorrectly, your radio may be damaged.

3. When you have properly set the POLARITY switch, connect the power cables. Connect cable with the in-line fuse holder to the accessory terminal on the ignition switch.

Adjustment of Antenna Trimmer

Fully extend the antenna and turn on the radio. Tune in a weak station near the top end of the AM band (1400 kHz or higher). Use a screwdriver to adjust the antenna trimmer for maximum volume.

Motor-Noise Elimination

Noise from your ignition may affect the operation of your AM car radio. This noise, if present, can be identified by a series of popping sounds which varies with the speed of the engine.

There are a number of things that you can do to reduce this kind of noise:

1. Use only the radio-suppression type of high-voltage ignition wire. Most new cars come already equipped with this type of wire.

2. Inspect the high-voltage ignition wire and its connections. If the wire is cracked, replace it.

3. If noise persists, install noise suppressors (See Fig. 30-9).

Chapter 31
Siren

This product is designed for emergency-service vehicles. Consult your local or state authorities before installing or operating the siren on a vehicle.

The Heath Model GD-18 electronic siren (Fig. 31-1) provides an automatic wail siren, a public-address (PA) system, and a radio-monitoring amplifier, all in one compact unit for emergency-service vehicles. The siren is powered by a 12-volt storage-battery system and is capable of delivering adequate sound levels on all of its five functions.

Instant switching from the siren mode to public address is an especially useful feature. This is accomplished by simply pressing the switch on the microphone.

The electronic siren may be used with either an external siren horn speaker or a concealed grille siren speaker.

INSTALLATION IN VEHICLE

Refer to Fig. 31-2 for the following steps:

NOTE: The gimbal bracket may be mounted above or below the electronic siren, as shown.

1. Determine the location for the electronic siren in your vehicle. Set the gimbal bracket in this location and use the bracket as a template for the holes for the mounting screws. Mark the holes and drill 1/8-inch diameter holes at these locations.

2. Mount the gimbal bracket using #8 × 1/2-inch sheet-metal screws. If you mount the microphone clip separate from the electronic-siren cabinet, choose a location for it and complete the following two steps.

3. Use the microphone clip as a template to locate the mounting holes, as shown in the inset drawing.

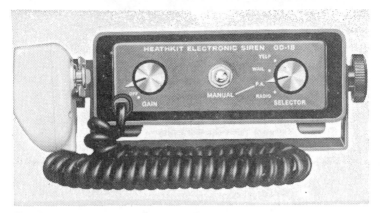

Fig. 31-1. The Heath GD-18 siren and PA.

4. Drill two 7/64-inch diameter holes at the mounting-hole locations and mount the clip with two #6 × 3/8-inch sheet-metal screws.

5. Determine whether your vehicle has negative-ground wiring (negative battery post connected to vehicle chassis) or positive-ground wiring (positive battery post connected to vehicle chassis).

For the following steps, refer to Fig. 31-3 if your vehicle has negative-ground wiring, or refer to Fig. 31-4 if your vehicle has positive-ground wiring.

Note that there are three drawings in the figure you have selected. Refer to the uppermost illustration if you intend to operate your siren from a foot switch. If you intend to operate your siren from a horn ring, you must first learn whether the horn ring is grounded or ungrounded. Then refer to the proper drawing.

NOTE: All wires to the electronic siren should be identified and taped to other cables in the vehicle for support. If possible, protect the cables against vandalism by keeping the cables concealed.

1. Attach the wires from the speaker system you are using to the SPEAKER terminals on the terminal strip on the backplate of the electronic siren. Be sure to position the #6 lockwashers *under* the lugs of the speaker wires. Route the speaker wires upward from the terminals.

2. Attach a wire from your remote switch, as shown, to the proper SWITCH terminal on the backplate of the electronic siren. Route the wire upward from the terminals.

3. Connect wires from the voice coil of the speaker of your 2-way radio to the RADIO terminals of the electronic siren. Be sure to position a #6 lockwasher under each lug of the voice coil wires. Two #8 solder lugs may be used for these wires. Route the wires upward from the RADIO terminals.

4. Install the electronic-siren cabinet in the gimbal bracket and secure it in place with two 10-32 plastic thumbnuts.

Power-Cable Installation

Refer to Fig. 31-5 for the following steps:

1. Connect the power socket of the power cable to the POWER plug of the electronic siren and thread the power cable from the electronic siren toward the battery in the vehicle. Leave enough slack in the cable in case you have to remove the electronic siren later.

2. If there is no existing hole in the firewall of the vehicle for the power cable, drill a 3/8-inch diameter hole and slide a 3/8-inch rubber grommet onto the free end of the power cable.

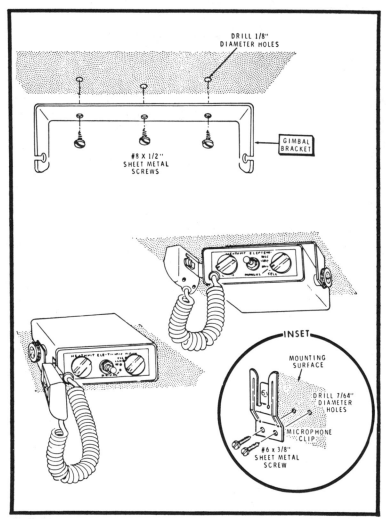

Fig. 31-2. Mounting the electronic siren and the PA microphone. (Courtesy Heath Company)

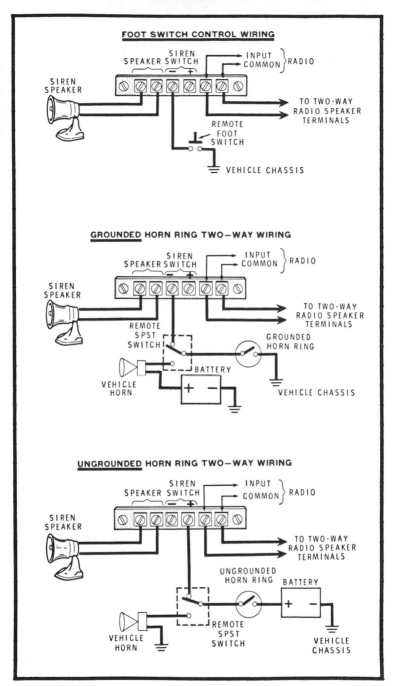

Fig. 31-3. Negative-ground wiring for the electronic siren.

3. Install the grommet in the firewall.
4. Cut the free end of the power cable to a length that will reach the power source in the vehicle.
5. Prepare new 8-inch wires on the power-source end of the power cable and permanently solder the large solder lugs on the new wire ends.

NOTE: If the power-cable lugs are attached directly to the battery clamps, route the power cable away from the battery to prevent corrosion by chemical deposits which may be present on the battery.

6. Install the lug ends of the power cable on the battery clamps (or on the battery side of the starter solenoid) and on a nearby ground of your vehicle, as shown. Be sure to observe the correct power-source and power-cable polarity.

Final Adjustments of Siren Pitch and 2-Way-Radio Level Input

Refer to Fig. 31-6 for the following steps:

1. Turn the GAIN control clockwise until it clicks.
2. Set the SELECTOR switch to the WAIL position.
3. Adjust the SIREN PITCH ADJUST control for the desired siren pitch. The most piercing sound of the siren can be obtained by turning the control in the range from the center of its rotation to a fully clockwise setting.
4. Turn the SELECTOR switch of the electronic siren to RADIO for radio monitoring through the PA system.
5. Turn on the 2-way radio in your vehicle.

    NOTE: If the electronic siren does not monitor the 2-way radio, or if a loud noise is present when the SELECTOR switch is in the RADIO position, reverse the two voice-coil wires connected to the RADIO terminal on the back of the electronic siren.

6. Set the volume of the 2-way radio to a normal listening level inside the vehicle.
7. Turn the GAIN control of the electronic siren fully clockwise.
8. Turn the RADIO LEVEL INPUT ADJUST control clockwise with a screw-driver until the PA sound outside the vehicle reaches a maximum volume with tolerable distortion.

NOTE: A small amount of noise from the vehicle's electrical system is unavoidable when the electronic siren is turned on with the selector switch in the PA or RADIO position and the vehicle engine is running.

OPERATION

The typical electronic siren is very simple to operate. Normal standby operation with the SELECTOR switch in the PA position and the GAIN control in the "on" position enables the operator to sound a short siren wail blast by pressing the MANUAL pushbutton siren switch. A remote switch, such as the horn ring or a foot switch, may also be used to sound the wail siren in this mode. The public-address feature is available simply by advanc-

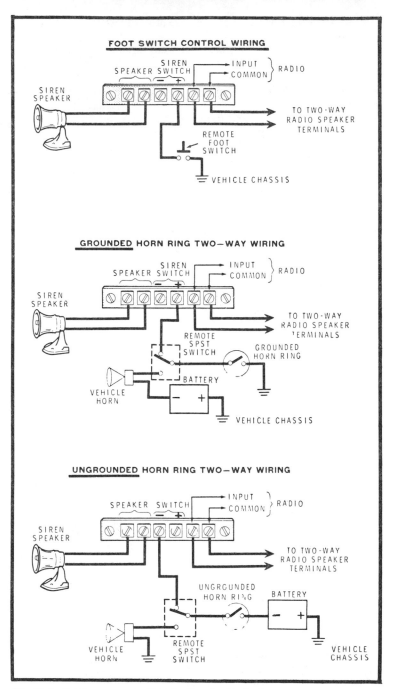

Fig. 31-4. Positive-ground wiring for the electronic siren.

ing the GAIN control and depressing the push-to-talk switch of the microphone.

To operate the PA system of the electronic siren with best results, hold the microphone slightly to the side of the mouth while speaking in a normal

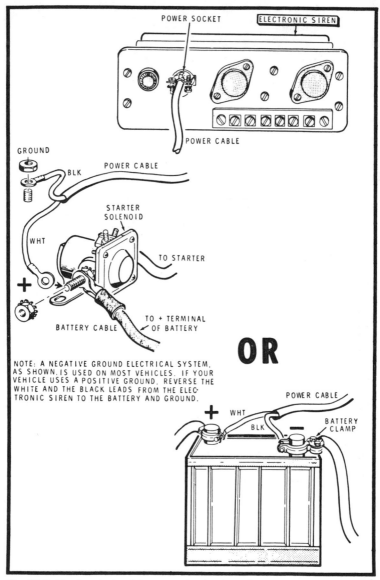

Fig. 31-5. The terminals of the power leads of an electronic accessory can be attached to threaded studs such as the ones on the starter solenoid or to the bolts on the battery-cable clamps. (Courtesy Heath Company)

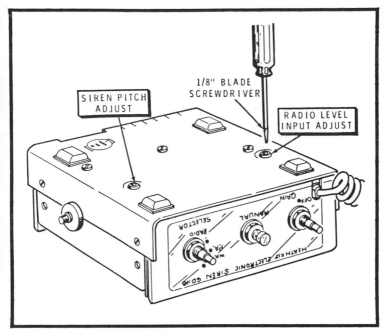

Fig.31-6. Adjustment of siren pitch and 2-way-radio level input. (Courtesy Heath Company)

voice. With the GAIN control fully advanced clockwise, a normal speaking voice will produce full PA output without objectionable distortion.

For clearing traffic or other situations requiring continuous siren operation, the automatic wail or yelp sirens may be sounded by advancing the SELECTOR switch to WAIL or YELP positions.

Incoming radio calls on a 2-way radio may be monitored outside the vehicle by turning the SELECTOR switch counterclockwise to RADIO and advancing the GAIN control for a sound level which can be heard at the desired distance from the vehicle.

When two vehicles use their sirens in the same area, one vehicle should use a wail siren and the other a yelp siren to alert traffic that there are two vehicles. When one vehicle follows another, the lead vehicle should use a yelp siren. In normal operation, no maintenance should be required for the electronic unit except to keep it clean and dry. Provide adequate ventilation for the back panel of the unit.

Chapter 32
Speakers

Speakers are among the most popular automotive accessories, and a speaker installation is often the first installation made by an automotive-electronics enthusiast. It's a good place to start, too, since speaker installations are relatively easy to make. There are a few complications you should know about—such things as flush-mount versus surface-mount speakers, 2-wire and 4-wire systems, and 2-speaker and 4-speaker installations. Speaker principles are illustrated using two speaker models from Radio Shack.

SURFACE-MOUNT SPEAKERS

The *Realistic* 12-1848 speakers are surface-mount speakers that feature a special instant-mount ring and a snapon padded-vinyl grille for easy installation.

Some popular locations for installation are shown in Fig. 32-1. A door installation is especially popular for this type of speaker. If you decide on this type of installation, route the wires as shown in Fig. 32-1B. Details of the car body and how to·remove panels appear in one of the previous, general chapters of this book.

If the speakers are to be mounted in the door panel, be sure to check that there is a depth of at least 2 3/8 inches behind the surface. To avoid unnecessarily damaging your upholstery, always remove the door panel and carefully check that there is ample room for a speaker installation.

Once the location is selected, mark the position for each speaker and grill mounting holes in the panel, using the mounting ring as a guide. Then, secure the mounting ring as pictured in Fig. 32-2. Secure the speaker to the mounting ring with the screws, as shown. Cover the mounted speaker with the snapon grille to complete the installation.

TWO-WAY SPEAKER SYSTEM

Some speakers come with an enclosure that permits them to be mounted on any convenient surface in a car without cutting any holes. This surface-mounting arrangement is illustrated by the *Realistic* 12-1847 in Fig. 32-3. Note that these speakers can also be flush mounted, in a hole, once the

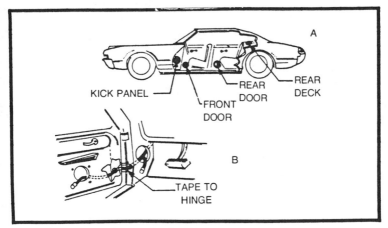

Fig. 32-1. Locations for speaker installation.

back of the enclosure is removed. These two-way speakers might be just the ticket if you are undecided about whether you want to cut holes in your car's interior to mount speakers.

Surface Mounting

1. Remove the speaker grille (speakers are attached to this grille) from the cabinet.
2. Attach the cabinet to the rear deck or other mounting surface with self-tapping screws and flatwashers. Use the grille as a template to mark and drill the holes. Be sure to use a drill size slightly smaller than the screws.
3. Connect the speaker wires from your tape player or radio through the cabinet hole and to the speakers, as shown in Fig. 32-4 or 32-5.
4. Then mount the speaker grille to the cabinet using the 6 self-tapping screws.

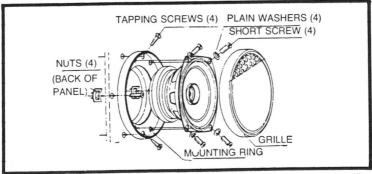

Fig. 32-2. A mounting ring supplied with the Realistic 12-1848 speaker simplifies the installation. (Courtesy Radio Shack)

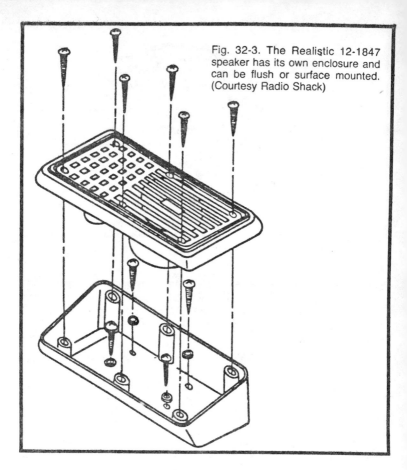

Fig. 32-3. The Realistic 12-1847 speaker has its own enclosure and can be flush or surface mounted. (Courtesy Radio Shack)

Flush Mounting

1. If the speakers are to be mounted in the rear deck, be sure to check that there is a depth of at least 1 3/4 inches behind the surface.

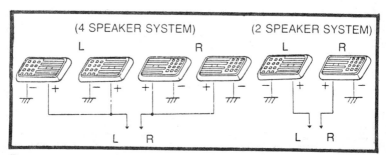

Fig. 32-4. Speaker hookup for 2-wire system.

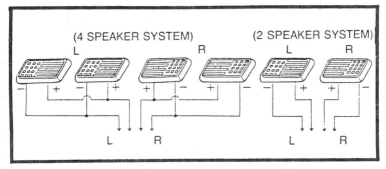

Fig. 32-5. Speaker hookup for 4-wire system.

2. Once the location is selected, mark the position for each speaker and drill mounting holes in the panel.
3. Cut the panel, using a sharp knife or razor blade.
4. Mount the speaker grille to the rear deck using self-tapping screws as shown in Fig. 32-6.

Speaker Hookup

Two-Wire System. If your tape player or radio comes equipped with only two speaker wires, one each for the left and right speakers, they should be connected as shown in Fig. 32-4.

Four-Wire System. If your unit comes equipped with four wires, two each for the left and right speakers, they should be connected as in Fig. 32-6.

NOTE: In 4-wire systems, one of the two wires for each channel will be color coded. It makes no difference which terminal this wire is connected to as long as you are consistent throughout the hookup.

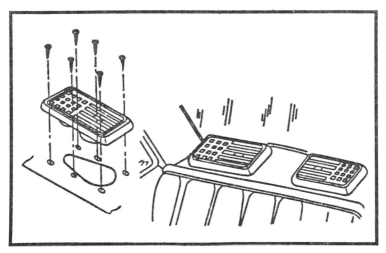

Fig. 32-6. Flush mounting. (Courtesy Radio Shack)

335

Chapter 33

Speaker-Selector Switch

A speaker-selector switch enables you to use one pair of stereo speakers in your vehicle (or boat) for connection to two stereo sources. For example, you have a stereo FM radio *and* a stereo tape player but you want to use only *one* pair of speakers. With a speaker-selector switch you can select to hear either the radio or the tape sound. Normally you'd add this switch when you install the second unit.

Installation requires that you cut and solder wires for both the radio and tape unit. It is very important that you make the correct connections, or the units can be damaged.

INSTALLATION

First, determine the location for mounting the switch. It should be:

- Convenient and safe to operate while you drive the vehicle.
- Convenient for wiring to the radio and tape units (make sure the wires will reach).
- Located where its mounting screws will not damage trim or go into existing wires in the vehicle.

Second, carefully study the required wiring connections to be sure you understand what needs to be done. Study the wiring for your radio and tape units, too.

You may want to mount the switch *after* you make all wiring connections. This way you can see all the wires, etc., while you are doing the work.

Using the switch bracket as a template, mark holes for drilling (under the dash or other carefully selected location). Drill holes and mount the switch with screws.

WIRING

You can use the switch either with two stereo units, or with a car radio which has two speakers (one front and one rear). The instructions are written assuming you are using stereo speakers; if your existing radio is an AM unit with front and rear speakers, just use one speaker for left-channel sound and the other for right-channel sound.

Turn ignition switch off to be sure power is not on while you do the wiring (don't use the ACC position of your ignition switch).

Power Connections

1. Locate the 12-volt power connection for the radio or tape unit.
2. Disconnect the wire(s) from the ACC screw or other location.

NOTE: For Radio Shack *Realistic* units, the following wires will be either red or blue (12-volt power-connection wires).

3. Connect the violet wire to the 12-volt power connection for the tape unit. (Refer to Fig. 33-1.)
4. Connect the blue wire to the 12-volt power connection for the radio.

NOTE: Be sure the in-line fuses remain between the switch and the radio and tape units (don't connect switch *between* fuse and radio/tape units).

5. Connect the orange wire to a 12-volt source (typically the ACC terminal on the vehicle's fuse block). If you want to protect the switch wiring, you may want to add an in-line fuse between the orange wire and the 12-volt DC sourse. Use an appropriate-size fuse (same value as the higher value fuse of the radio or tape unit—don't add values, just use the higher rating of the two).

These instructions are written assuming you already have a stereo radio connected and that you are adding the tape unit at this time. If your radio is an AM unit with two speakers, let one be for left channel and the other for right channel. If you only have one speaker, you must add a second.

Left-Channel Speaker Connections

1. Locate the "hot" wire for the radio's left-channel output. (For Radio Shack *Realistic* units, this will be green or white.)

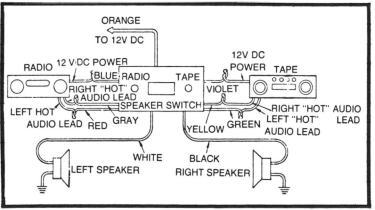

Fig. 33-1. Connections for a speaker-selector switch.

2. Cut (or disconnect) this wire.
3. Connect the wire from the radio to the red wire from the switch.
4. Connect the white wire to the wire which goes to the left speaker.
5. Locate the "hot" wire for the tape unit's left-channel output. (For Radio Shack *Realistic* units, this will be green or white.) Connect this wire to the green wire from the switch.

Right-Channel Speaker Connections

1. Locate the "hot" wire for the radio's right-channel output. (For Radio Shack *Realistic* units, this will be gray or brown.)
2. Cut (or disconnect) this wire.
3. Connect the wire from the radio to the gray wire from the switch.
4. Connect the black wire to the wire which goes to the right speaker.
5. Locate the "hot" wire for the tape-unit's right-channel output. (For Radio Shack *Realistic* units, this will be gray or brown.) Connect this wire to the yellow wire from the switch.
6. Very carefully recheck all your connections before you try it all out.
7. Then, before applying power, you must insulate all of these connections. By the way, to ensure good connections, you should solder them (insulate the bare wire ends with electrical insulating tape). Or, use wire nuts. Be sure all connections are well insulated—from each other and from any metal surfaces—then tuck the wires up under the dash and out of the way.

USING THE SWITCH

Turn on the ignition switch and set the speaker switch to TAPE. Turn your tape unit on and listen to the sound from the tape unit through your speakers. Now set the speaker switch to RADIO. Turn on your radio and listen to the radio's sound through the speakers.

There is no need to turn the radio or tape unit on and off since the power of these units is switched by the speaker switch. Just select whichever unit you want to listen to and adjust that unit's controls for the desired sound.

If you do not hear any sound, check the fuses to be sure they have not blown. Before you replace a blown fuse, recheck your wiring. Recheck all connections by following the illustration and the instructions. Make sure all leads and bare wire ends have been carefully and completely insulated.

338

Chapter 34

Tachometers

Basically, tachometers come in two types. The older, meter-type tach has a needle that swings in an arc over a scale as in a conventional speedometer. How far the needle swings depends on the speed being read. That is, the amount of needle travel is the analog of the speed, and this type of tach is also referred to as the *analog* type.

The digital type, on the other hand, indicates the engine speed by means of a lighted numerical display somewhat like the display on a digital clock. Often the speed will be indicated by just two numerals—40 to 4000 rpm, for example. It is no problem to mentally add the two missing zeros on the end.

This chapter describes the installation of a digital tachometer, using a product of the Heath Company for example. Procedures for other products are similar. The text emphasizes power wiring and the connection of a tachometer to modern electronic ignitions.

DIGITAL TACHOMETER

The Heath Model CI-1079 digital tachometer (Fig. 34-1) is an accurate, easy-to-read tachometer that operates well with 4-, 6-, or 8-cylinder, 4-cycle and 2-, 3-, or 4-cylinder, 2-cycle spark-ignition engines. The intensity of the 2-digit display is adjustable at the front panel so you can compensate for variations in ambient lighting. The tachometer will operate on any negative-ground, standard ignition system and on most solid-state systems.

An induction-pickup accessory is available to allow you to connect this tachometer to ignition systems where the points are not accessible.

INSTALLATION

As shown in Fig. 34-2, you can mount the tachometer on top of or beneath the dash, and with or without the mounting bracket. Decide where

Fig. 34-1. Heath Model CI-1079 digital tachometer.

you want to mount the tachometer in your vehicle, noting that most on-top-the-dash locations will require that you drill a 1/4-inch hole in the dash for the cable.

Perform the following steps that pertain to the type of installation you have chosen, either *With Bracket* or *Without Bracket*.

With Bracket

Refer to Fig. 34-3 for the following steps:

1. Mount the mounting bracket to the tachometer. Slide each bracket slot between the screw head and the large lockwasher on the tachometer.
2. Set the tachometer in the position in which you want it to be mounted. Then, while you hold the mounting bracket firmly in place, lift the tachometer off the bracket and set the tachometer aside.
3. Use a pencil to mark the three bracket holes.
4. Use the mounting bracket as a guide and drill holes. Then mount the bracket with sheet-metal screws. Use a lockwasher on one of the screws as shown.
5. Mount the tachometer to the bracket. If your location requires a hole in the dash for the cable, temporarily remove the tachometer, drill a 1/4-inch hole, route the cable through the hole, and remount the tachometer.

Proceed to *Power Wiring.*

Without Bracket

Refer to Fig. 34-4 for the following steps:

1. Set the tachometer in the position in which you want it to be mounted. Then, make a faint pencil line around the tachometer.

340

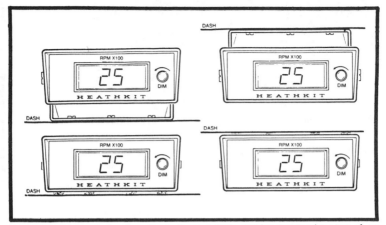

Fig. 34-2. Small electronic units such as a tach can be mounted on top of, or under the dash, with or without a bracket.

Make sure the line is far enough away from the tachometer so that it can be erased after the tachometer is mounted.

2. Cut four equal-sized pieces of double-stick foam tape as shown.
3. If your mounting location requires a hole in the dash for the cable, carefully drill a 1/4-inch hole at a suitable location as show in the drawing.

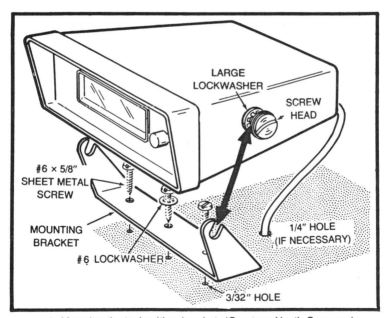

Fig. 34-3. Mounting the tach with a bracket. (Courtesy Heath Company)

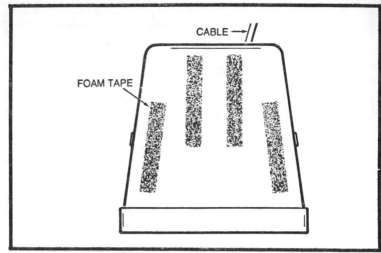

Fig. 34-4. Mounting the tach with foam tape. (Courtesy Heath Company)

NOTE: In the following steps you will stick the foam tape to the cabinet, and then stick the cabinet to the dash.

4. Remove the protective paper backing from one side of the foam tape and press the tape in place on the tachometer. Put it on top of the tachometer for a beneath-the-dash installation or on the bottom of the tachometer for an on-top-of-the-dash installation.
5. In a similar manner, install the other three pieces of foam tape.
6. Remove the remaining paper backing from the pieces of tape, route the cable through the cable hole (if you drilled one), center the tachometer over the penciled outline, and carefully press the tachometer into place.
7. Erase the penciled outline.

Proceed to *Power Wiring.*

POWER WIRING

Because there can be a large difference between vehicles, the following information is general. Read all of it before you perform any steps. Two groups of steps are given below. Use the first group if your vehicle has a fuse block. Use the second group if your vehicle does not have a fuse block. In these steps you will connect the power wires as follows:

If your vehicle has a fuse block:

1. Cut the large red and black wires to a length that (when routed as desired) will be long enough to reach and connect to the fuse terminals. Keep the large black wire as short as possible.
2. Remove 1/4 inch of insulation from the red and the black wires.
3. Refer to Fig. 34-5 and connect a pushon connector to the red wire.
4. Refer to Fig. 34-6 and connect a terminal connector to the black wire.

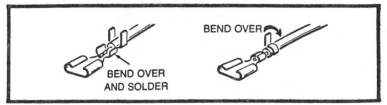

Fig. 34-5. Heath Company supplies handy terminals for connecting to existing lugs on car's fuse block.

5. Push the connector on the red wire onto a fuse-block lug marked FUSE ACC, ACC, or RADIO. (See Fig. 34-7.)
6. Connect the connector on the black wire to a screw that is connected to chassis ground. (This is usually a metal part of the dash, etc.)

Proceed to *Breaker-Point Connections.*

If your vehicle does not have a fuse block, refer to Fig. 34-8 for the following steps:

1. Cut the red and the black wires to the shortest length that will allow them to reach their intended connection points.
2. Refer to Fig. 34-6 and connect a terminal connector to the black wire.
3. Connect and solder the red wire to the wire that carries power to the radio or other accessory that is connected after the ignition switch.
4. Connect the connector on the black wire to a screw that is connected to chassis ground. (This is usually a metal part of the dash, etc.)

BREAKER-POINT CONNECTION

This section is divided into several types of electronic ignition systems. Use the steps that pertain to your particular installation.

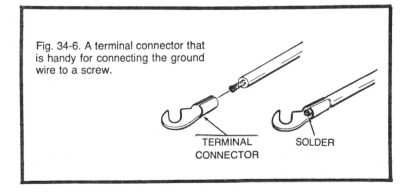

Fig. 34-6. A terminal connector that is handy for connecting the ground wire to a screw.

TERMINAL
CONNECTOR

SOLDER

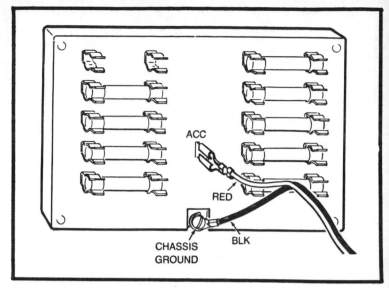

Fig. 34-7. Connecting an accessory's power leads to a car's fuse block. (Courtesy Heath Company)

GM High-Energy System

Refer to Fig. 34-9 for the following steps:

1. Route the shielded sensor cable to the point where it will be connected.

2. Cut the sensor cable so there is ample length to reach from where the tachometer is mounted to the point where the cable will be connected.

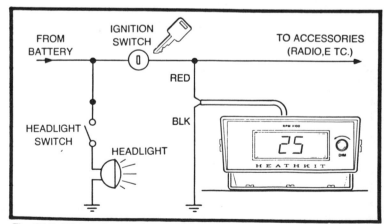

Fig. 34-8. Wiring diagram for supplying power to an electronic tachometer. (Courtesy Heath Company)

3. Remove 8 inches of outer insulation from the free end of the cable. Do not cut off the shield lead.

4. Remove 1/4 inch of insulation from the end of the inner wire of the cable.

5. Refer to Fig. 34-5 and solder a pushon connector on the end of the inner lead.

6. Refer to Fig. 34-6 and solder a terminal connector on the end of the shield lead.

7. Connect the pushon connector to the terminal marked TAC on the distributor.

8. Connect the terminal connector on the shield lead to a nearby ground.

This completes the tachometer installation.

Ford Electronic System

Refer to Fig. 34-10 for the following steps:

1. Route the shielded sensor cable to the point where it will be connected.

2. Cut the cable so there is ample length to reach from where the tachometer is mounted to the point where it will be connected.

3. Remove 6 inches of outer insulation from the free end of the cable. Do not cut off the shield lead.

4. Remove 1/4 inch of insulation from the end of the inner wire of the cable.

5. Refer to Fig. 34-6 and solder a terminal connector on the end of the shield lead.

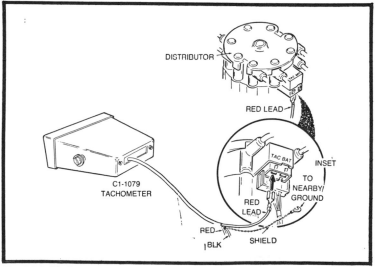

Fig. 34-9. Tachometer connection to General Motors car.

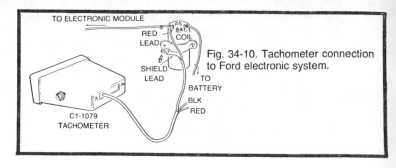

Fig. 34-10. Tachometer connection to Ford electronic system.

6. Connect the inner lead to the ignition coil terminal that is *not* marked BAT. Use a terminal connector, or, if necessary, splice this lead to the other wire already connected to that terminal.

7. Connect the terminal connector on the shield lead to a nearby ground.

This completes the tachometer installation.

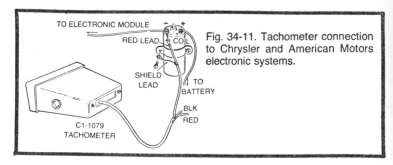

Fig. 34-11. Tachometer connection to Chrysler and American Motors electronic systems.

Chrysler and AMC Electronic Systems

Refer to Fig. 34-11 for the following steps:

1. Route the shielded sensor cable to the point where it will be connected.

2. Cut the cable so there is ample length to reach from where the tachometer is mounted to the point where it will be connected.

3. Remove 6 inches of outer insulation from the free end of the cable. Do not cut off the shield lead.

4. Remove 1/4 inch of insulation from the end of the inner wire of the cable.

5. Refer to Fig. 34-6 and solder a terminal connector on the end of the shield lead and the inner lead.

6. Connect the terminal connector on the end of the inner lead to the negative (−) ignition-coil terminal.

7. Connect the terminal connector on the shield lead to a nearby ground.

This completes the tachometer installation.

Chapter 35
Tape Players

Basically, there are three different speaker hookups for audio systems in cars; these are illustrated by Fig. 35-1.

Part A shows a typical rear-seat speaker hookup for a single-channel (monaural) radio. Note how the negative and positive terminals are connected together, each to the like terminal on the other speaker. Connecting the speakers thus is necessary to ensure that they will be in phase, i.e., working together.

In Fig. 35-1B and C, typical hookups of stereo tape players are shown. In the hookup in B, it is important to have a wire from the plus terminal of one speaker connected to the plus terminal of the other. In the hookup in C, the two wires running to the speaker plus terminals are usually the same color.

The two complete stereo hookups in Fig. 35-2 are typical. The hookup in Fig. 35-2A is used with Muntz, Audio Stereo, Automatic Radio, Ranger, Kraco, Tenna, Bowman, and Auto-Sonic units. The orange wire is present only in the case of those Muntz and Audio Stereo units having a remote-track-change feature and leads to the remote switch. Note that the black lead and one lead of each speaker must be connected to a good chassis ground (in a negative-ground car), and the red power lead must be fused. This lead may be connected to the accessory terminal of the car's ignition switch or fuse block.

Figure 35-2B shows another common hookup, used for Craig, Taiko, and Gibbs (332A, 332B, and 664) units. Note that in this installation the speakers are not grounded.

The pin configurations for the wiring plugs used with various stereo units are shown in Fig. 35-3. In using the drawings, imagine that the pins of the plugs shown are projecting toward you.

An example will clarify and refine the installation procedures for a tape player. The unit to be considered is Radio Shack's *Realistic* Model 12-1836

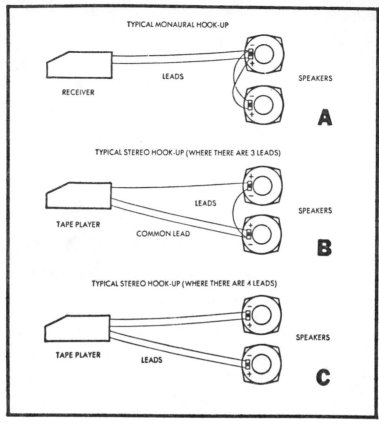

Fig. 35-1. Speaker hookups for audio systems in cars.

(Fig. 35-4), which is a complete auto music center. It combines an AM/FM stereo radio with a cassette tape player—all in a case little larger than the AM radio found in most cars. It comes with all the hardware for either in-dash or underdash mounting.

The tape player features pushbutton eject, a lighted tape-play indicator, and a fast-forward button.

The radio has a lighted dial and an FM stereo beacon. A local-distant FM selector provides maximum sensitivity without overloading.

The integrated circuit, 23 transistors, 9 diodes, and 3 ceramic filters produce superb sound at a fraction of the original-equipment price. And since you'll probably mount it yourself, you'll be saving even more.

INSTALLATION

It is a good idea to make all the electrical connections before you mount the unit. However, before making connections, determine how you will mount the unit (in dash or under dash).

1. Connect the single black wire to the frame of the vehicle or to the negative side of the battery.
2. Connect the red wire (with the in-line fuseholder) to an accessory terminal on the vehicle's fuse block.
3. Connect the brown wire to the marked terminal on the left speaker (see Fig. 35-5).
4. Connect the gray wire to the marked terminal on the right speaker.
5. Connect the gray wire to the marked terminal on right speaker.
6. Check all the connections. Put the wiring-harness plug into the socket at the end of the wires coming from the unit.
7. Plug the lead from your vehicle's antenna into the antenna receptable.

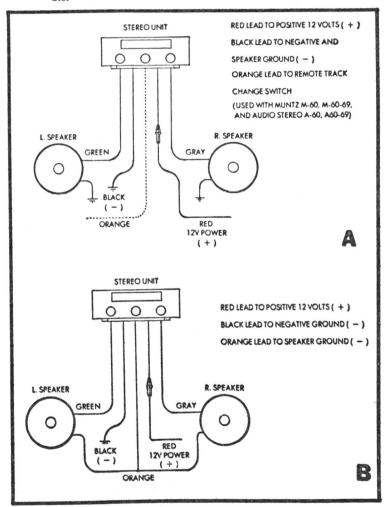

Fig. 35-2. Stereo-unit hookups.

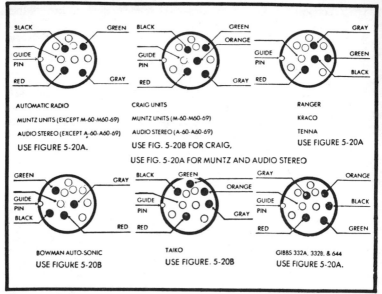

Fig. 35-3. Stereo-connector configurations.

Underdash Mounting

Determine the best location, considering safety and passenger convenience. Be sure the location will be easy for the driver to reach and that the wiring will not interfere with the vehicle's controls.

Mount the two L-brackets to the sides of the unit as shown in Fig. 35-6. Hold the unit under the dash in the location you have chosen and mark the drilling holes.

Drill the appropriate-size holes, being careful not to drill into the existing wires, etc. Fasten with hardware as shown in Fig. 35-6.

For a secure installation and a good negative-ground electrical connection, fasten the rear-support strap between the rear of the unit and a convenient screw or bolt on the vehicle's chassis.

In-Dash Mounting

If your vehicle (or boat) has suitable space in the dash, you may want to mount your radio/tape player in the dash. The unit should come with a trim plate designed for in-dash mounting, along with required hardware. Remove the transit screw on the top of the unit.

Check your dash and cutouts provided to be sure the radio/player will fit. Use the trim plate as a template to see if there is adequate space. The two control shafts can be adjusted to the appropriate widths.

1. Carefully pull control knobs off.
2. Carefully remove the existing nuts, washers, and front panel. You will not require the front panel for in-dash mounting, but keep the nuts and washers handy for the next steps.

g. 35-4. A stereo-cassette player with AM-FM radio—the Realistic 12-1836
ⁿm Radio Shack.

3. Determine the required spacing between the centers of the control shafts. If their spacing needs to be changed, loosen the remaining control-shaft nuts and fit the locating tabs into one of the other sets of slots. (Each pair of slots is numbered: 1, 2, 3, or 4.) Use the pair of slots which will provide proper control-shaft spacing. Tighten the nuts.

4. Mount the radio/player from inside the dash.

NOTE: Extra nuts and washers may be provided to place over the shafts directly behind the dash cutout. These can be positioned on the threaded shafts so the trim plate will mount flush with front of the dash cutout. Use the washers and nuts if needed.

5. Place trim plate over the control shafts. If holes don't line up, you can file (or drill) slotted holes for proper control-shaft spacing. Drill or file from the back of the trim plate.

6. Fasten trim plate in place with washers and nuts previously removed.

7. Press control knobs back in place.

For the remainder of the installation, refer to Fig. 35-7.

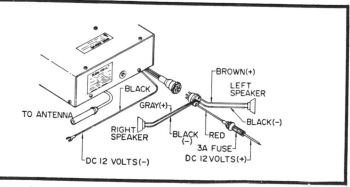

g. 35-5. Connections to speakers, antenna, and power.

351

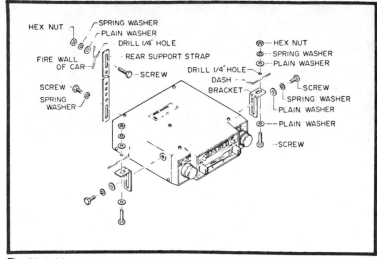

Fig. 35-6. Mounting hardware for a tape unit.

LISTENING TO TAPES

Rotate VOLUME clockwise to turn the unit on. Holding a cassette with side 1 up and the open side of the cartridge to your right, insert into the cassette slot and press all the way in. The TAPE light will come on and the tape will begin to play. When that side is complete, the TAPE light will go out. Press the eject button, turn the tape end over end, insert again. Adjust VOLUME, TONE, and BALANCE for the desired sound.

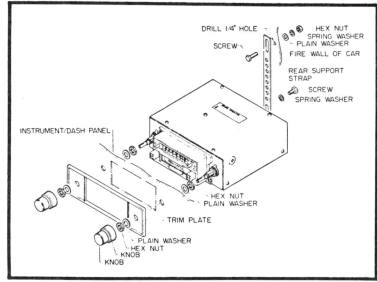

Fig. 35-7. In-dash mounting with rear-support strap. (Courtesy Radio Shack)

To move tape rapidly in a forward direction, press FF button. Press again to return to normal speed.

To remove cassettes, merely press the eject button. When not in use, eject the cassette. Do not leave a cartridge loaded all the way in when power is off or you are not using the unit. Always eject the cartridge.

LISTENING TO FM

Turn the unit on by rotating VOLUME clockwise. Press FM/AM button in. Adjust TUNING for the desired station. The STEREO light will come on if you are tuned to a station broadcasting in stereo. Adjust VOLUME, TONE, and BALANCE for best sound.

For normal listening, leave the LOCAL/DX button out. If a very strong FM station begins to overload the radio, causing distortion, press this button in. This button has no effect on FM reception.

If you are listening to a weak or distant FM stereo station, the sound may be noisy and fluttery. This means either the station signal is too weak or you are too far away or in a poor location for stereo. In such a case, press VOLUME in. This will defeat the stereo function (you'll receive only a monaural signal), but the noise and flutter should improve. Press VOLUME again to return to stereo.

LISTENING TO AM

Follow the instructions for FM, except you must press the FM/AM button so it is out. The MONO/STEREO function and LOCAL/DX button has no effect on AM.

The radio will not operate while a tape is playing. Press EJECT button to remove the tape and permit radio operation.

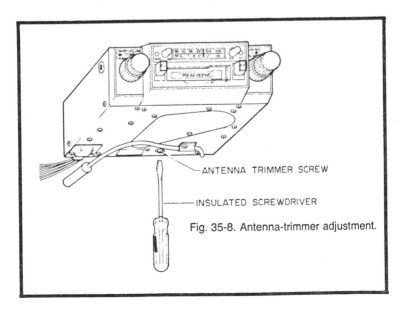

Fig. 35-8. Antenna-trimmer adjustment.

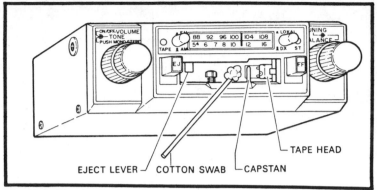

Fig. 35-9. Cleaning the tape head.

ANTENNA TRIMMER

For most sensitive reception of both AM and FM signals, there is an internal antenna-trimmer adjustment you can make. After installation is complete, extend the auto antenna to 30—32 inches (optimum length for FM reception). Then turn on unit for AM reception and tune in station around 1400 kHz.

Look at the bottom of the unit and use an insulated screwdriver to carefully adjust the screw at the right rear (see Fig. 35-8).

Adjust for maximum sound.

MAINTENANCE

If the in-line fuse blows, don't replace it with a higher rating fuse. Use only a 3-ampere fuse. If the fuse blows again, carefully check all electrical connections.

The cartridge door protects the mechanism from dust and dirt. Never play a dirty or dusty cartridge; wipe it off first.

After repeated playing, residue from the tape and dust from the surroundings will build up on the tape head and handling surfaces. To ensure troublefree performance (especially from tape wrapups or breakage), clean the tape head and other tape-handling parts after every 25-30 hours of use. Use a cotton swab and recorder cleaner (obtainable at Radio Shack). This will improve tape handling, frequency response, and reduce sound dropouts.

To ensure maximum frequency response, demagnetize the tape head. Use a demagnetizer after every 50 hours of use. Or, by using a cassette damagnetizer/cleaner cartridge, you can both clean and demagnetize in one simple operation.

Tape units require very little attention, but you will be assured of top performance only if you follow the above notes. Also, about once a year, a single drop of high-grade machine oil on the capstan bearings will ensure proper lubrication. Open the cassette door and press the eject lever inside the opening. This will expose the tape head and capstan. After cleaning is completed, press the EJ button.

Chapter 36
Vapor Detector

The fuel-vapor detector is a warning system that consists of a control unit, sensing element, and interconnecting cable. This warning system, which is used on a boat for detecting a combustible condition in the engine comparment, has an audible alarm and a meter to indicate a safe, dangerous, or explosive condition. An external warning device can also be wired to the control unit.

The control unit is mounted near the wheel of the boat, and the sensing element is mounted in the engine compartment. The element is completely enclosed in a steel-mesh shield. This will prevent the element from causing an explosion if it should be surrounded by explosive fumes.

The Heath Model MI-25 fuel-vapor detector has three circuit safety features that are important in a warning system such as this. In case of a faulty sensing element or faulty part in the control unit, the alarm will sound and the meter will indicate EXPLOSIVE. This assures you that any failure in the system will not go unnoticed. Another feature is a voltage-regulator circuit that maintains accurate operation regardless of battery-voltage fluctuations. The third feature is the TEST position of the ON-OFF switch. The purpose for this position is to check all circuits for proper operation and to burn off the oxide that may have accumulated on the filament of the sensing element.

INSTALLATION

Refer to Fig. 36-1 for the following steps:

1. Insert two nylon speednuts in the square holes on each side of the case
2. Make sure all wires are positioned away from the mounting holes on each side of the chassis. Then install the case on the chassis with the slanted side of the case toward the front panel. Use four #6 × 3/8-inch screws.

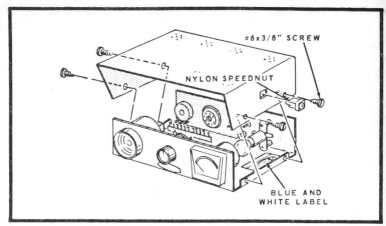

Fig. 36-1. Case and chassis of Heath MI-25 fuel-vapor detector.

Refer to Fig. 36-2 for the following steps:

1. Find a location for the control unit near the boat's helm where it can easily be seen, but away from the boat's compass. The magnet in the meter could affect the compass accuracy.
2. Install the case mounting bracket on the mounting surface of the boat. Position the bracket so the open end of the slot is as shown. Fasten the bracket with three #6 × 3/8-inch sheet-metal screws.
3. Install the control unit on the mounting bracket with #10 fiber washers and #10 × 5/8-inch wood screws.

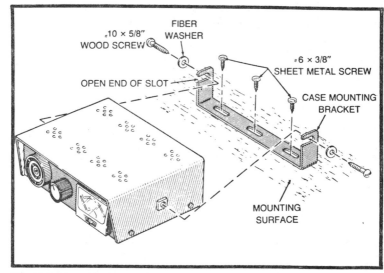

Fig. 36-2. Mounting the control unit of a fuel-vapor detector in a boat. (Courtesy Heath Company)

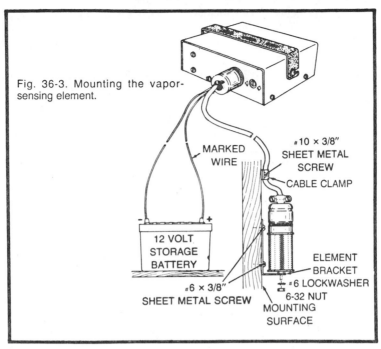

Fig. 36-3. Mounting the vapor-sensing element.

MARKED WIRE

#10 × 3/8" SHEET METAL SCREW

CABLE CLAMP

12 VOLT STORAGE BATTERY

ELEMENT BRACKET

#6 LOCKWASHER

6-32 NUT

#6 × 3/8" SHEET METAL SCREW

MOUNTING SURFACE

Refer to Fig. 36-3 for the following steps: The mounting location for the sensing element will depend upon individual boat layout. However, do not mount the element where water or spray can come in contact with the shield. The best location is near the engine, under the carburetor and approximately 1 to 2 inches above the highest water level in the bilge.

1. After finding a location for the element, install the long end of the element bracket in a vertical position on the mounting surface. Use two #6 × 3/8-inch sheet-metal screws.

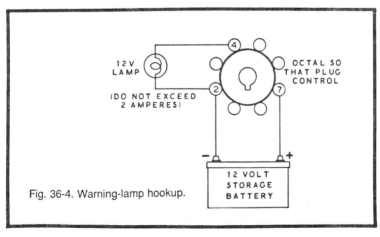

12 V LAMP

(DO NOT EXCEED 2 AMPERES)

OCTAL SO THAT PLUG CONTROL

12 VOLT STORAGE BATTERY

Fig. 36-4. Warning-lamp hookup.

2. Mount the sensing element on the bracket with the plug end up as shown. Use a #6 lockwasher and a 6-32 nut.
3. Plug the cable (the end *without* the two battery wires) onto the sensing element.

NOTE: The length of this cable is important for the proper operation of the fuel-vapor detector. However, if necessary, it could be shortened, but no more than 1 1/2 ft. If the cable between the control unit and sensing element is too long, coil the excess length.

4. Route the shielded cable and battery wires to the control unit and plug the socket onto the plug at the rear of the unit. Position the cable and wires away from the exhaust manifold or other source of heat. Fasten the cable with the six cable clamps and #10 × 3/8-inch sheet-metal screws. Use one clamp near the sensing element, one near the control unit, and the others as required along the length of cable. The battery wires can be taped to the shielded cable.

CAUTION: Do not attempt to operate the fuel-vapor detector in a boat unless the element shield is fastened to the sensing element.

5. Connect the marked wire to the positive (+) side of the battery. Connect the other wire to the negative (−) side of the battery.

EXTERNAL LAMP AND BLOWER HOOKUP

The socket that plugs onto the control unit can be wired to an external lamp or other warning device, as shown in Fig. 36-4. However, the warning device should not draw more than 2 amperes of current. If this amount is exceeded, the relay inside the control unit could be damaged.

Figure 36-5 shows a blower hookup using an external relay that will handle over 2 amperes of current. The relay is wired to the same socket that plugs onto the control unit.

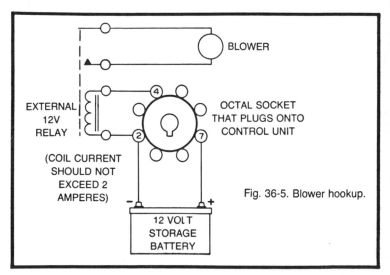

Fig. 36-5. Blower hookup.

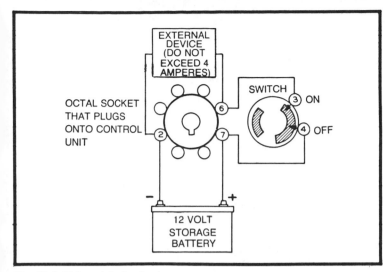

Fig. 36-6. External-device hookup.

Figure 36-6 shows how to connect an external device to lugs 2 and 6 of the octal socket that plugs onto the control unit. This device would be turned on with the switch in the control unit.

OPERATION

As a safety precaution, this procedure should be followed whenever you board your boat.

Turn the fuel-vapor detector switch ON upon boarding your boat and before starting the engine. If a combustible mixture is present in the bilge, the alarm will sound and the meter will give an indication of DANGEROUS or EXPLOSIVE. If no danger exists, the alarm will not sound and the meter will indicate SAFE.

NOTE: When the fuel-vapor detector is first turned ON, the alarm will sound momentarily. This is normal and should not be confused with an unsafe condition.

If the meter indicates SAFE, the following check should also be performed. Turn the switch to TEST for approximately 5 seconds. The alarm will sound and the meter will indicate EXPLOSIVE. This check indicates that the control unit, the cable, and the element are functioning properly. Also, any oxide that may have accumulated on the element will be burned away. Then turn the switch to ON and leave it there while you are on the boat.

Always turn the fuel-vapor detector on before refueling your boat. Refueling can be dangerous. As an example, a half-cupful of gasoline spilled in the bilge could increase the vapor content to an explosive condition.

Chapter 37

Windshield-Wiper Delay

This is a very simple and useful device (see Fig. 37-1). Often, no doubt, while driving in a very light rain or mist, you wished that your windshield wiper could be set to a lower speed (or you just decided to turn it on once in a while just to keep the windshield clear). This electronic control unit will solve that problem, for it permits you to delay the wiper action to a variable number of sweeps with a variable interval of time between each group of sweeps.

MOUNTING

Choose the position for mounting your wiper delay. Be sure it is in a place where the driver can reach it with ease and it will not interfere with any normal driving functions. Also consider the routing of wires. Position the unit as desired and mark for drilling the mounting holes, using the mounting bracket as a template. Drill holes with care (don't drill into existing wiring or trim) and fasten in place with the hardware supplied.

WIRING

The control of electrical windshield motors is accomplished in one of two ways:

1. Switching the "hot" lead on and off.
2. Switching the ground-return lead on and off.

The type used in your vehicle will determine how you connect the windshield-wiper-delay wires. General Motors vehicles use the second type noted above. Almost all other vehicles use the first type.

Connections for the two types are slightly different. With the first type, the wiper delay must be installed in *series* with the hot wire to the wiper motor. The second type required installation in *parallel* with the wiper motor.

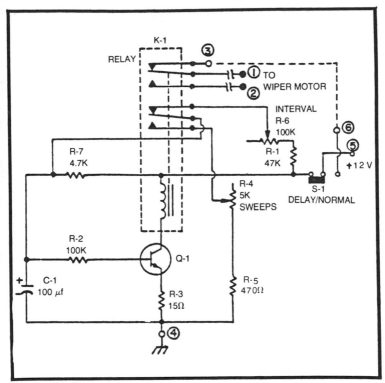

Fig. 37-1. Circuit of Archerkit windshield-wiper delay.

The black and red wires are to supply power to the wiper delay and can be connected to any convenient fused course of 12-volt power (e.g., fuse block). Connect the red wire to the + side of the vehicle's 12-volt electrical supply and connect the black wire to the negative side (typically the metal frame of the vehicle).

NOTE: The Radio Shack unit can be used with either negative- or positive-ground 12-volt electrical systems (some foreign cars and some old U.S. cars use positive-ground systems), providing you observe correct polarity in the connection of the red (to +) and black (to −) wires. All U.S. and most foreign cars produced since 1956 use negative-ground electrical systems.

The green and white wires must be connected to the leads going to the wiper motor as noted below.

General Motors Vehicles (Parallel Installation)

The easiest method of connection is right at the windshield-wiper control swtich, mounted in the vehicle's dashboard. This control will have two or more wires connected to it. If just two wires are connected, solder the unit's green wire to one and the white wire to the other. If there are more than two wires, determine which wire is the common and which is for the slow wipe. (Refer to the manufacturer's service literature or use a voltmeter to determine which wires receive voltage when the windshield wiper switch is turned on.) You may trim the green and white wires to an appropriate length.

For Vehicles Other Than GM (Series Installation)

On vehicles which use series hot-wire switching for windshield-wiper control, the green and white wires must be connected in series with the hot wire to the wiper motor. Series connection means you must cut the hot wire and then splice the green to one end and the white to the other. The important thing is to identify the hot wire. This can be done either by referring to the manufacturer's service literature or by using a voltmeter.

Locate a hole in the firewall so you can thread the green and white wires into the engine compartment. Now, identify the hot wire going to the wiper motor. If you do not have the manufacturer's service literature, use a voltmeter and turn the windshield-wiper control on. Carefully pierce the wires going to the motor and check which wire has voltage applied to it. If more than one wire has voltage applied to it, perform this brief test: With the meter still connected, turn the windshield-wiper control off. If the meter drops to zero and stays there, that is the correct wires. If the meter drops slightly and then briefly swings back up before dropping back to stay at zero, this is not the wire.

When you have identified the hot lead as noted above, cut it. Now splice the green wire to the end going to the motor, and the white wire to the other end. Solder these leads and then cover with insulating tape.

USING THE WIPER DELAY

When you leave the slide switch in the NORMAL position, your windshield wipers will function normally. In the DELAY position, when you turn your windshield wipers on, you can obtain adjustable intervals of wiper sweeps. INTERVAL determines the amount of time between periods of windshield wiping operation. SWEEPS determines the number of sweeps which will occur when the windshield wiper will operate. Experiment with these controls a little to be sure you understand their function.

NOTE: With GM vehicles, the wipers will automatically return to the "park" position. With other vehicles, due to the wiring of the wiper delay, the wipers will not stop in the normal part position when you turn the windshield-wiper control off. To bring the wipers to their normal position, set the wiper-delay switch to NORMAL and operate your wipers in a normal fashion for one cycle.

Index

364